JOËLLE

DUBOIS

HANNIBAL

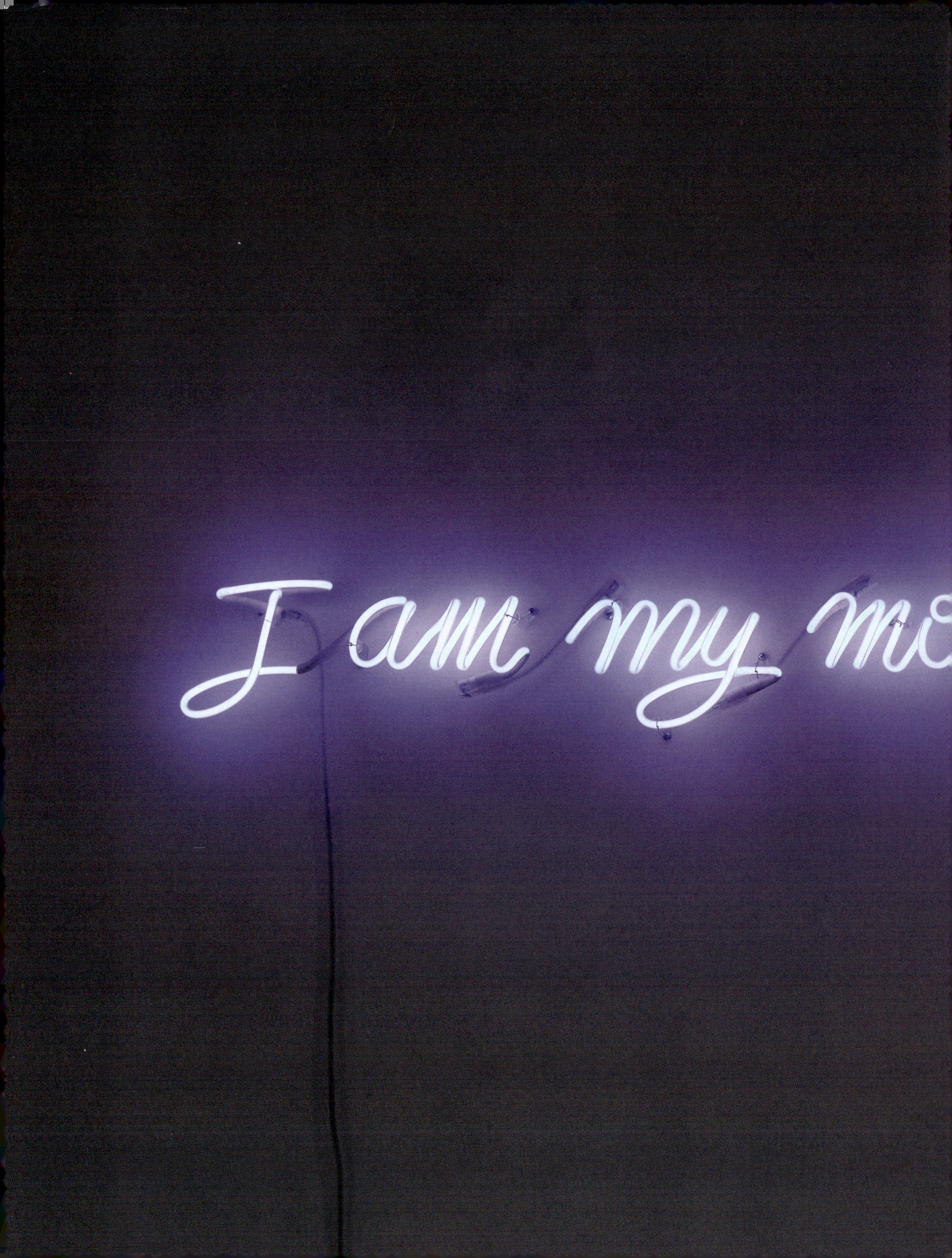
I am my

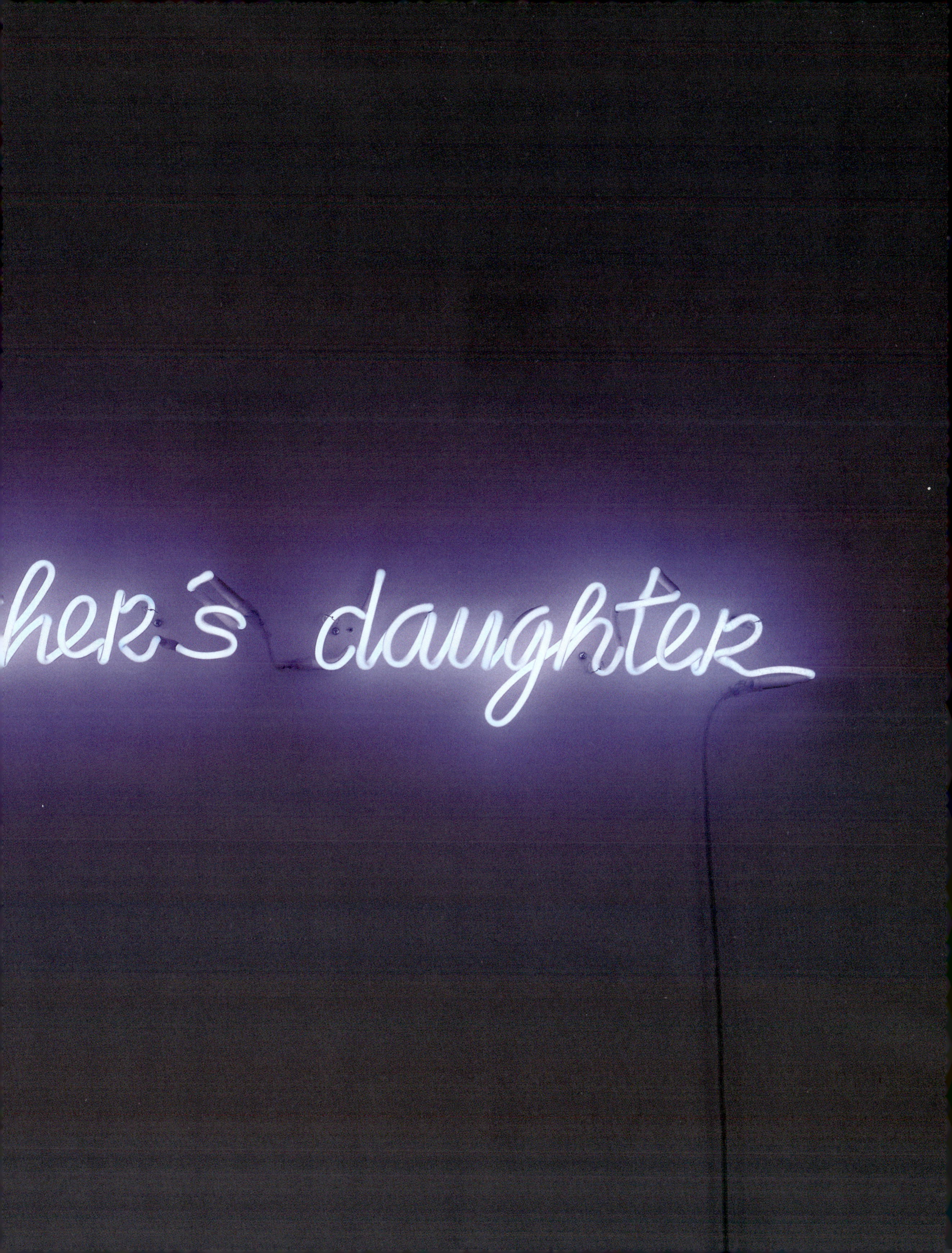
her's daughter

THE BUTTERFLY,

THE ALCHEMIST

AND

THE PAINTER

It's a sunny day and I am sitting on a bench waiting for Joëlle Dubois. In front of me, a butterfly is whirling from flower to flower and the soft ballet movements of the scarlet red-winged insect bring to mind *An Omen*, the self-portrait with the enormous moth on the artist's forehead. Knowing the deeply personal story of the painting, I wonder if the presence of the butterfly is a coincidence? While in an artist residency in Gargilesse-Dampierre, France – the picturesque *village d'adoption* of novelist George Sand in the Indre – a giant moth took refuge for several days in front of Dubois's door, so fearless and trusting, to a point that it even allowed itself to be touched. When it decided to leave, news from Belgium arrived requesting the artist's presence at her mother's bedside.

Dubois is known for her edgy, vibrant and colourful paintings. They usually depict groups of intimidating people or stern-looking individuals. Either alone or engaged in activities of explicit sexual intercourse, her characters are frequently absorbed by a screen of some sort. In these compositions, Dubois fleshes out the codes and symptoms of interpersonal relationships in an age of advanced technology, self-optimisation and heightened desirability. She exposes the fakeness of the promises of friendships and relationships made on social media, and pinpoints the loneliness that permeates contemporary society. Dubois is bold enough to include herself in her work, but even then, she eerily manages to stay in the observer's safe space.

Now, a softer side is unveiled. Addressing the sickness and loss of her mother, Dubois delivers a highly personal and fragile – yet universal and emancipatory – body of work which alternates between numbness, anger, distress, but also hope and deliverance. In *Let Me Finish My Drink First (Homage to Nicole Eisenman)*, a scene reminiscent of Bergman's *The Seventh Seal*, the mother-figure is seen in a game of seduction with Death, holding a glass of wine, in a conversation that will delay and hopefully rescue her from her plight. With her black and white ceramic vases, the artist toys with the idea of vials that contain the elixir of eternal life. The painted umbilical cords, tunnels and hourglasses are a testament to the efforts to keep the mother-figure alive and sound in body and mind. Dubois tries desperately, like an alchemist, to work out the formula for immortality. But the outcome is inevitable.

Paint is the medium *de préférence*. Nonetheless, Dubois is unafraid to step out of her comfort zone and explore other artistic forms. In her latest experiments she explores the moving image and, in collaboration with Florinda Ciucio, has created a video installation, *The Memory Machine*, which makes use of the endless hours of footage of her mother she accumulated over the years. A digital vault against the evanescence of memory.

Dubois talks of her artistic process in this latest body of work as being cathartic. A visceral and therapeutic exercise that brought acceptance and closure with the reality of death. She allowed space for her suffering, stayed attuned to messages that came in her dreams, and filled the canvas with symbols, metaphors and allegories.

The art historical references are multiple: Dalí, Botero, Lucas, Emin… even Aztec codices are referenced in the *Reincarnation* series, an intimate and delicate series of pencil drawings, a probe on internal struggles and the circle of life. But the fairy godmother must be Frida Kahlo, even if Dubois is not thinking of her during this process. Her first encounter with Kahlo occurred when her mother took her, at a young age, to an exhibition in London. Then, when she was an adult, her mother gifted her with a book on the Mexican painter. An omen! Dubois's paintings are vibrant in colour. Her work is autobiographical, with a visual lexicon of signs and symbols, but mostly it is unafraid to speak of suffering in total and disarming honesty.

By addressing the psychological states one goes through when losing a parent, Dubois continues to explore loneliness. Whilst in her previous works she kept her distance as an observer, here, her embodiment of loneliness is palpable. Her paintings and drawings exude an other-worldly presence that cannot be missed, and we feel almost uneasy to be witnesses to this extremely private moment. Yet, sharing this personal journey is intentional. Like Joan Didion, Dubois writes her story using a wide variety of media, with the aim of healing – herself as much as the viewer – from the crushing realisation of the fleeting nature of life and the parting from the people we love most.

Christel Tsilibaris,
Curatorial Project Manager at Bozar, Brussels

My Mother

2022

100 × 80 cm

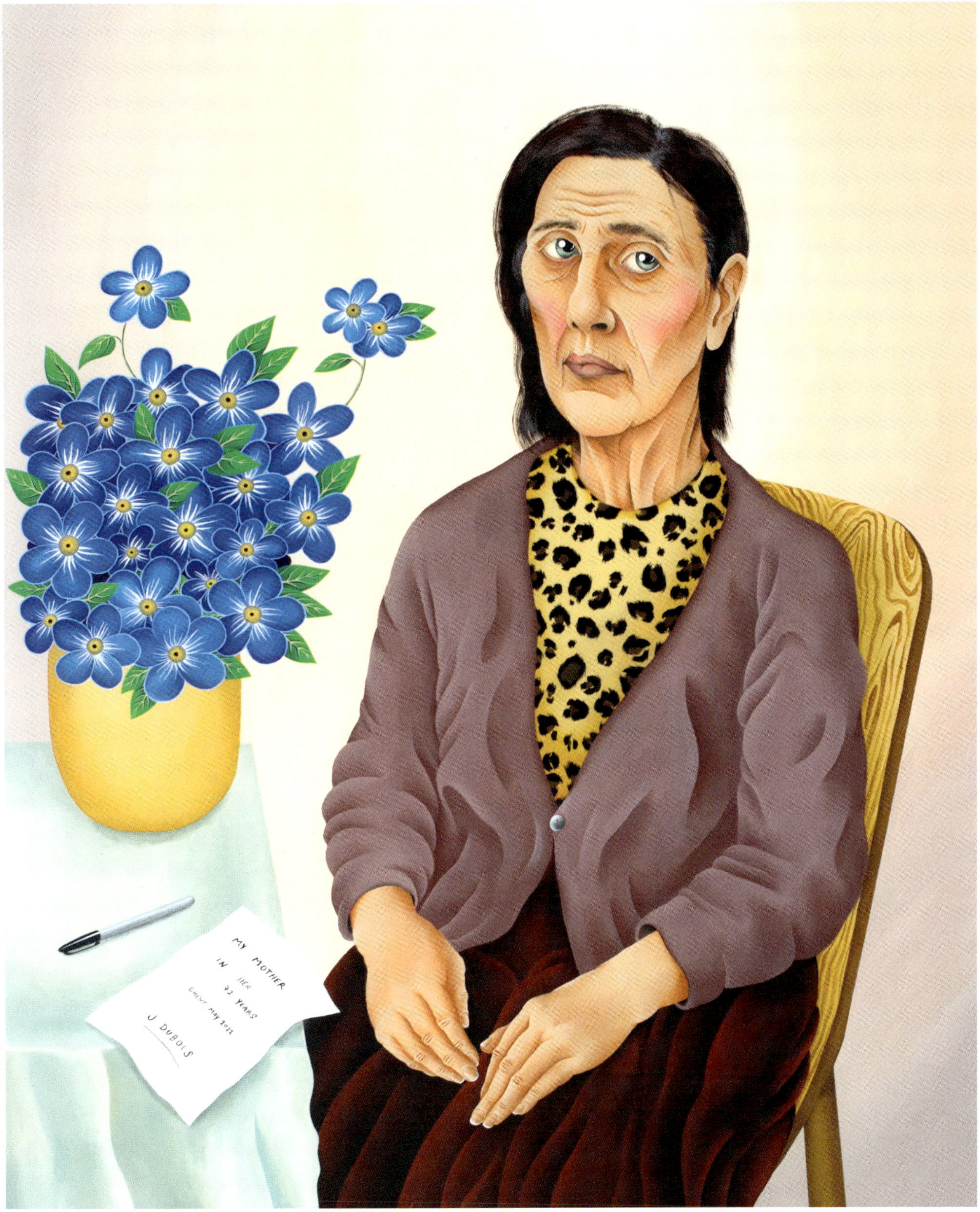
MY MOTHER
IN HER 72 YEARS
GHENT, MAY 2022
J DUBOIS

ME

FORGET

NOT

30 × 30 cm

Taking Notes

2022

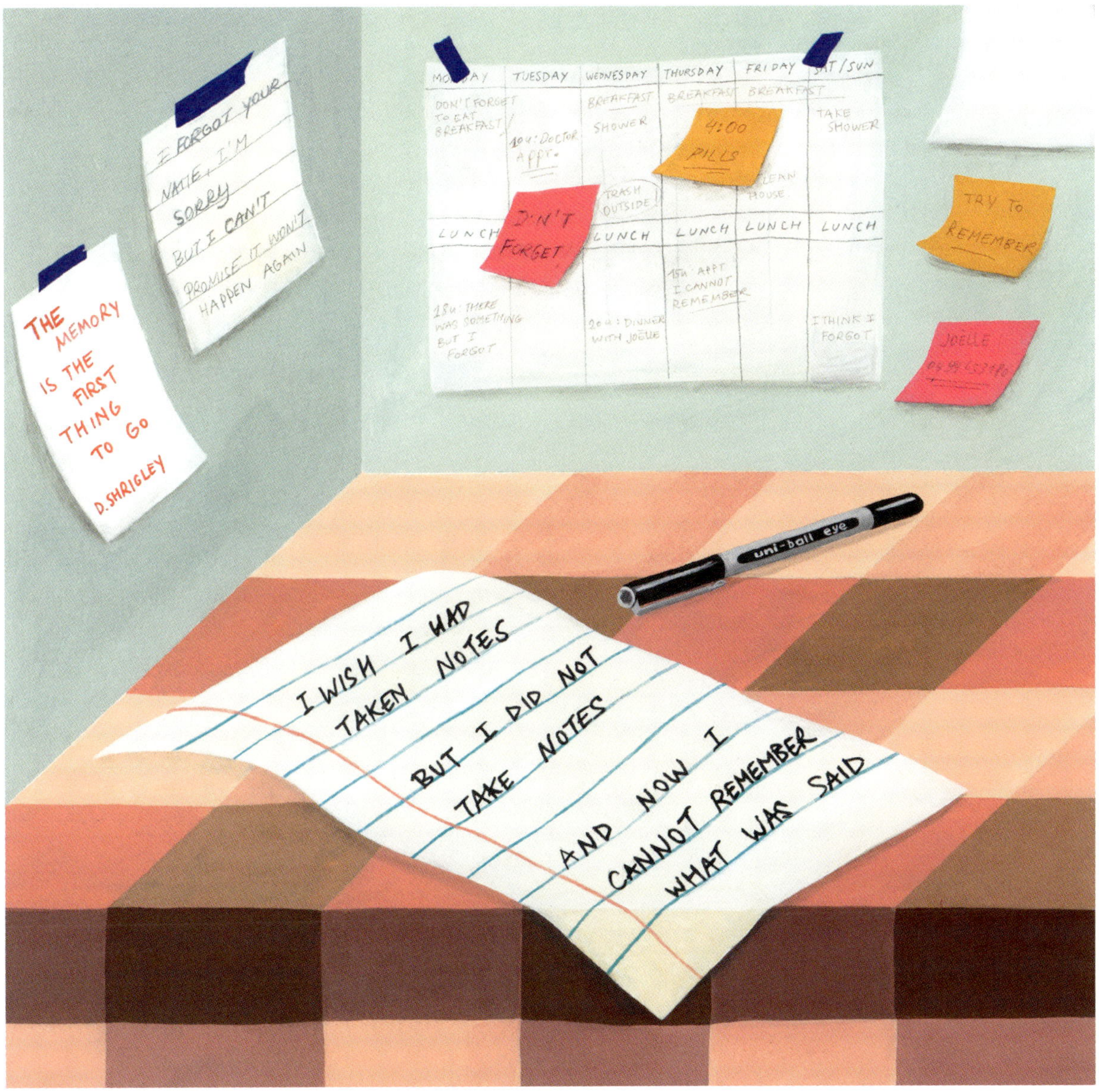
THE MEMORY IS THE FIRST THING TO GO
D.SHRIGLEY
I FORGOT YOUR NAME, I'M SORRY BUT I CAN'T PROMISE IT WON'T HAPPEN AGAIN
TUESDAY
WEDNESDAY
THURSDAY
FRIDAY
SAT/SUN
DON'T FORGET TO EAT BREAKFAST
BREAKFAST
SHOWER
TAKE SHOWER
4:00 PILLS
DON'T FORGET
LUNCH
LUNCH
LUNCH
LUNCH
TRY TO REMEMBER
uni-ball eye
I WISH I HAD TAKEN NOTES
BUT I DID NOT TAKE NOTES
AND NOW I CANNOT REMEMBER WHAT WAS SAID

21.4 × 30.5 cm

Fooling Death with the Elixir of Immortality | *Women in the Family Tree*

2022

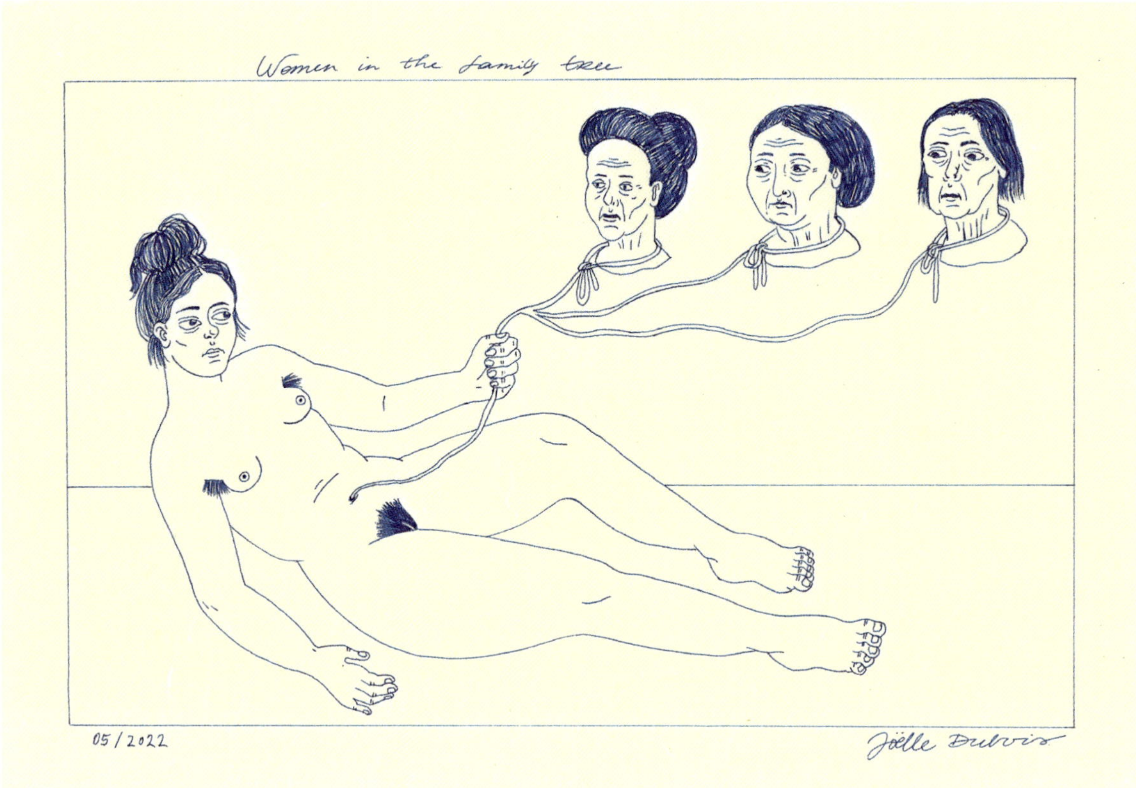

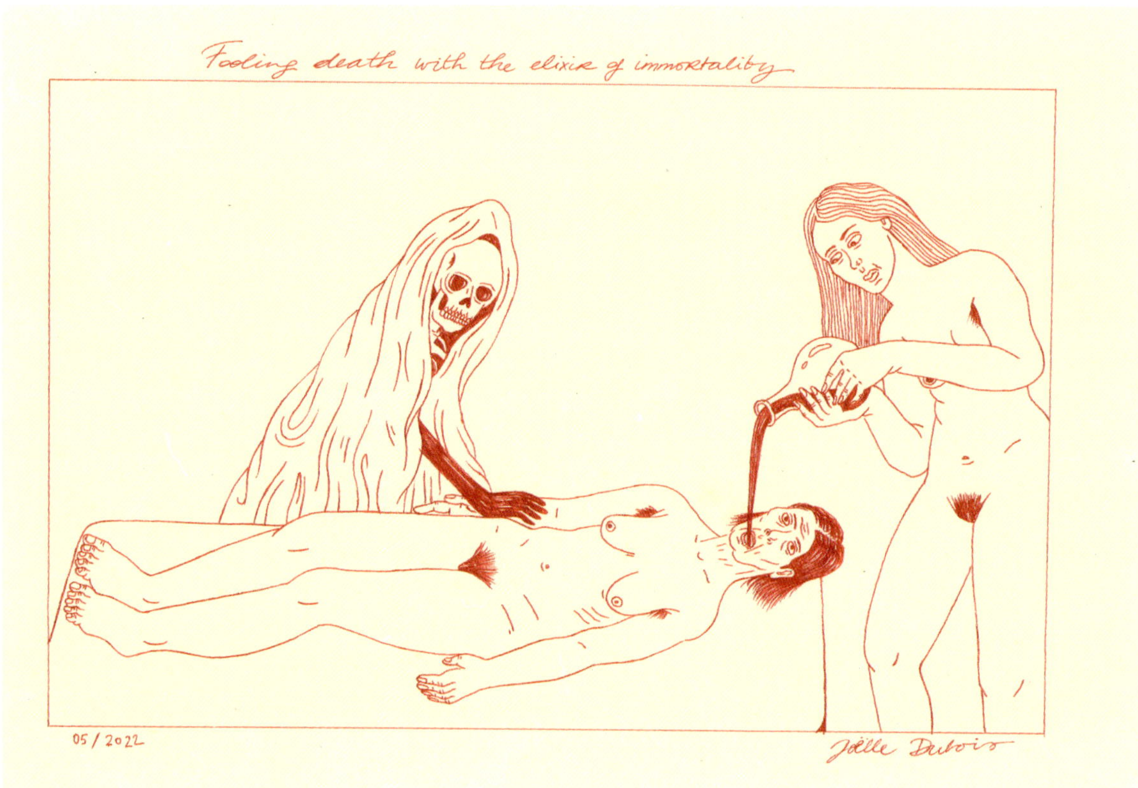

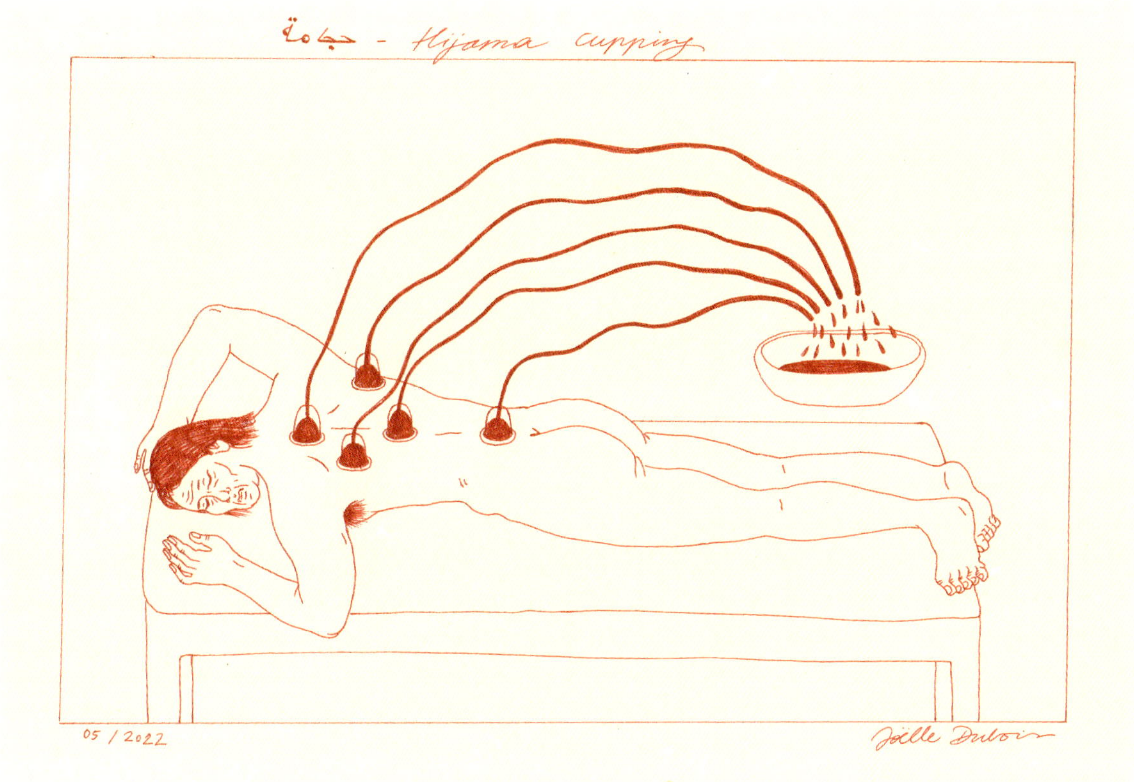

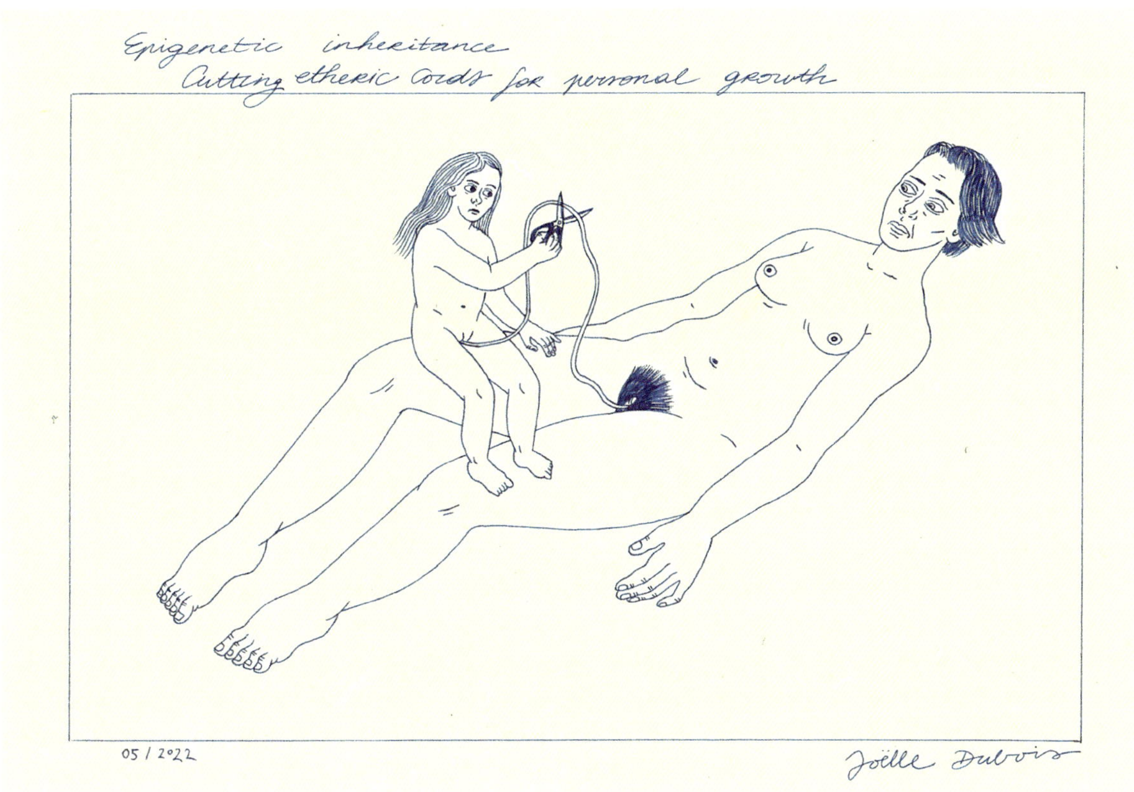

Hijama Cupping | *Epigenetic Inheritance, Cutting Etheric Cords for Personal Growth*

2022

21.4 × 30.5 cm

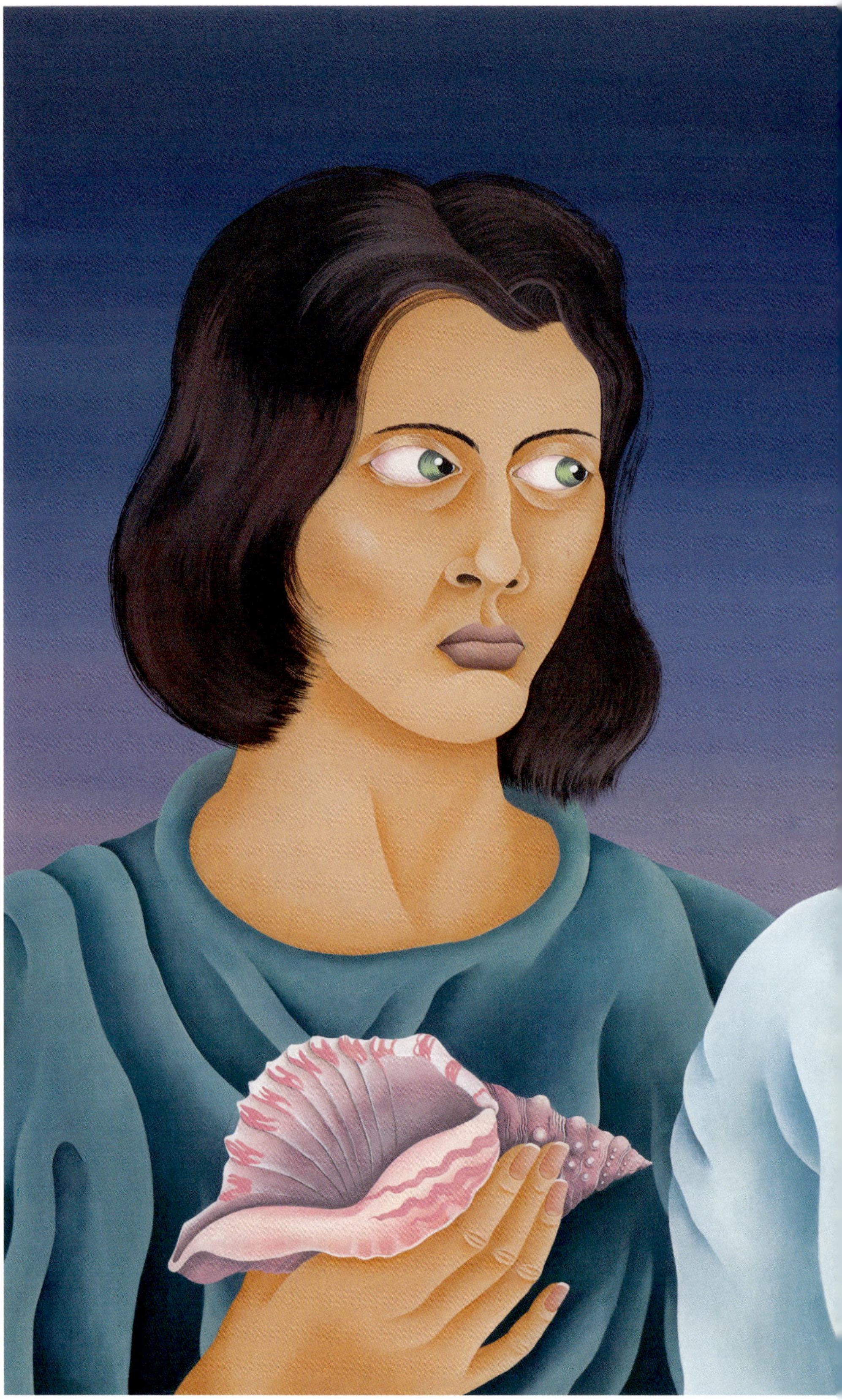

2022

Three Mothers

102 × 162 cm

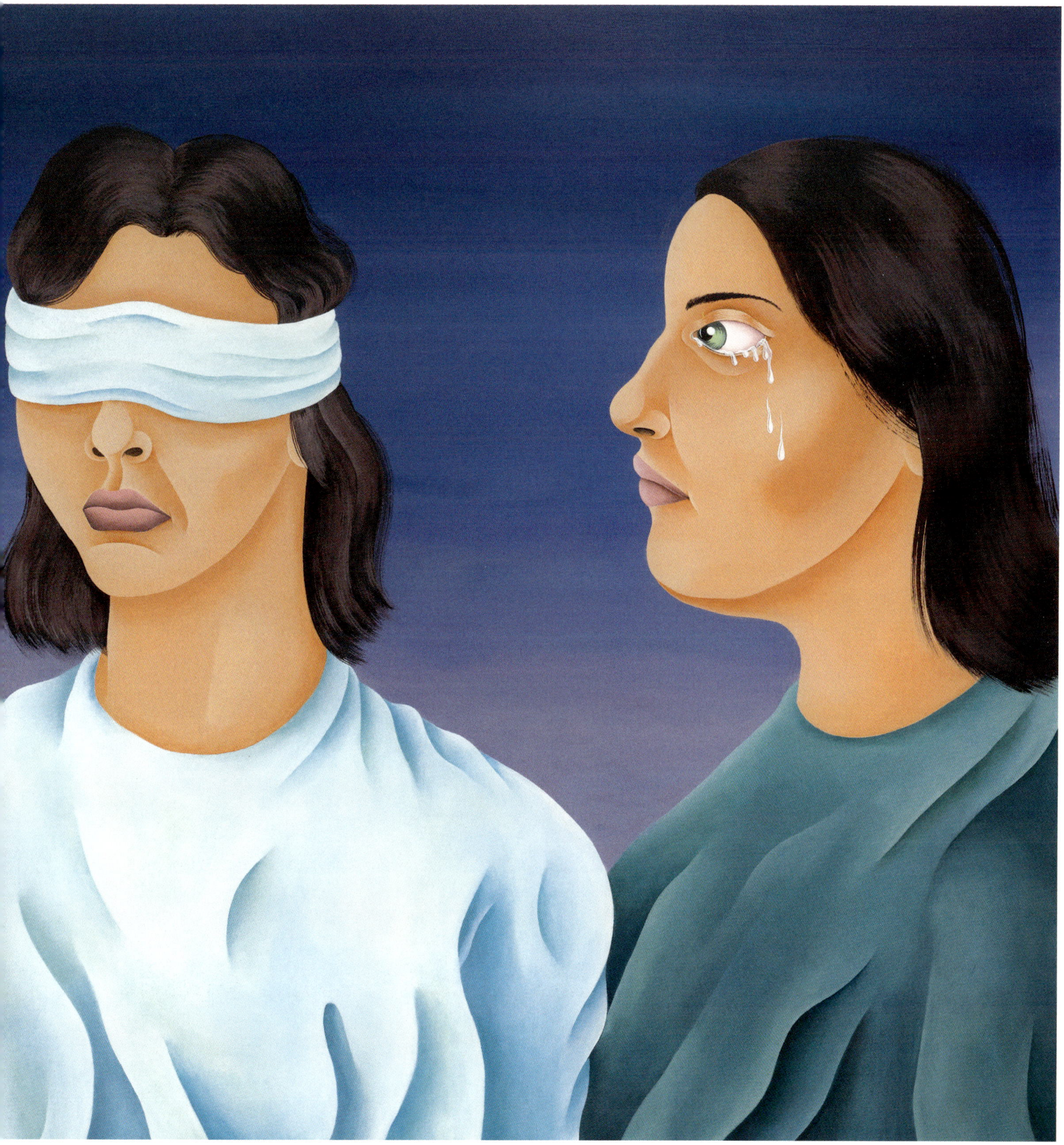

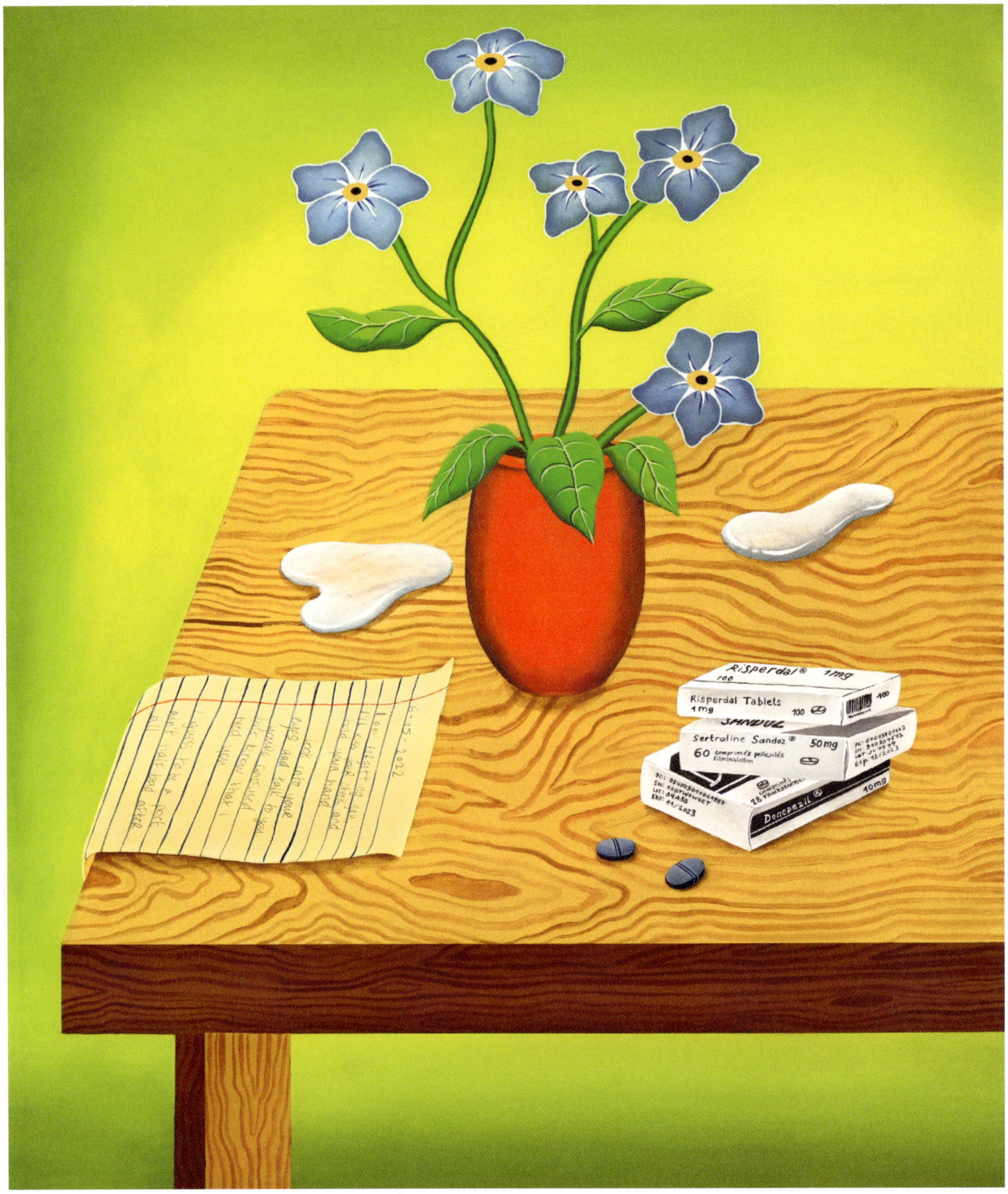

Memorabilia

2022

60 × 50 cm

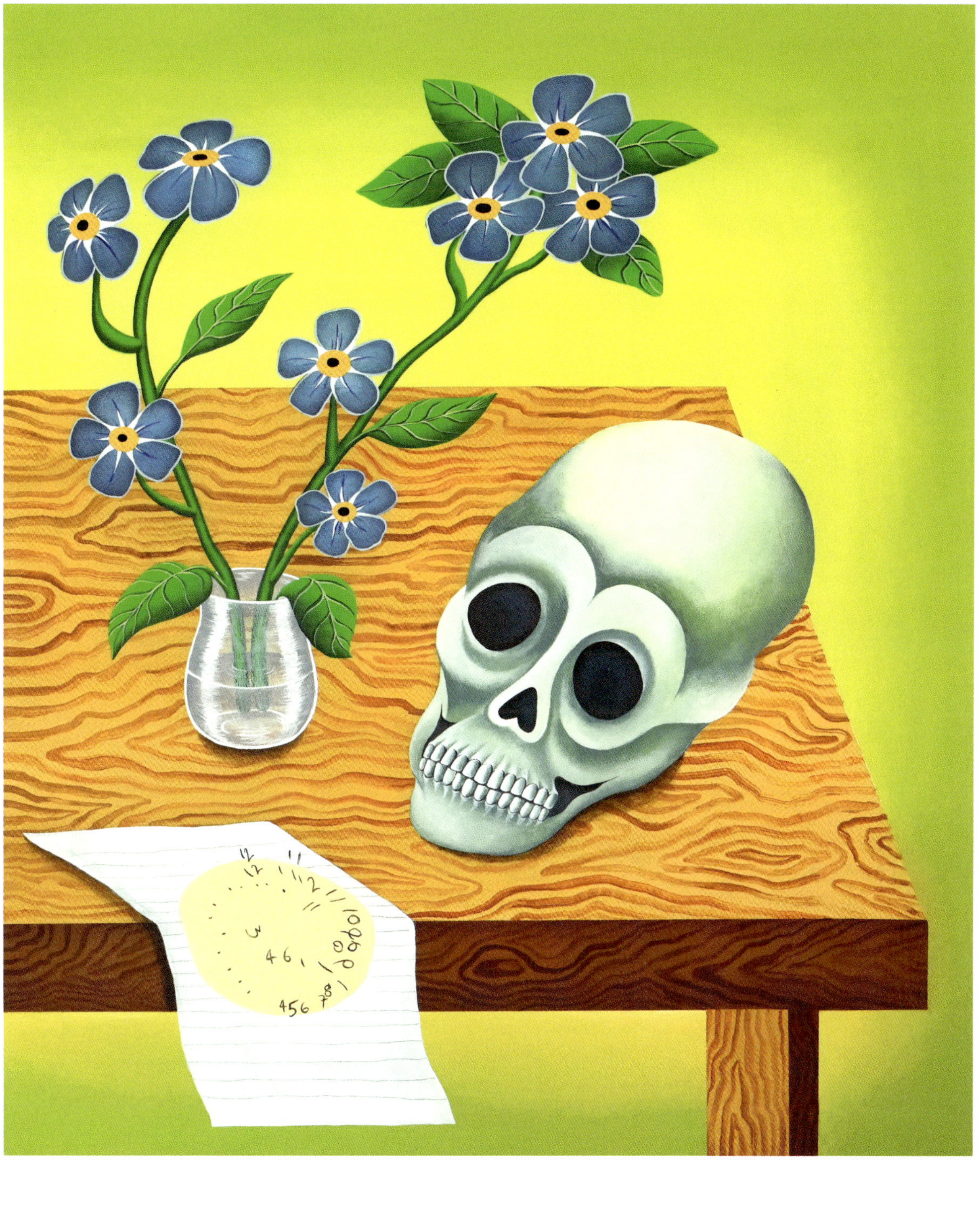

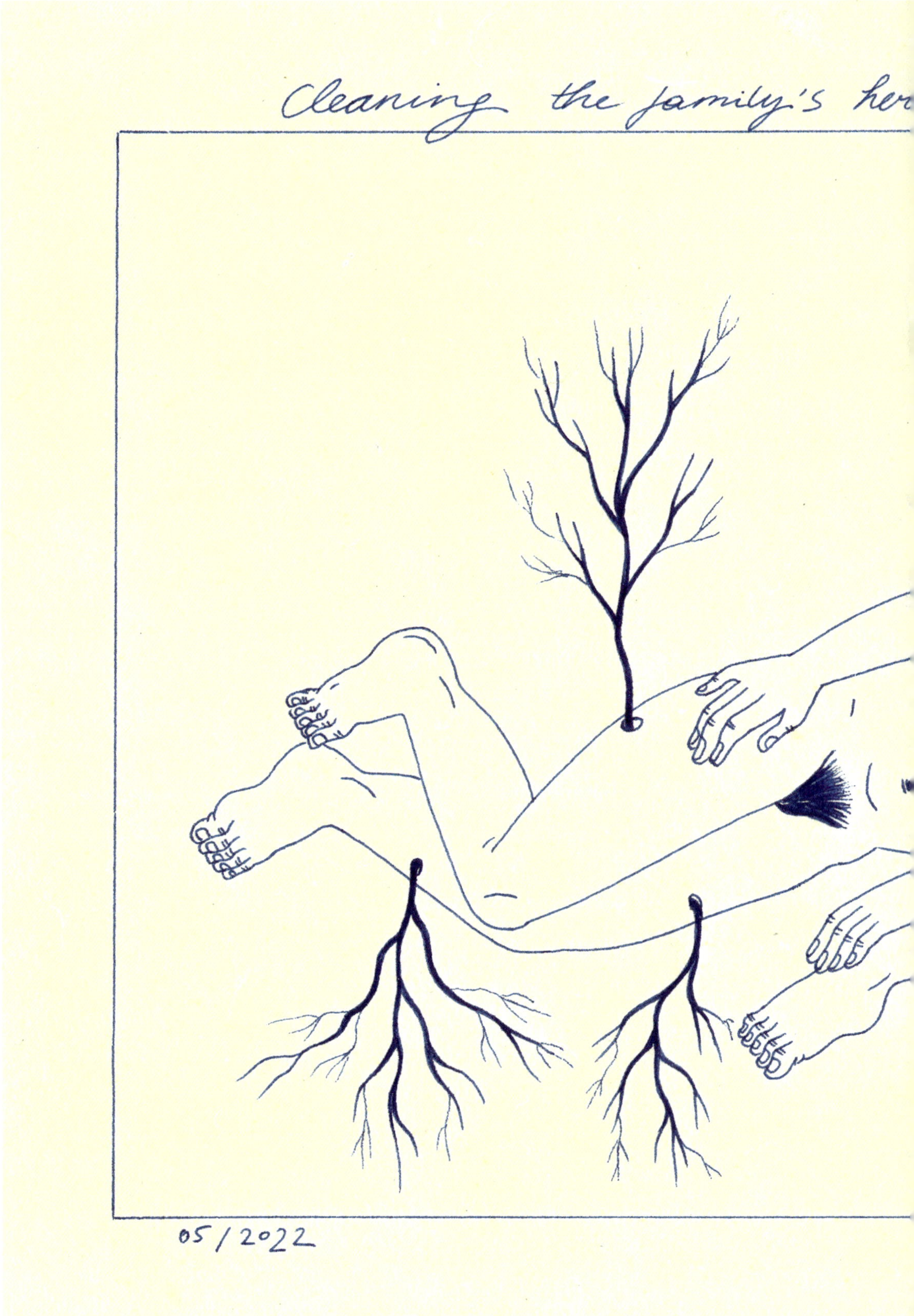

Cleaning the Family's Heritage for Future Generations

21.4 × 30.5 cm

2022

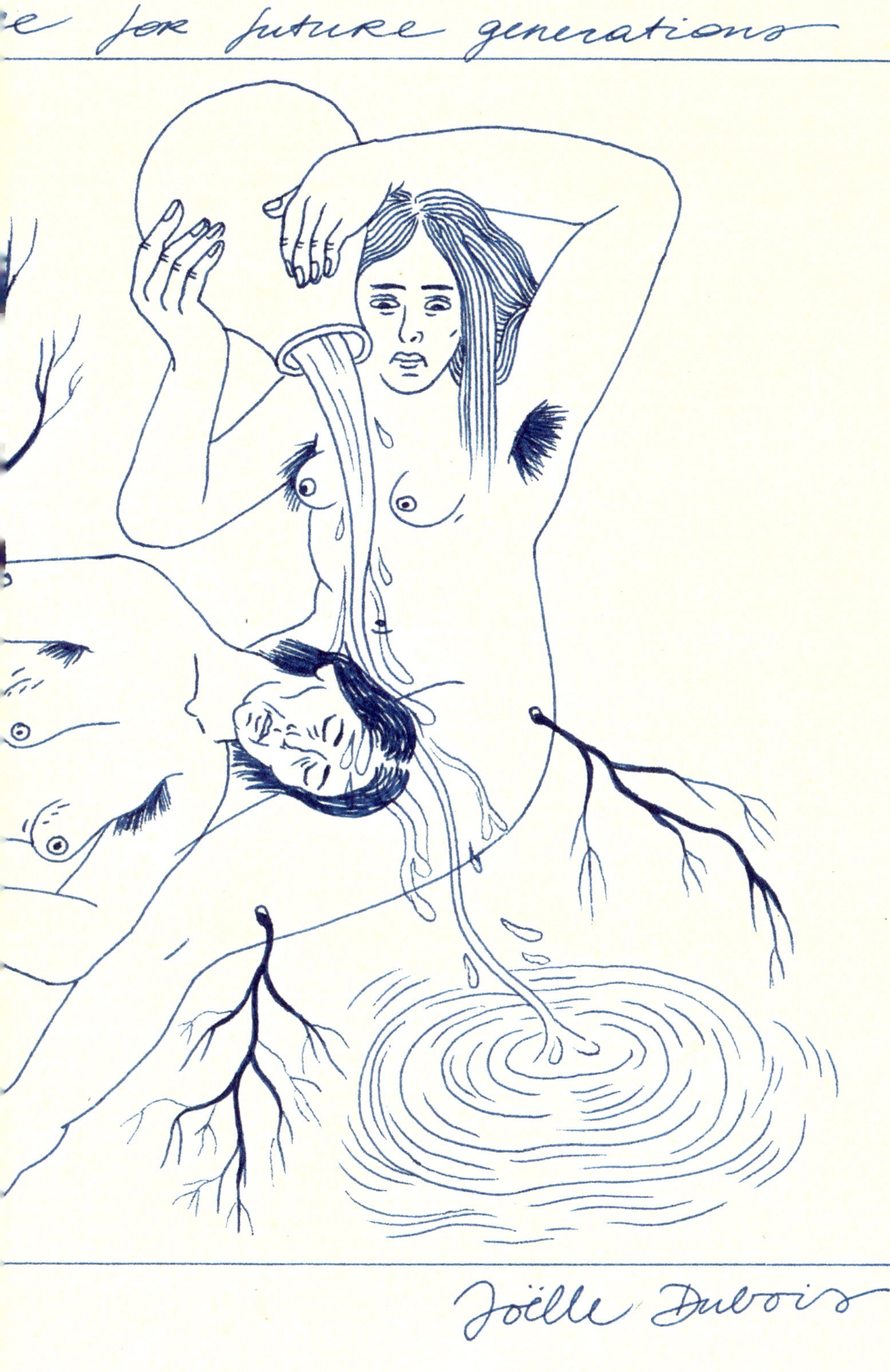
for future generations
Joëlle Dubois

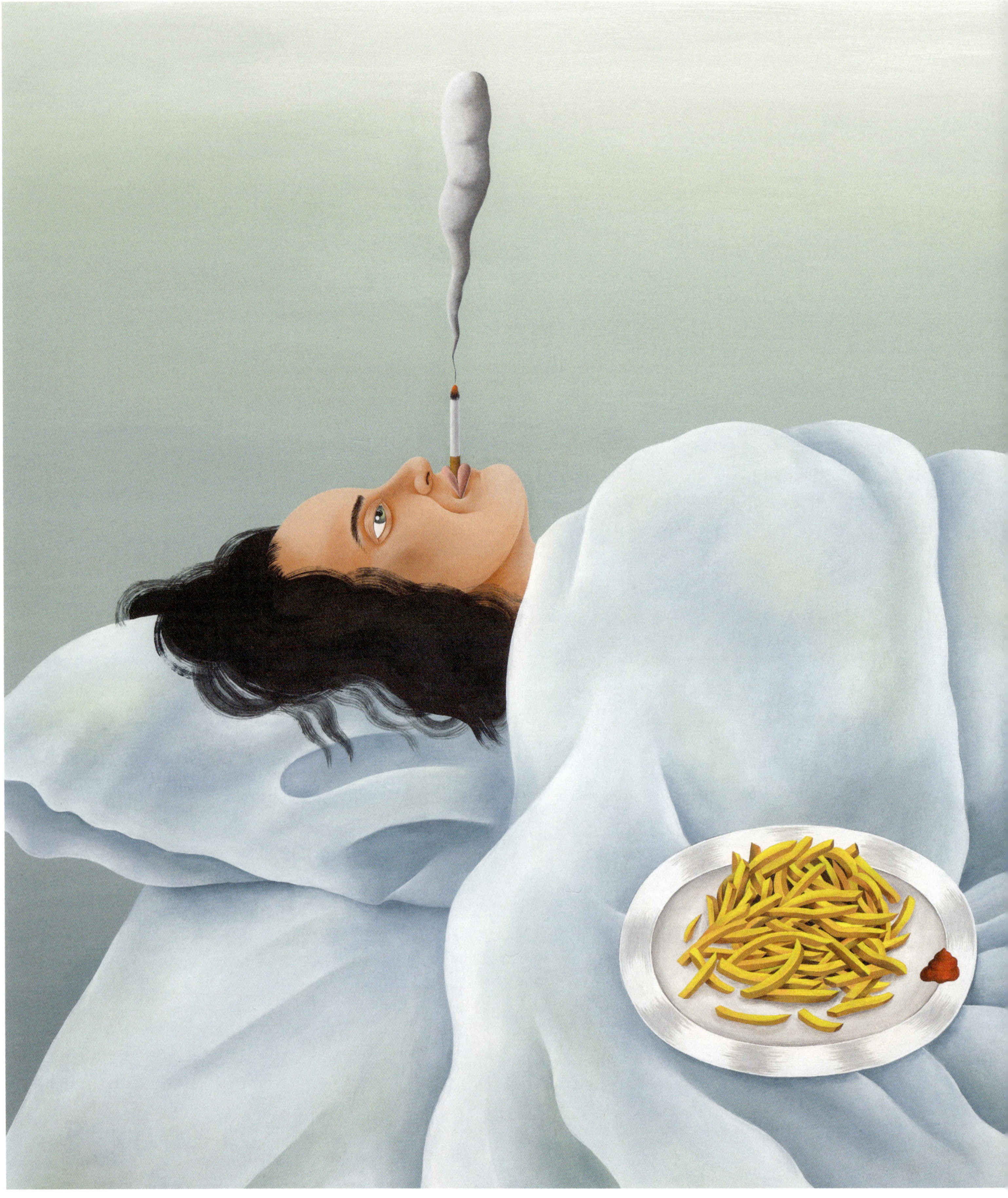

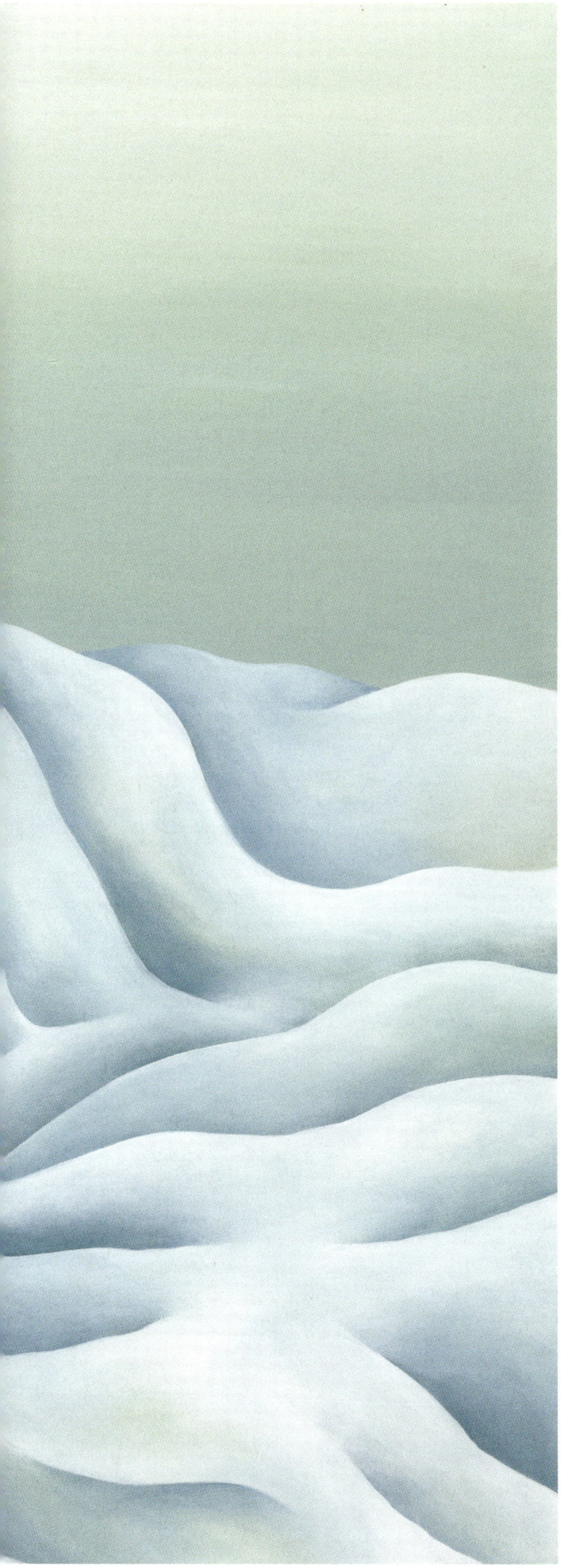

Bed Habits (Hommage to Annette Lemieux and Philip Guston)

2022

80 × 100 cm

60 × 50 cm *Death for Breakfast* 2022

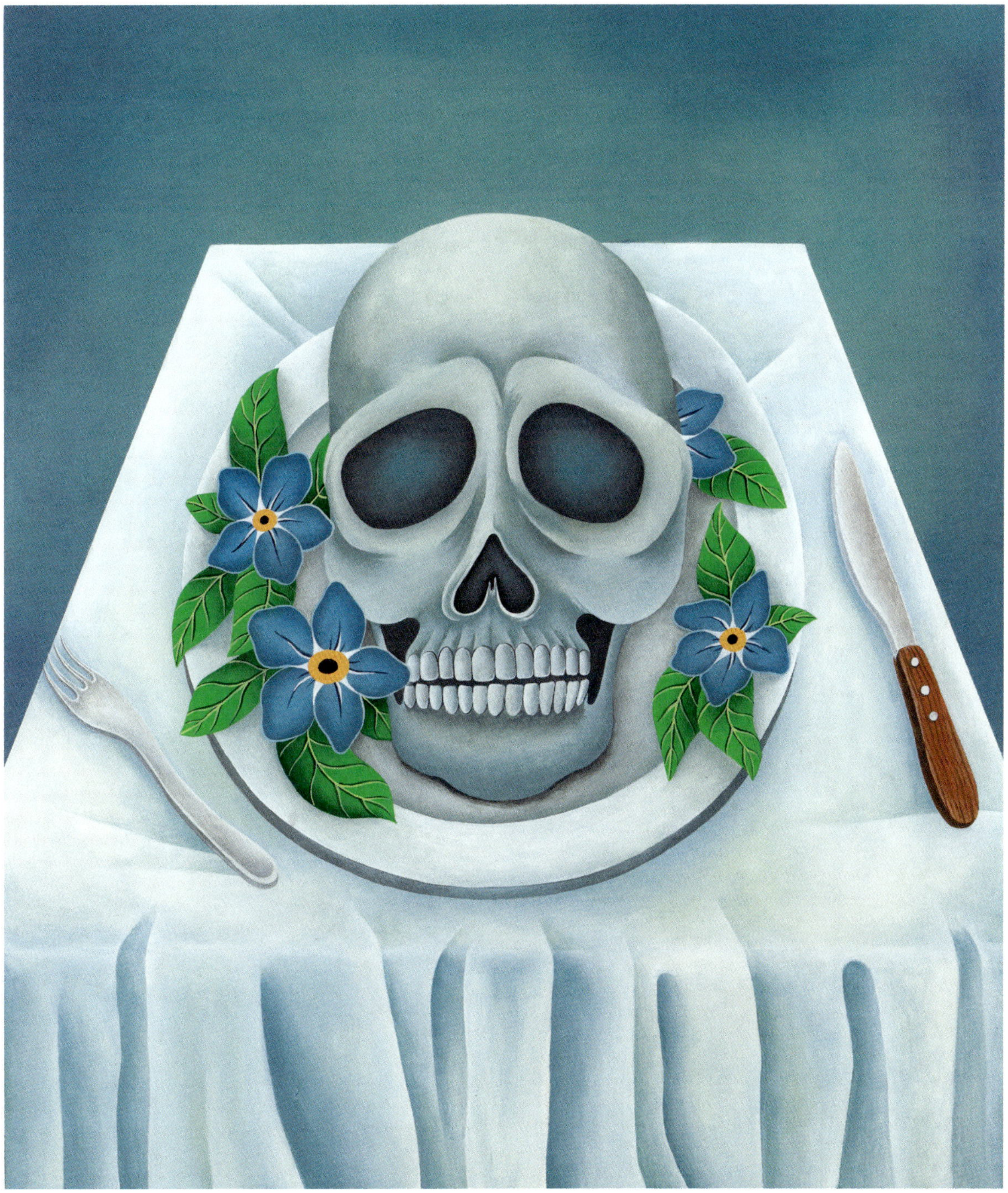

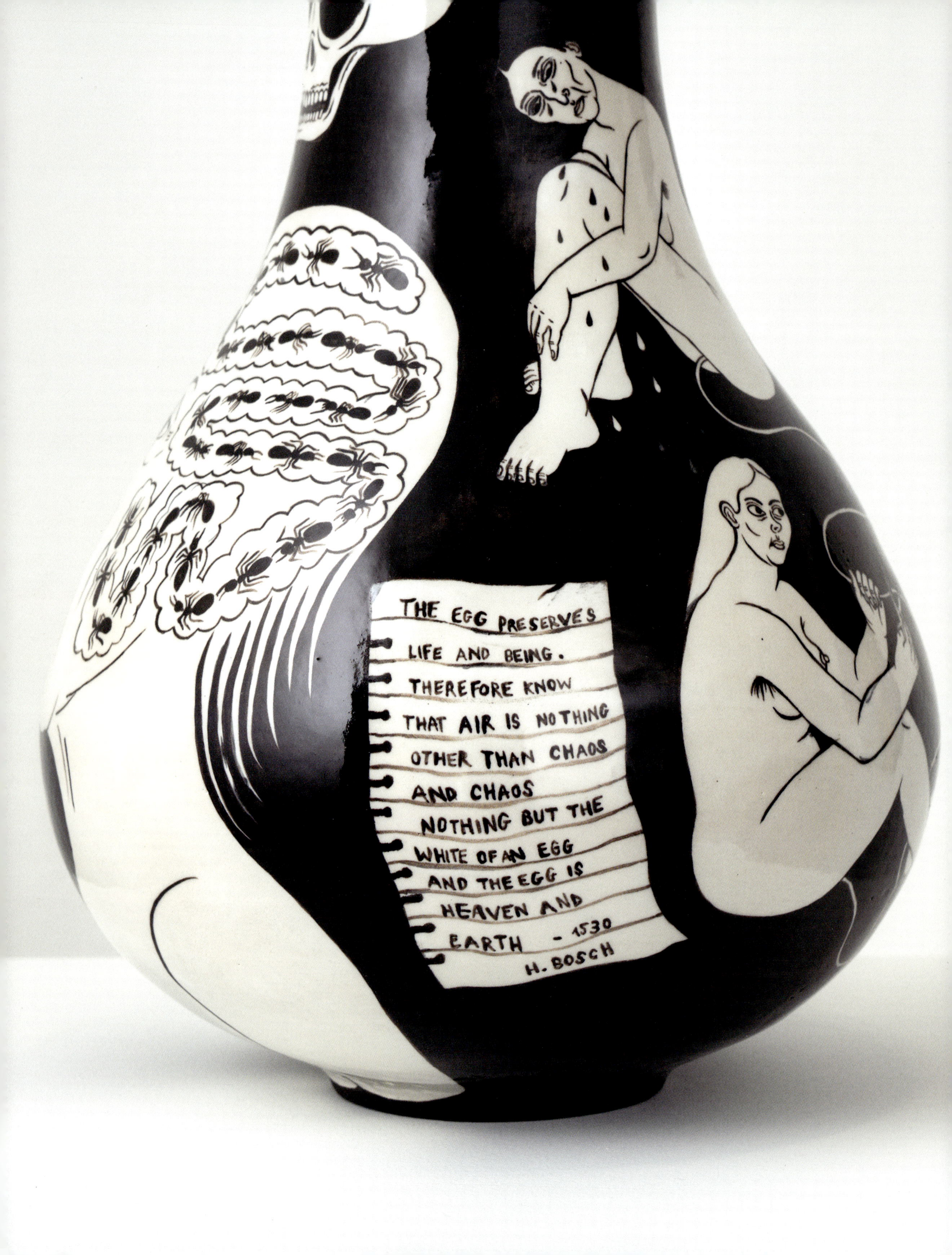
THE EGG PRESERVES
LIFE AND BEING.
THEREFORE KNOW
THAT AIR IS NOTHING
OTHER THAN CHAOS
AND CHAOS
NOTHING BUT THE
WHITE OF AN EGG
AND THE EGG IS
HEAVEN AND
EARTH - 1530
H. BOSCH

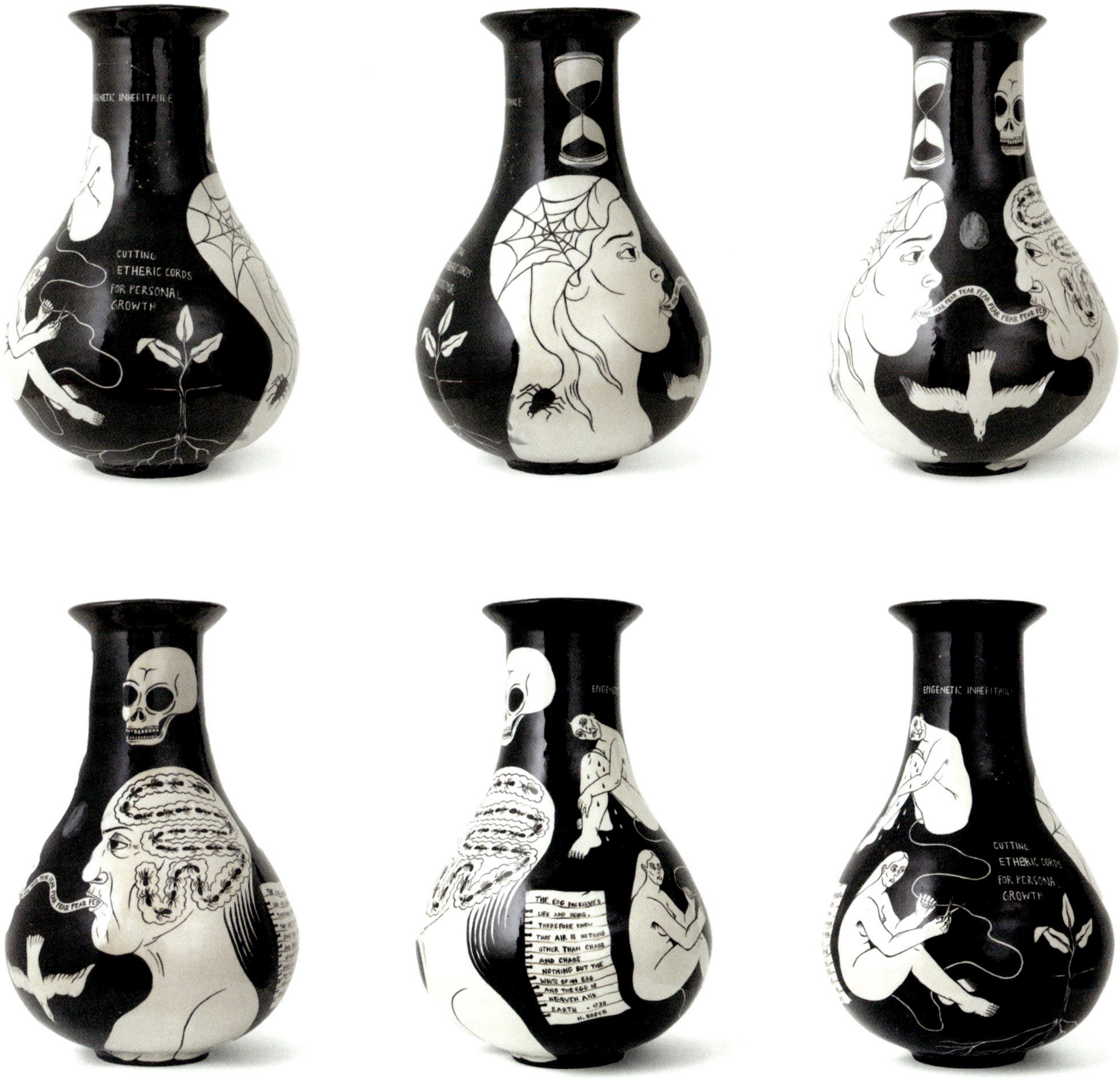

Elixir of Life

2022

38 × 25 × 25 cm

2022

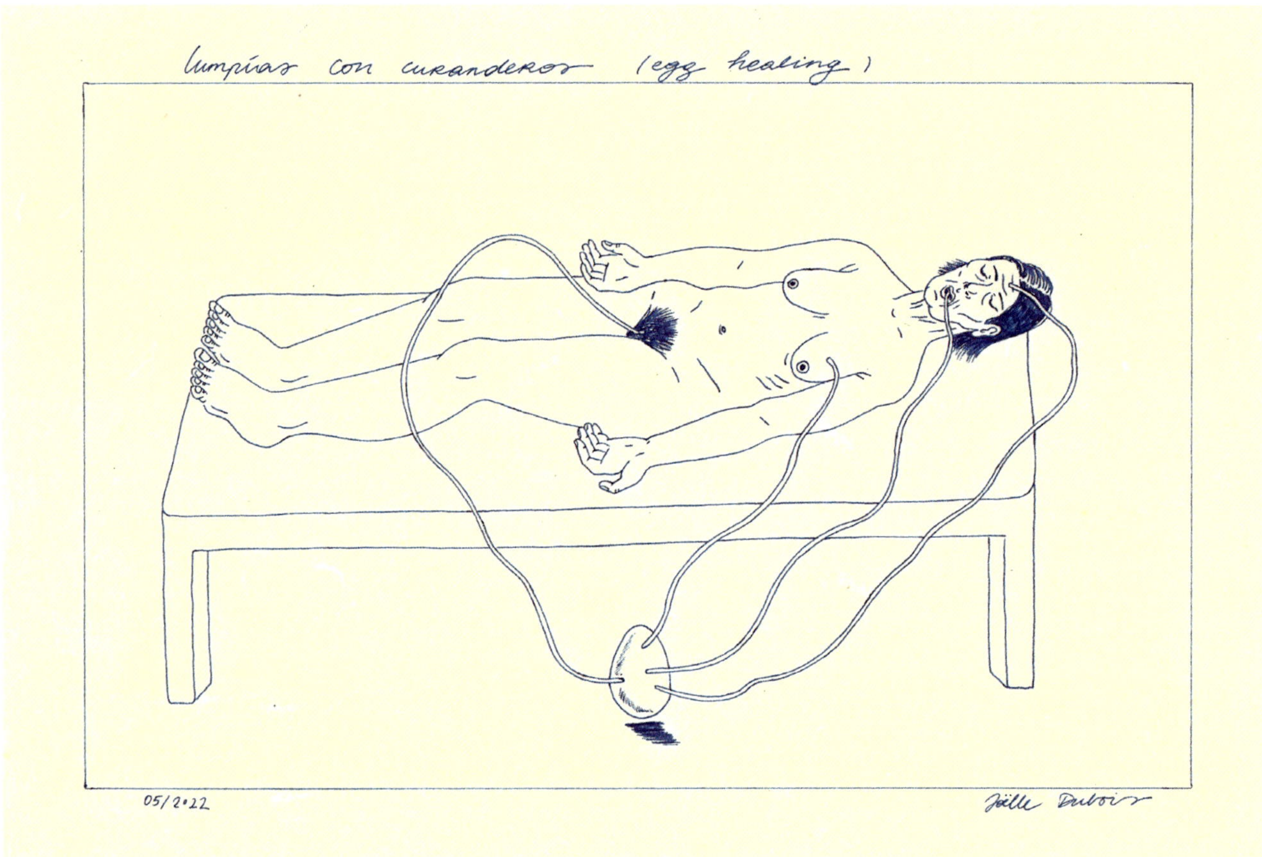

Lumpias con Curanderos (Egg Healing)

21.4 × 30.5 cm

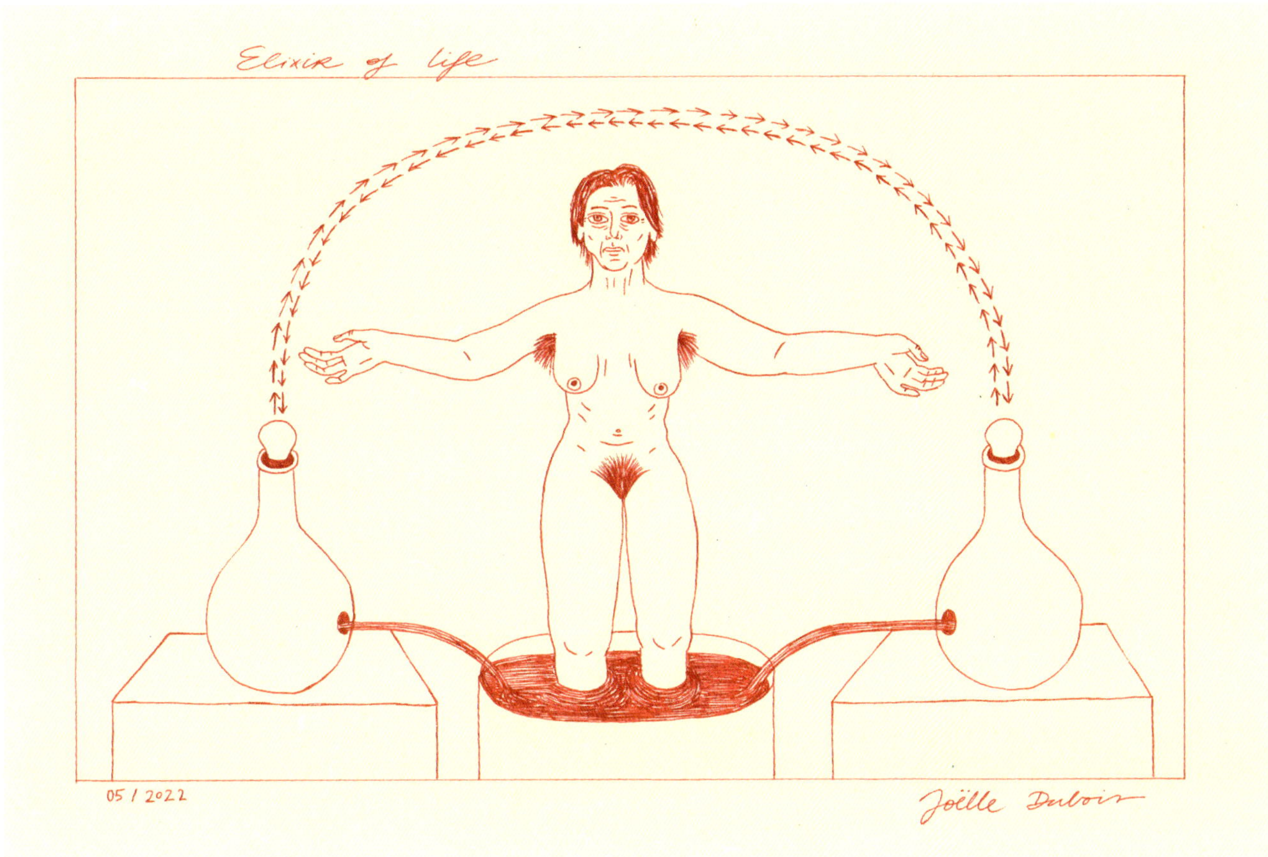

2022

Elixir of Life

21.4 × 30.5 cm

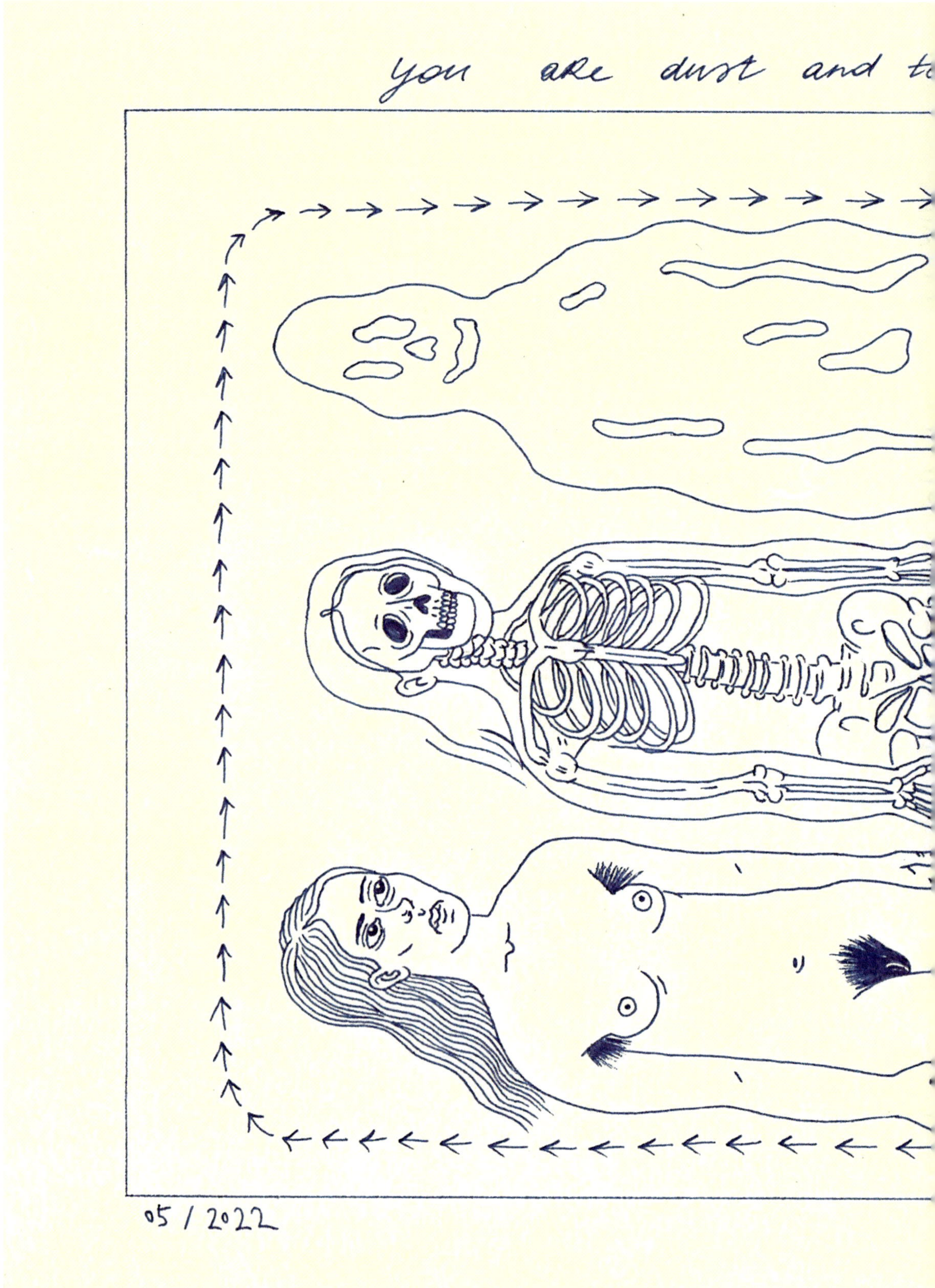

You Are Dust and to Dust You Shall Return

2022

21.4 × 30.5 cm

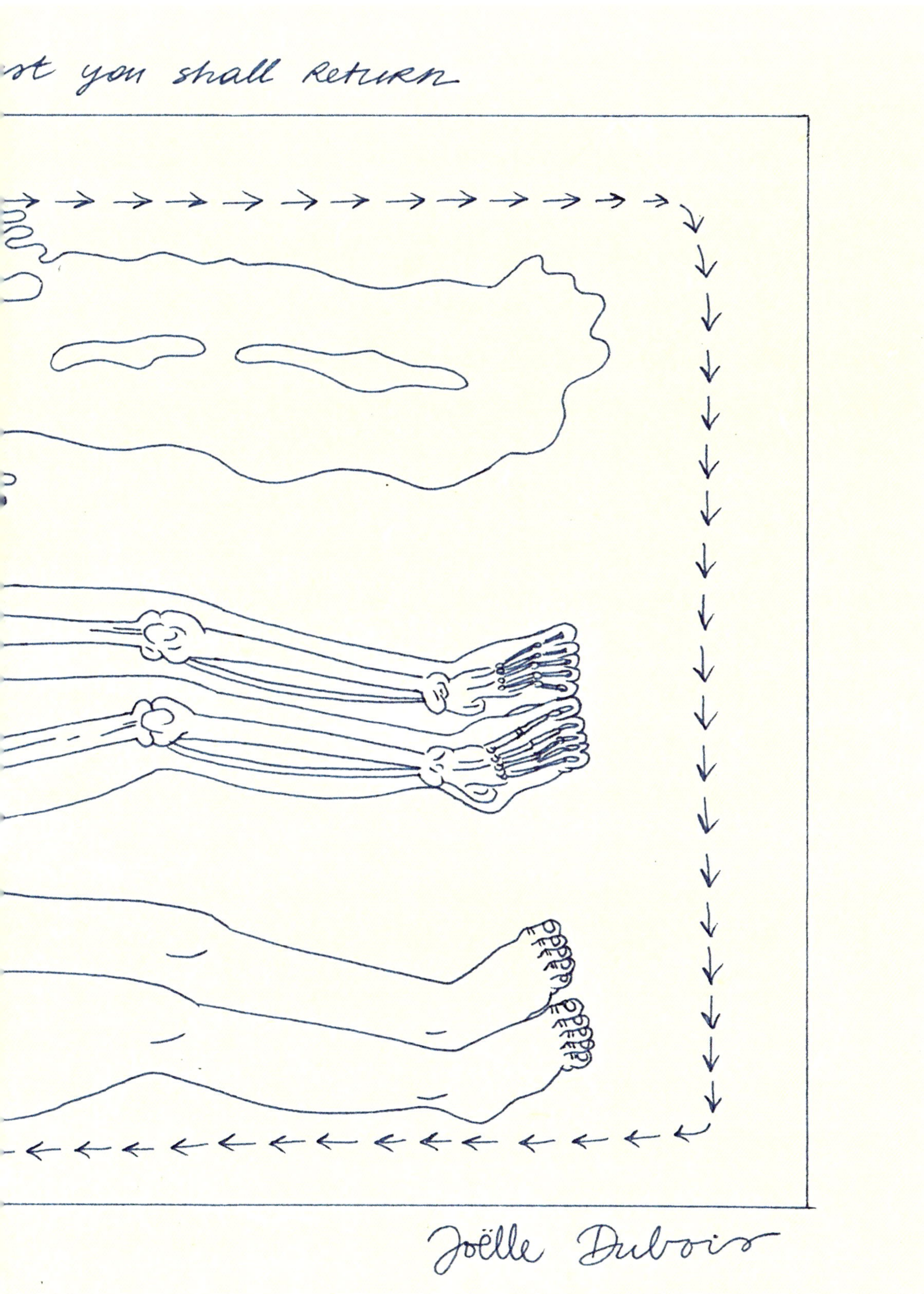
st you shall Return
Joëlle Dubois

2023

Glooming Days

150 × 110 cm

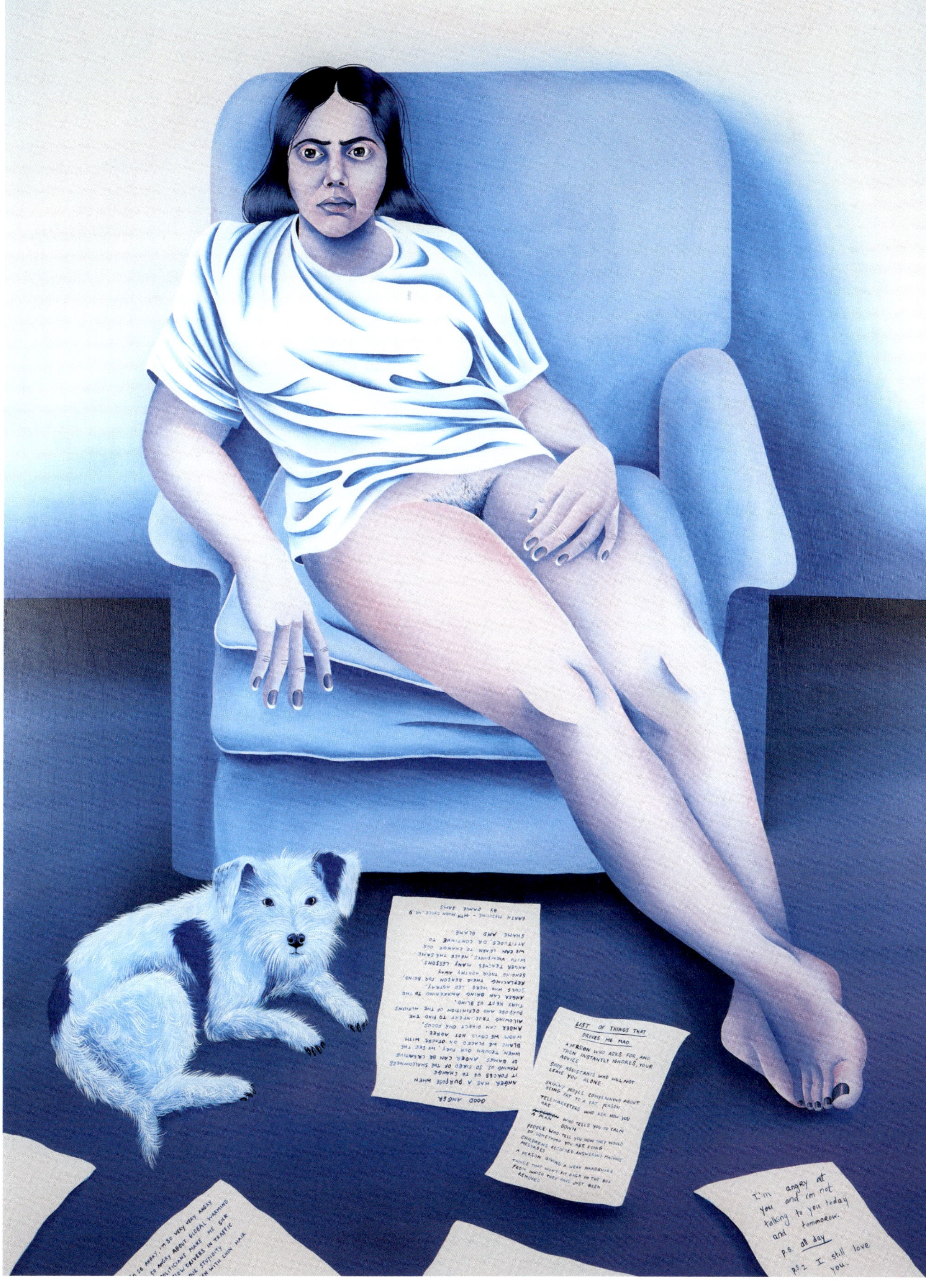
LIST OF THINGS THAT DRIVES ME MAD
A PERSON WHO ASKS FOR, AND THEN INSTANTLY IGNORES, YOUR ADVICE
SHOP ASSISTANTS WHO WILL NOT LEAVE YOU ALONE
SKINNY PEOPLE COMPLAINING ABOUT BEING FAT TO A FAT PERSON
TELEMARKETERS WHO ASK HOW YOU ARE
A MAN WHO TELLS YOU TO CALM DOWN
PEOPLE WHO TELL YOU HOW THEY WOULD DO SOMETHING YOU ARE DOING
CHILDRENS RECORDED ANSWERING MACHINE MESSAGES
A PERSON GIVING A WEAK HANDSHAKE
THINGS THAT WON'T FIT BACK IN THE BOX FROM WHICH THEY HAVE JUST BEEN REMOVED
I'm angry at you and i'm not talking to you today and tommorow.
p.s. all day
p.s.2 I still love you.

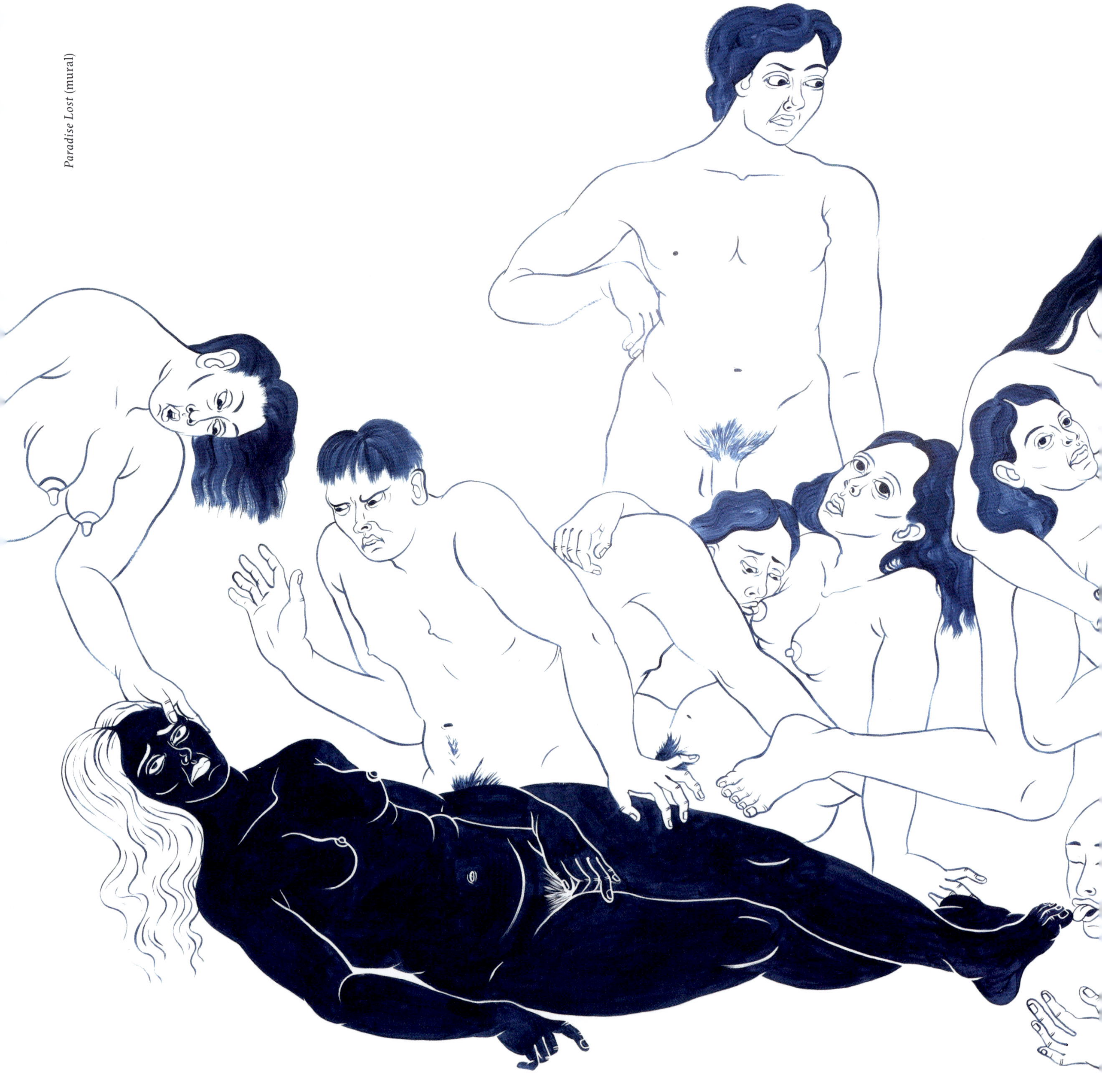

Paradise Lost (mural)
2023
272 × 1640 cm

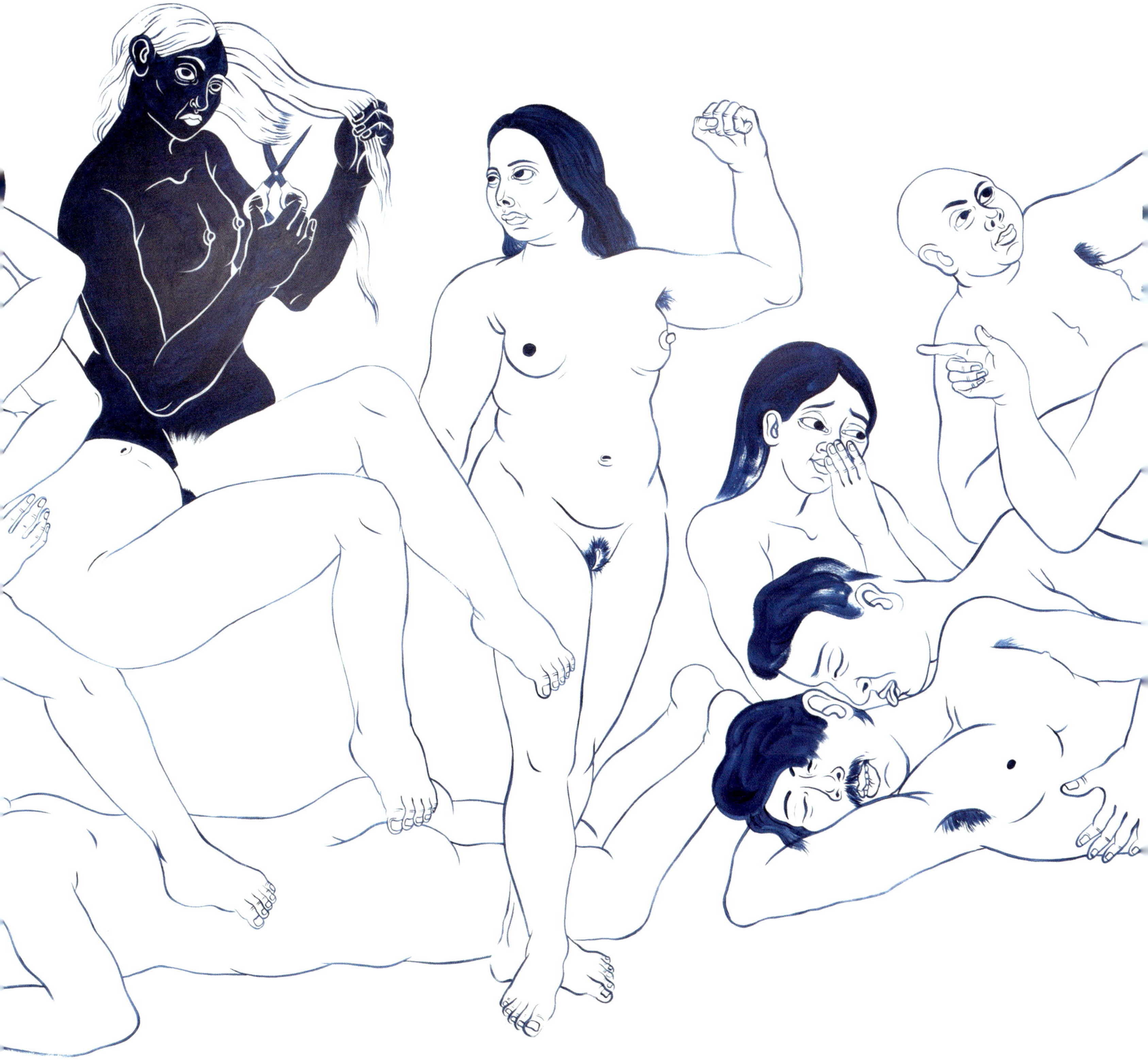

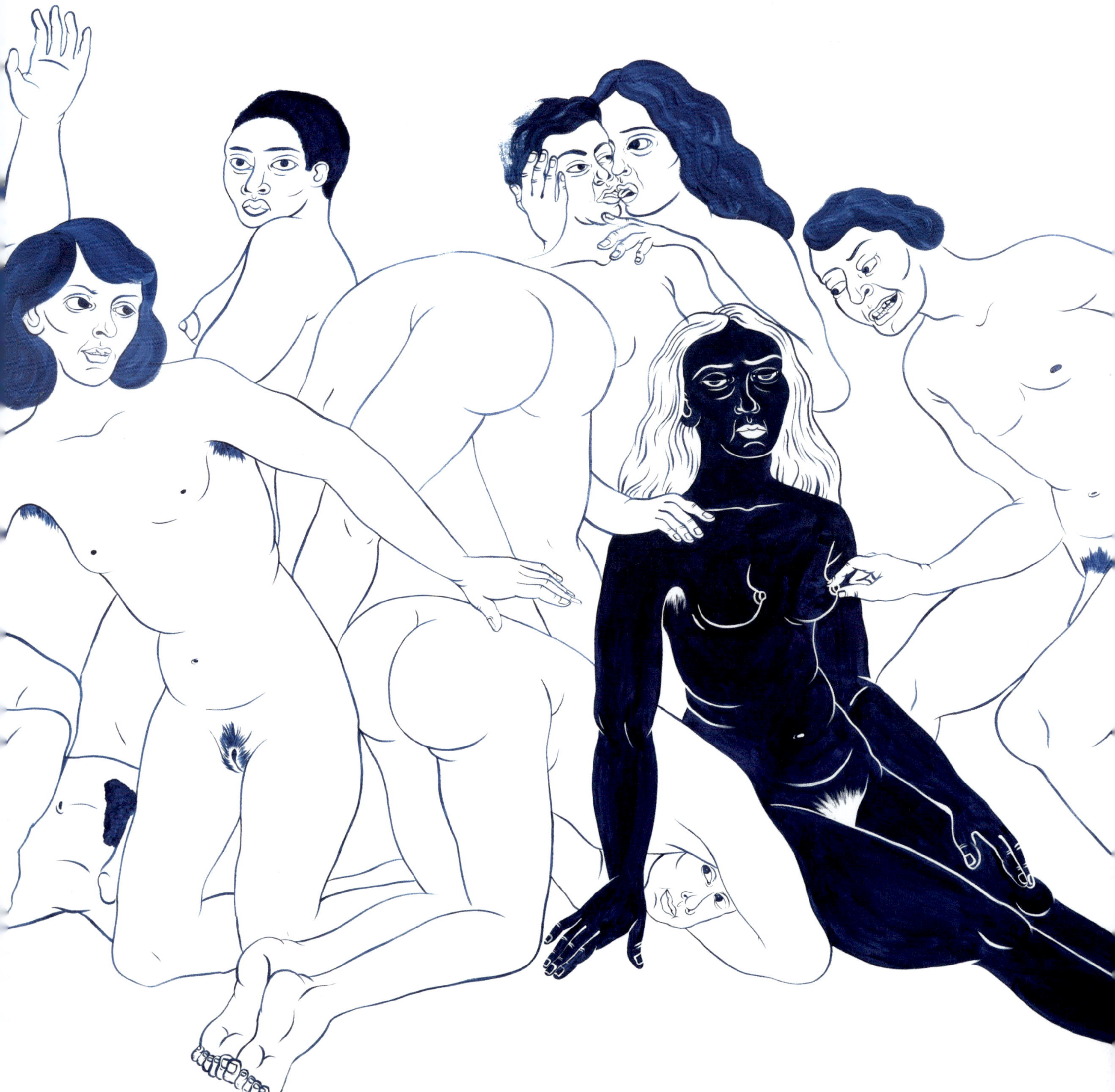

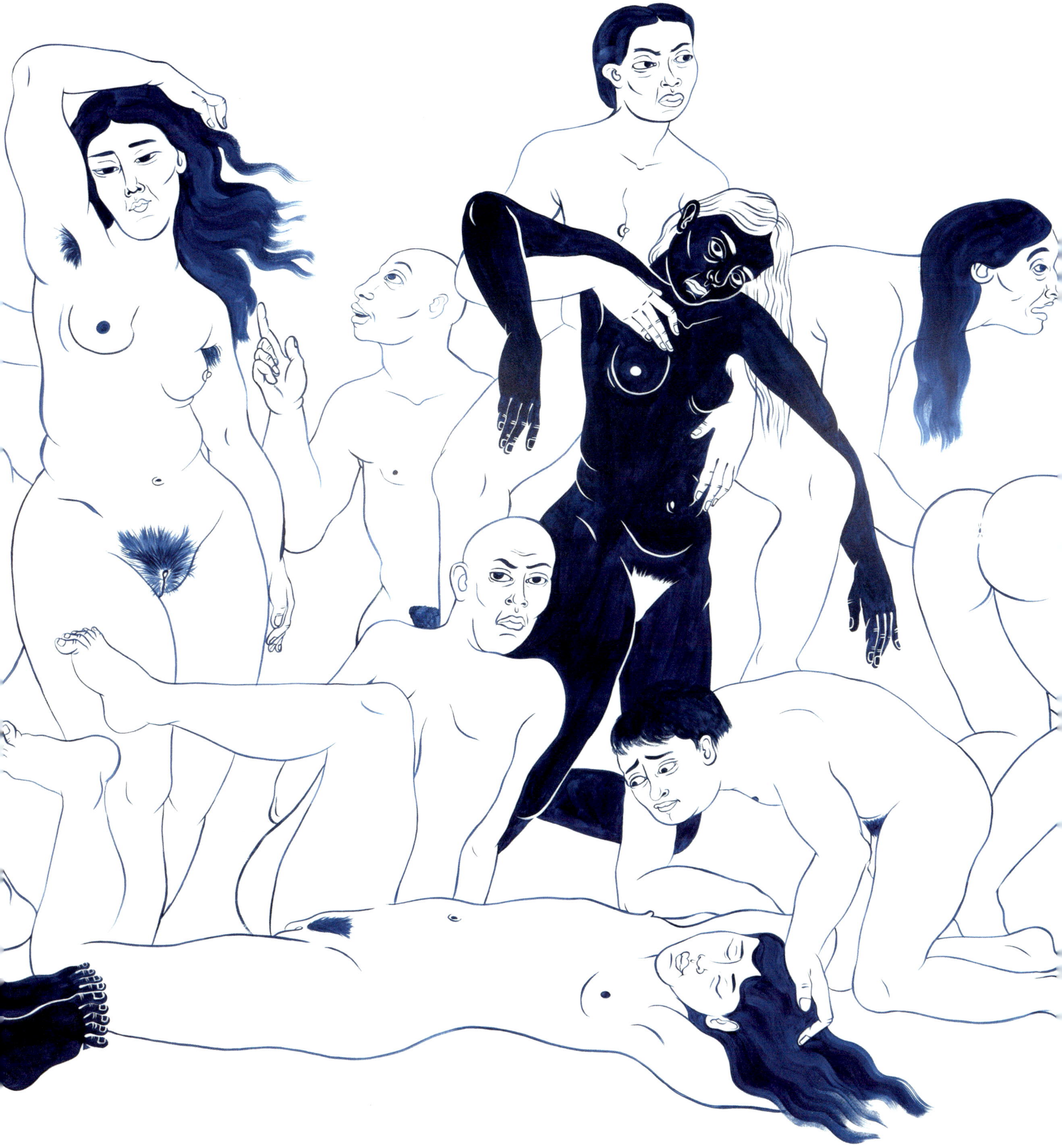

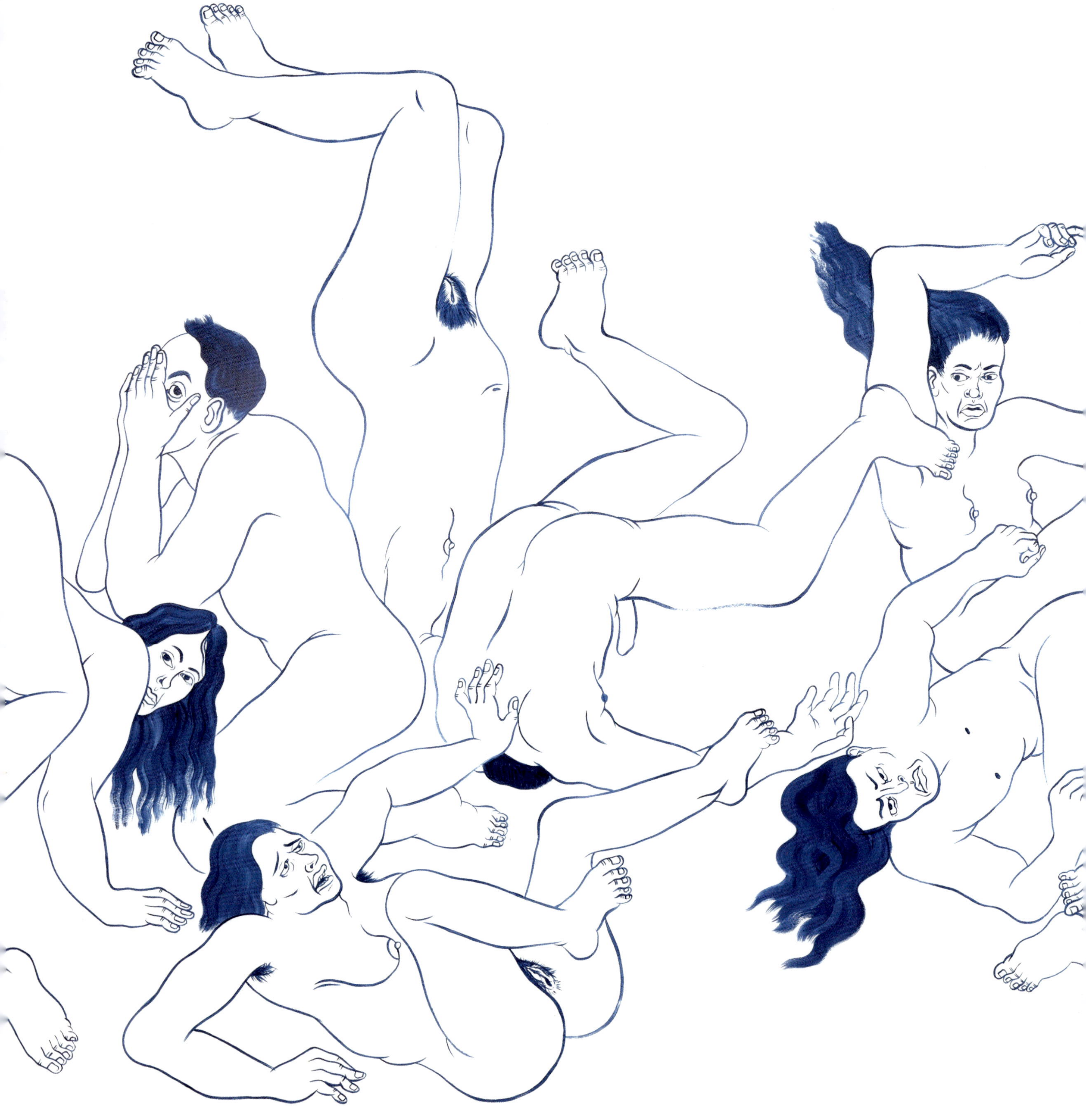

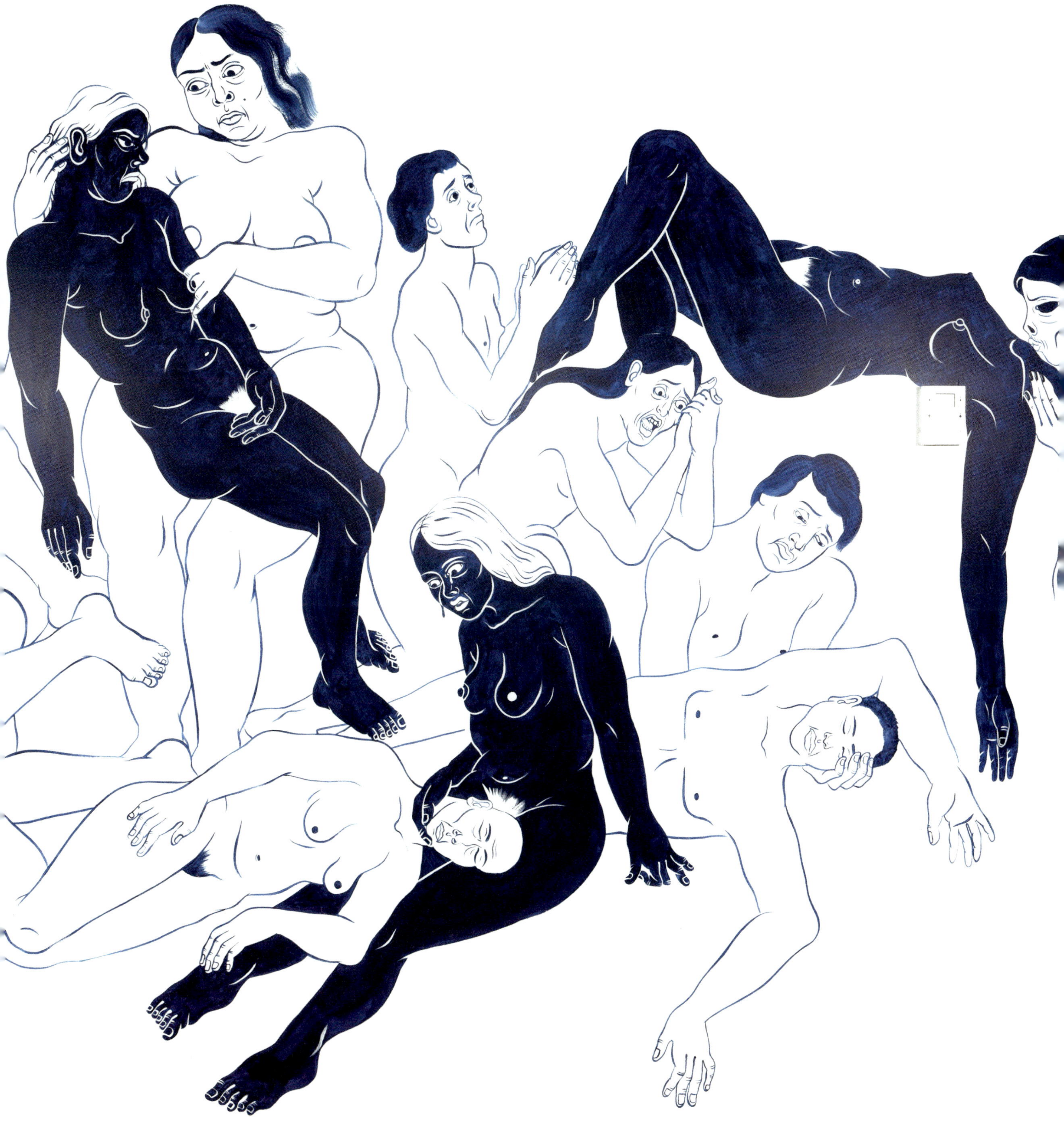

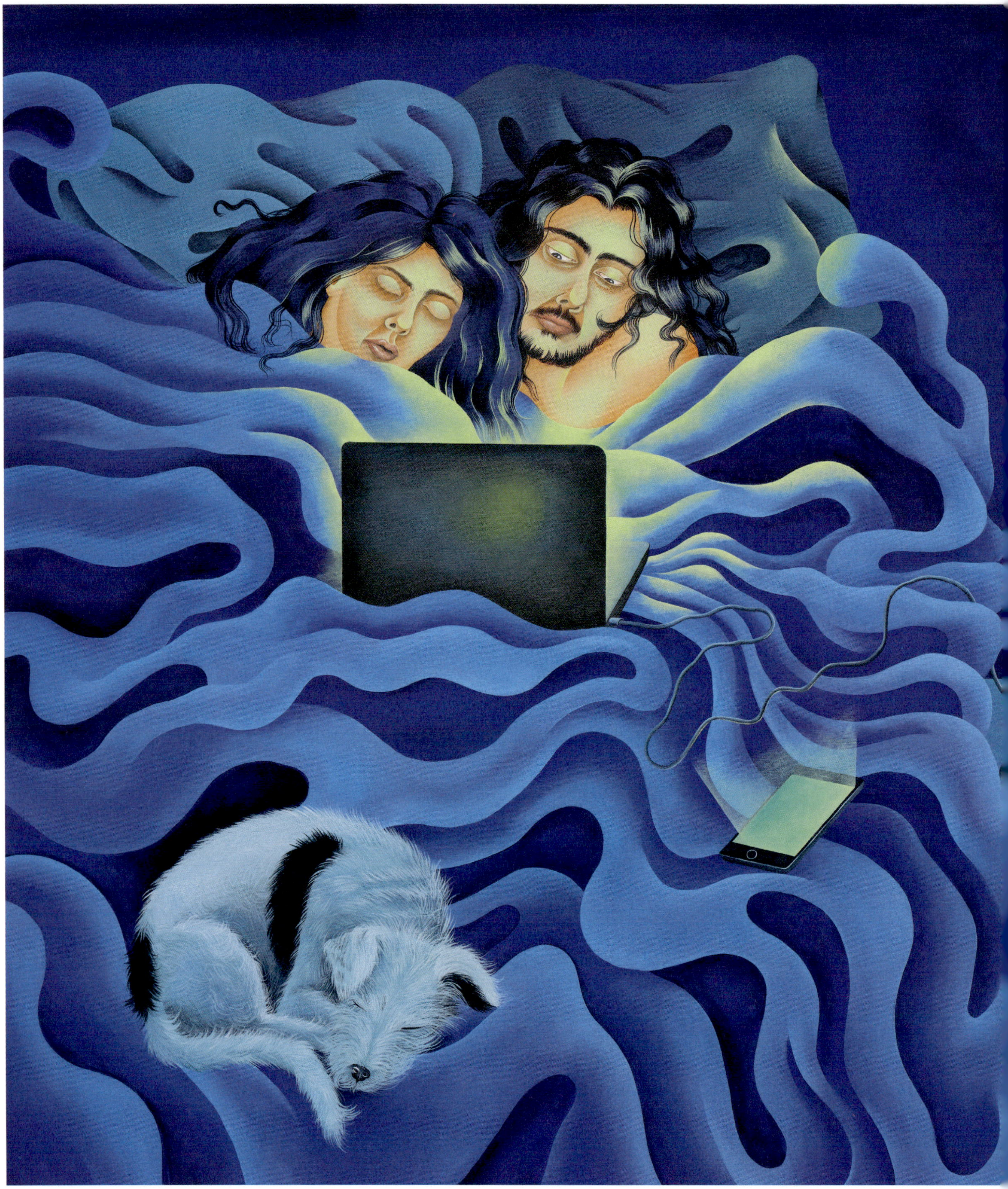

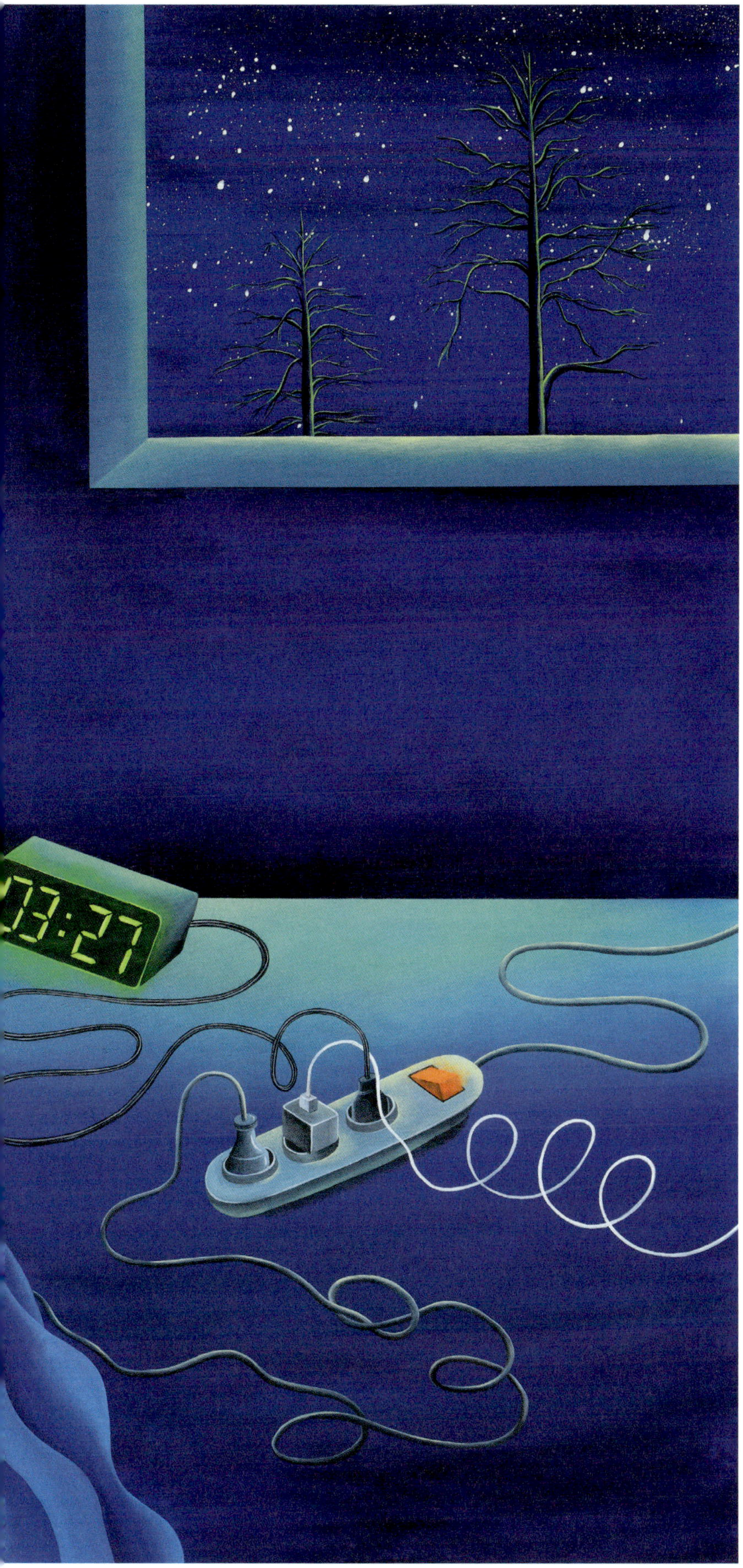

2023

Liminal Space

150 × 110 cm

40 × 30 cm

Moon Cave

2022

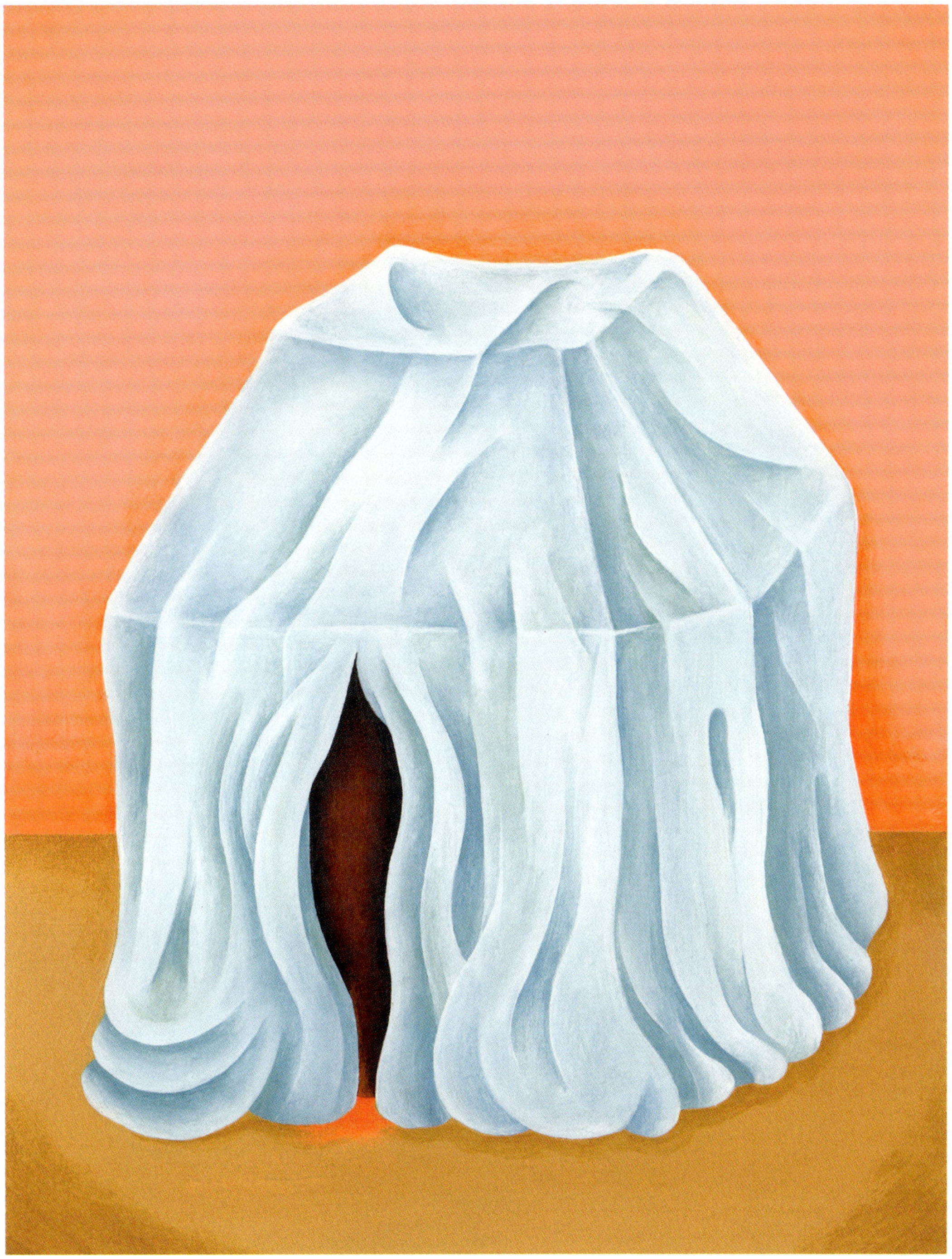

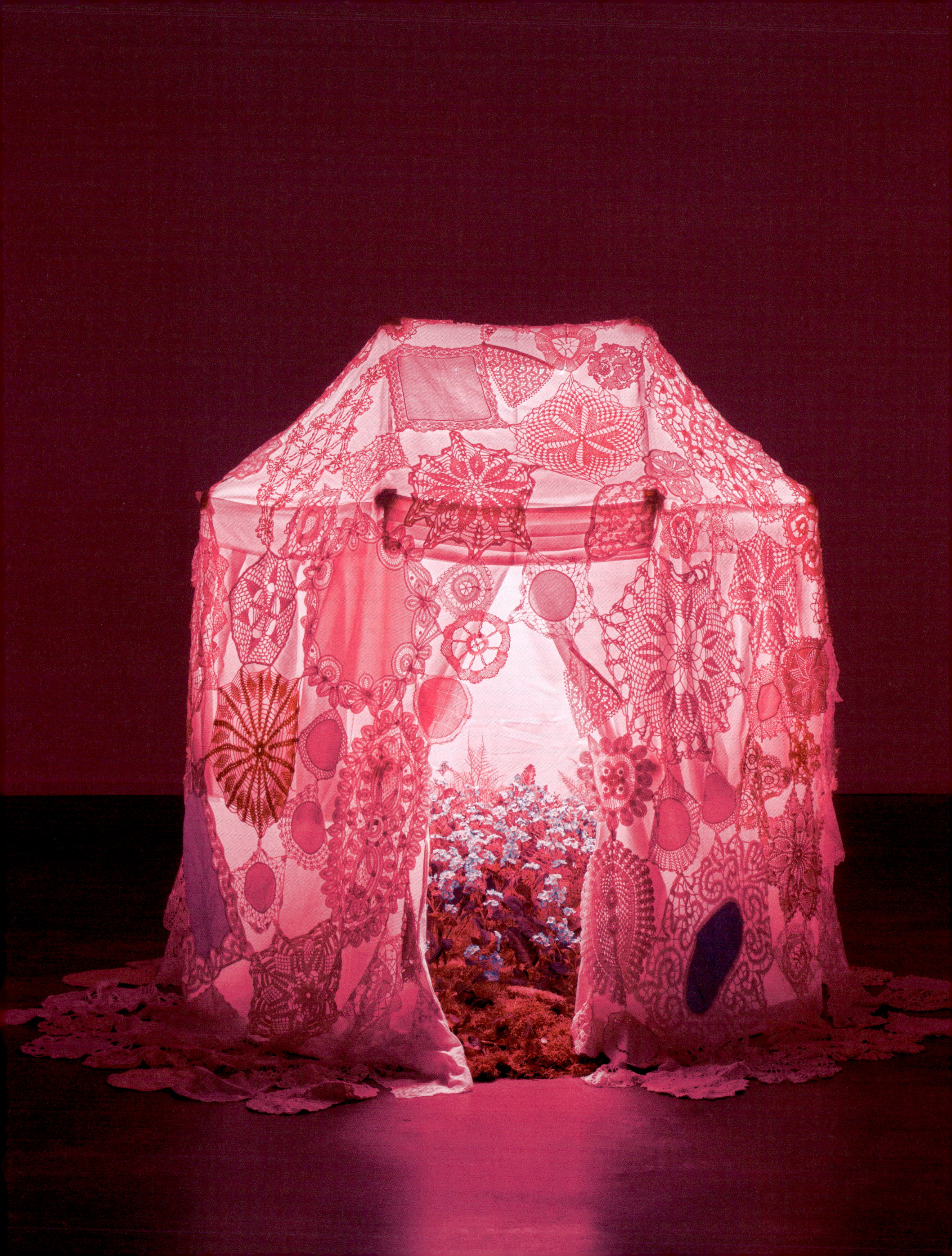

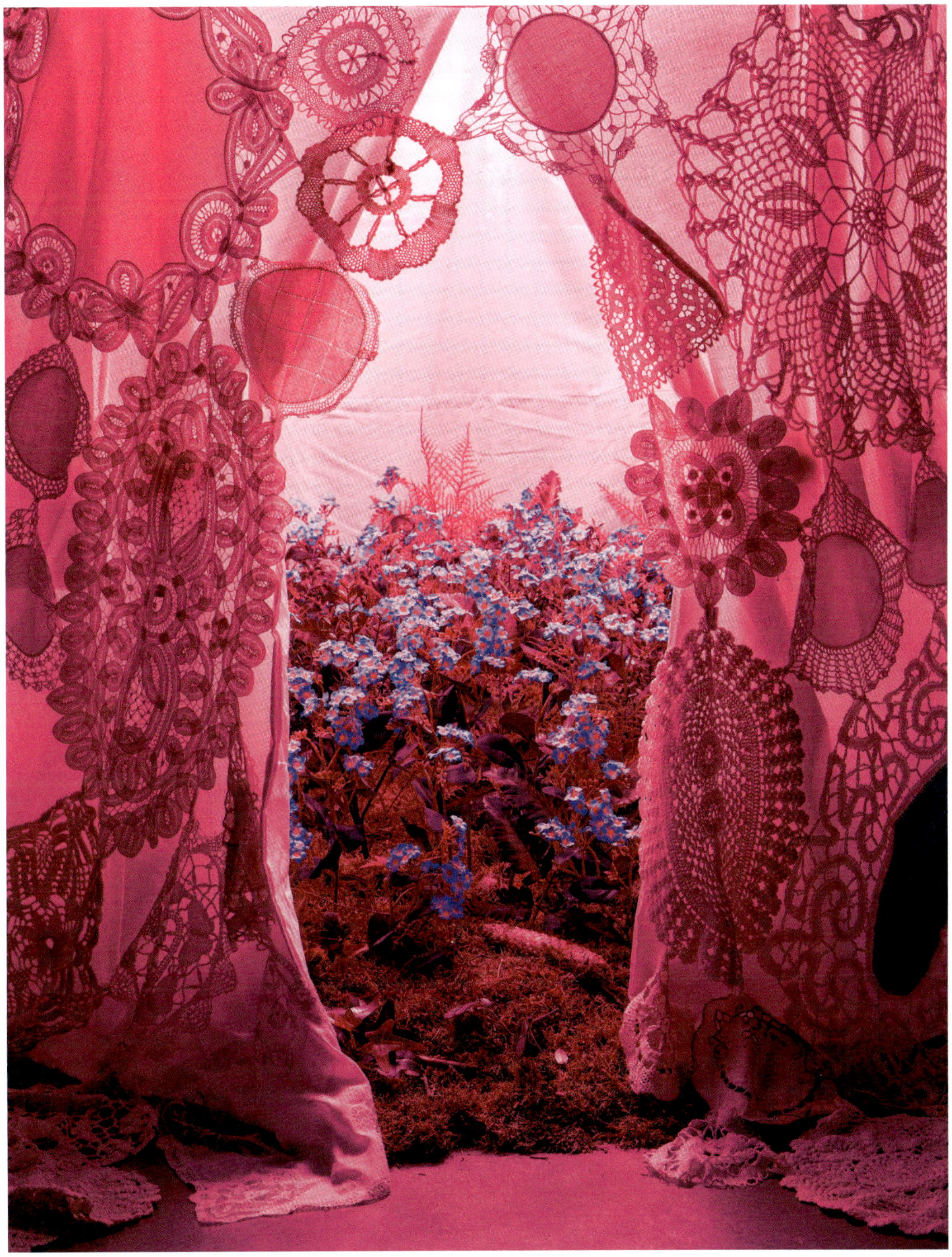

2022

Forget Me Not

135 × 130 × 150 cm

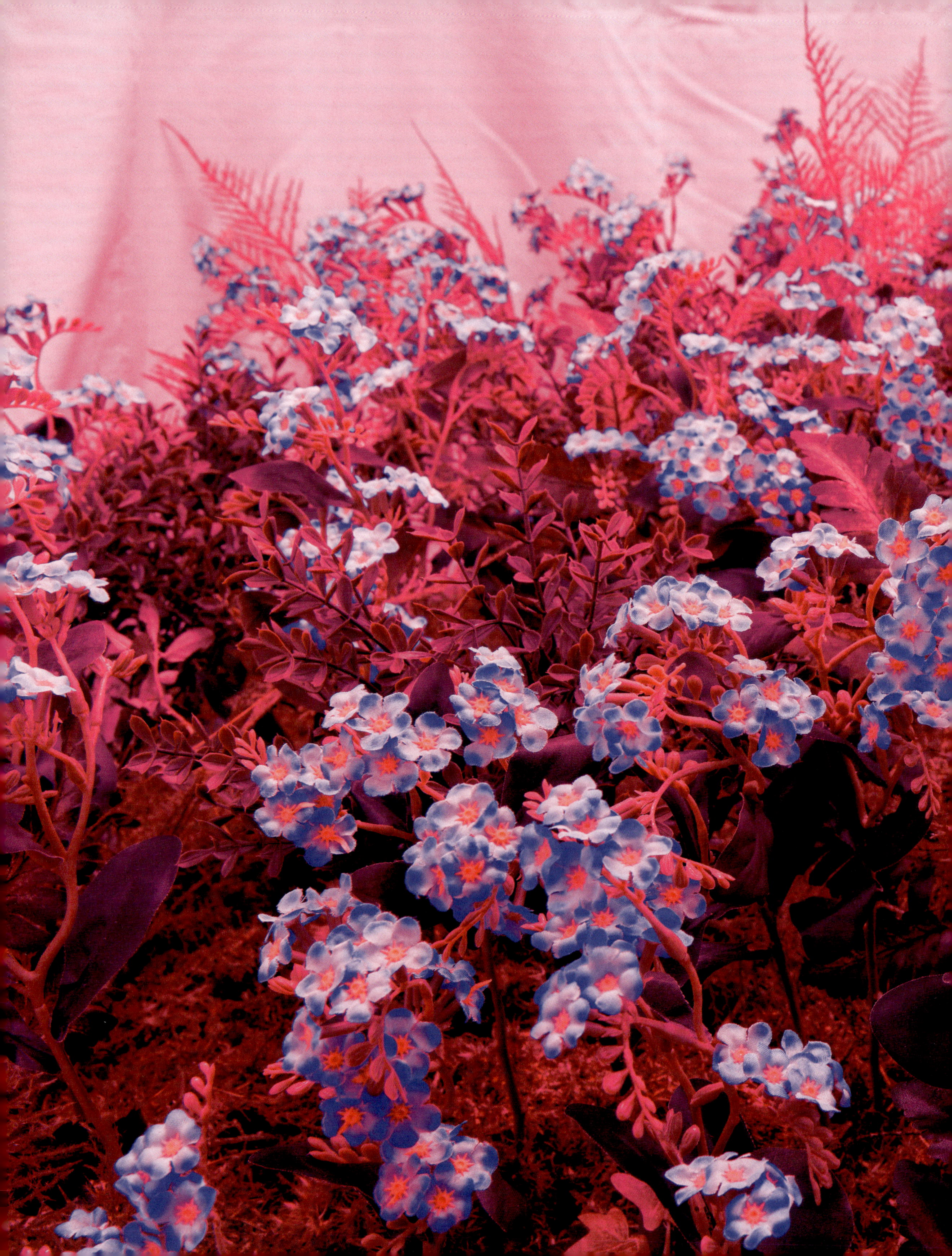

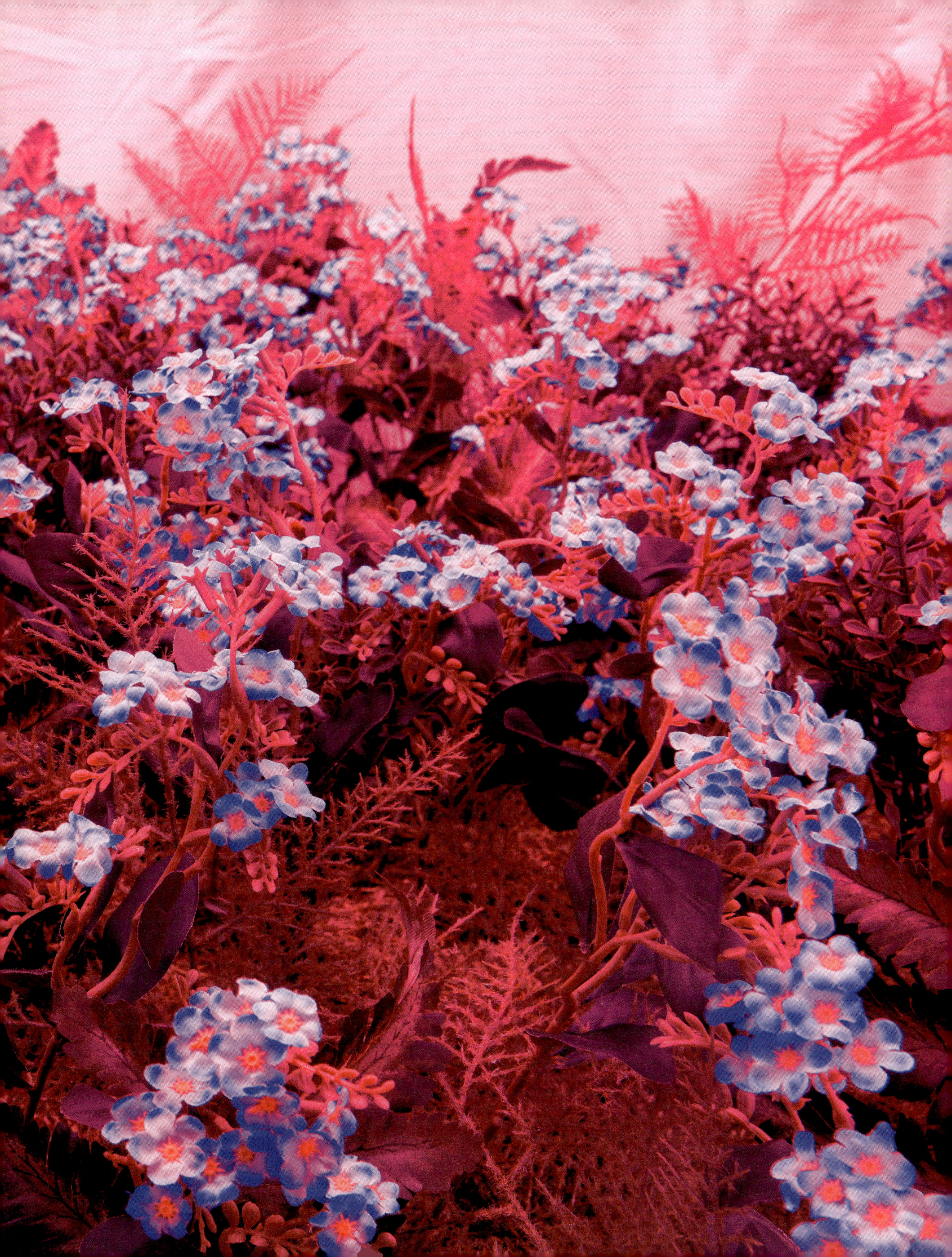

50 × 40 cm

Mother with Egg

2022

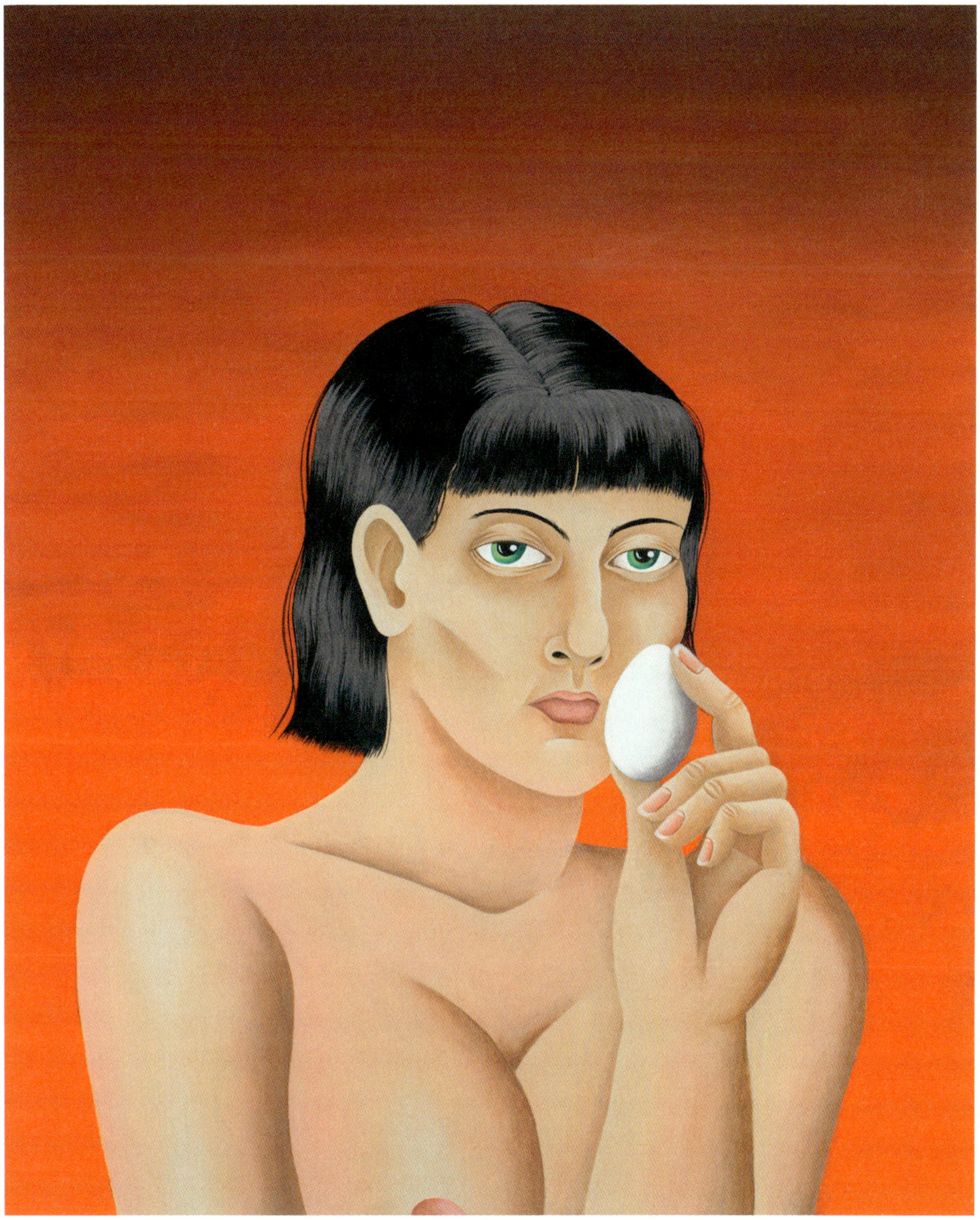

Egg Series

2022

31 × 25 cm (each)

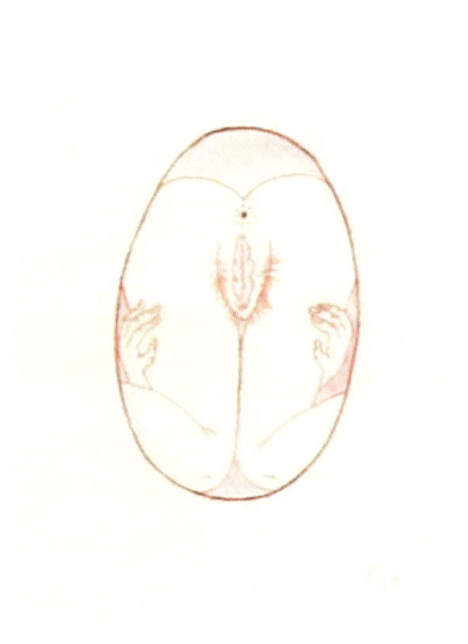

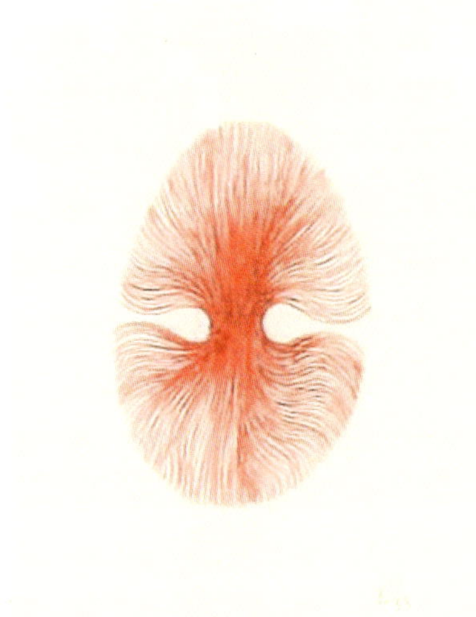

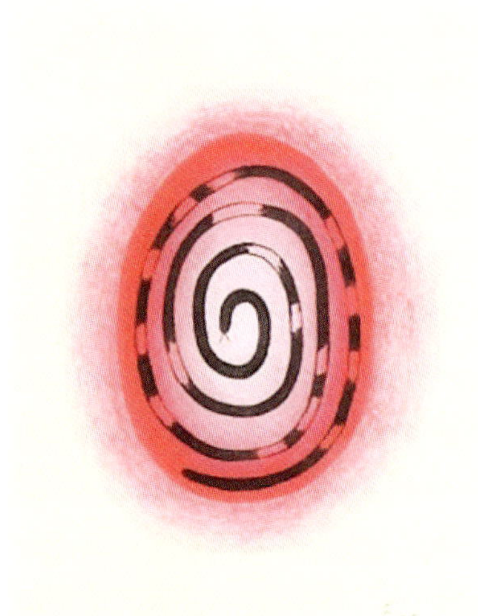

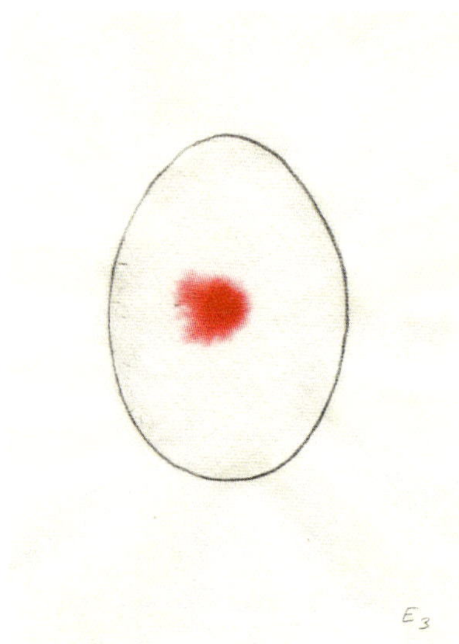

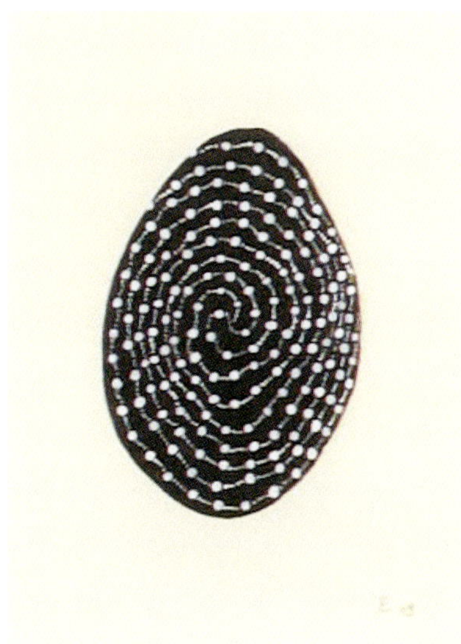

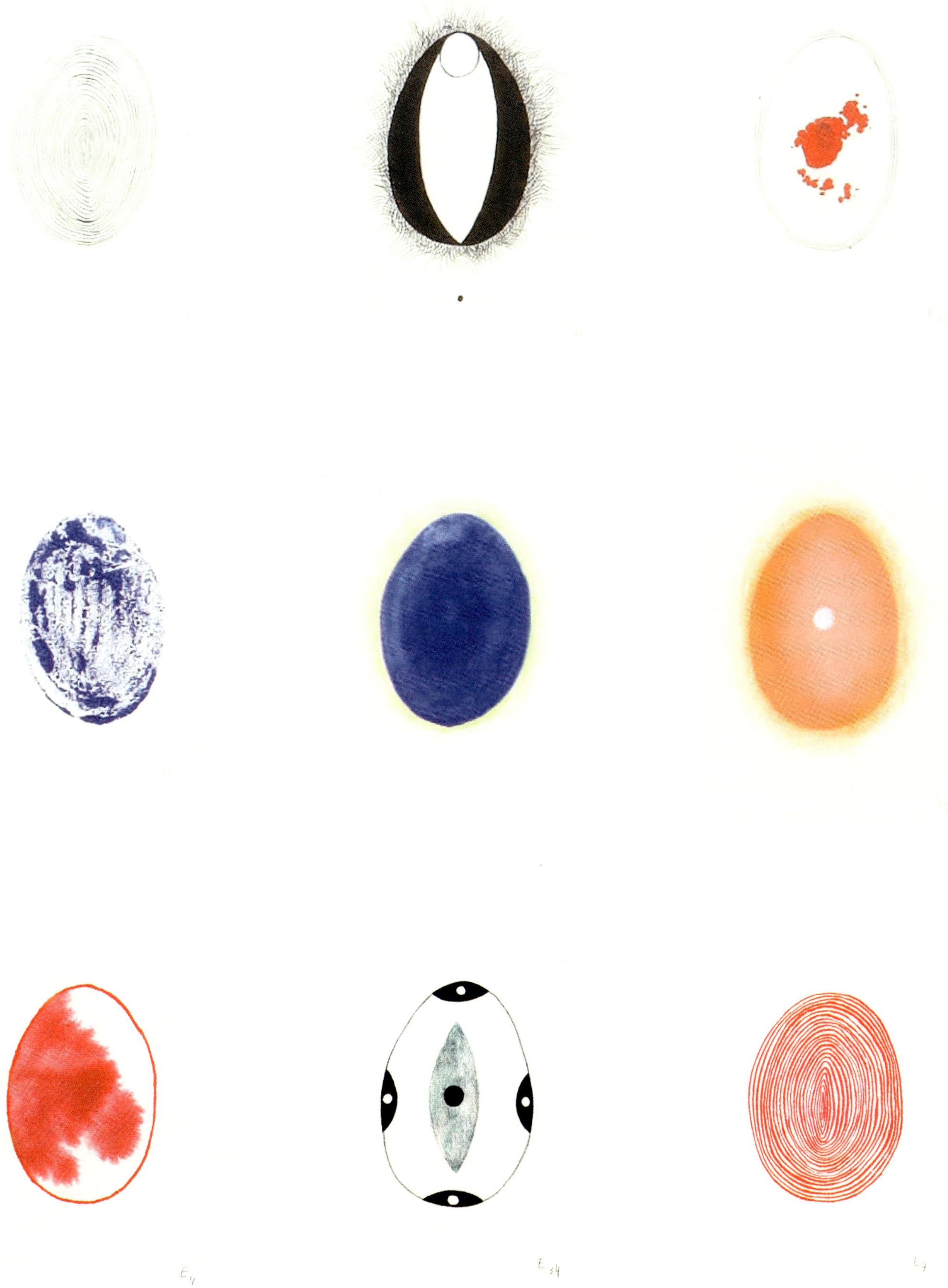

76 × 56 cm

Viva la Vida

2023

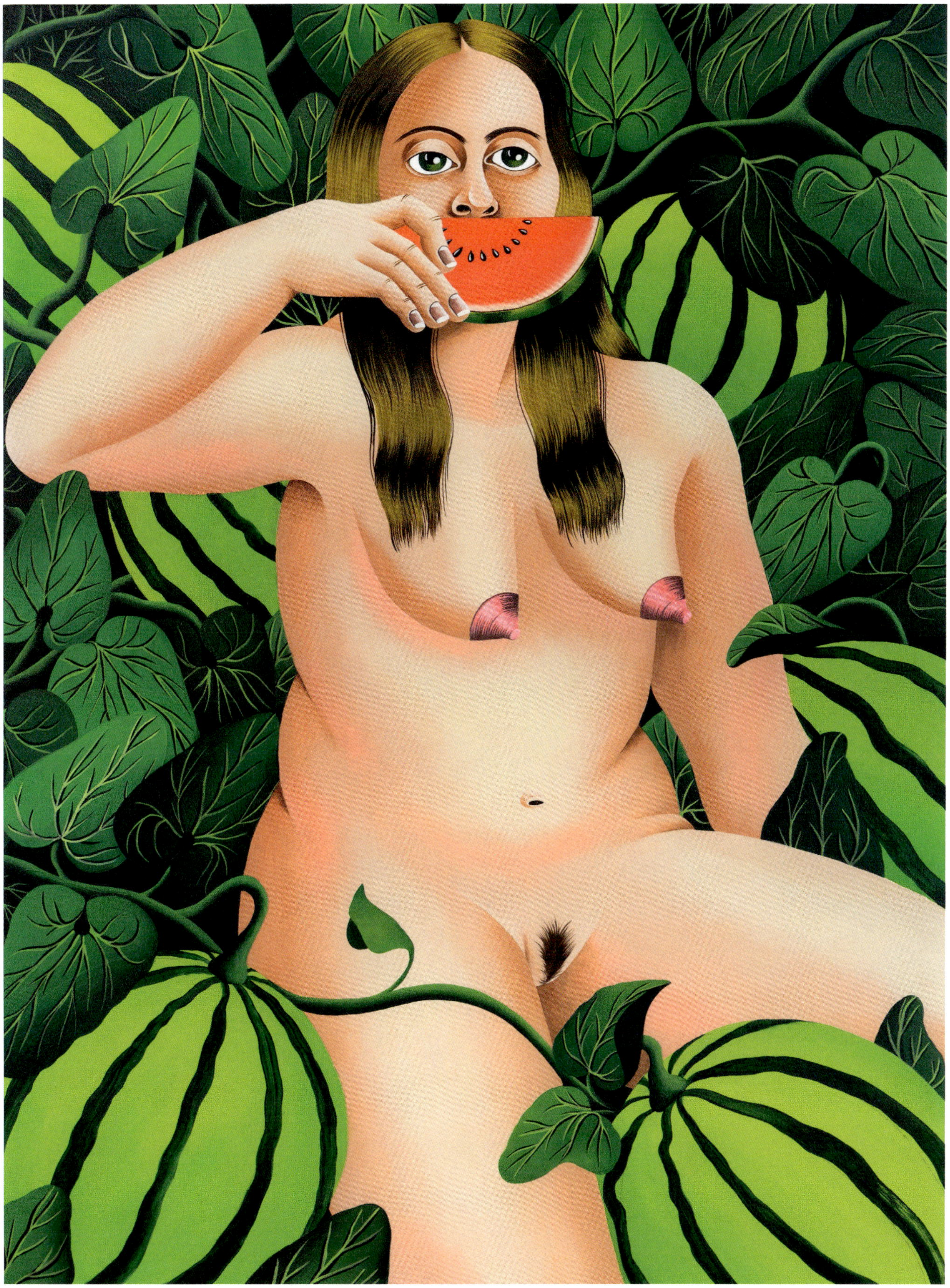

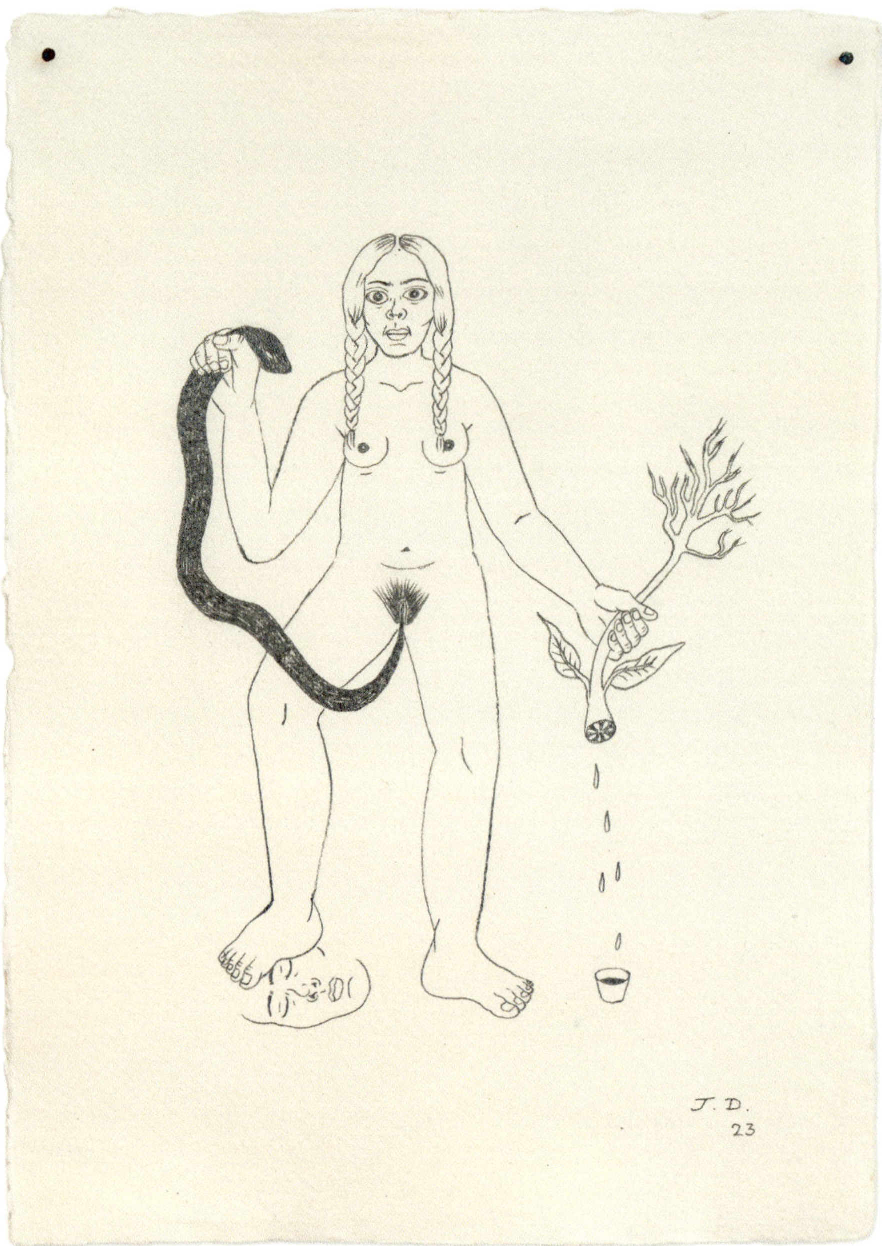

29.7 × 21 cm / 21 × 29.7 cm (each)

Reincarnation (series) [pp. 52–9]

2023

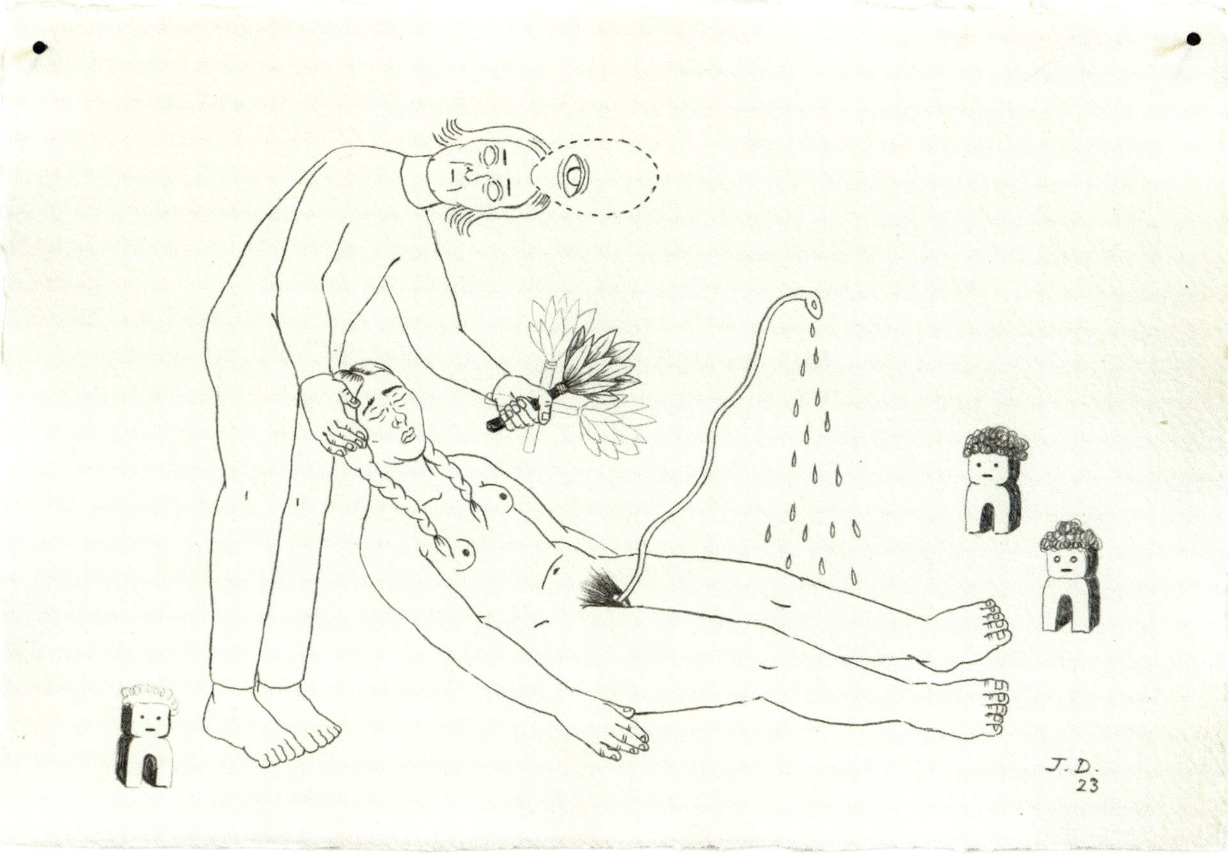
J.D.
23

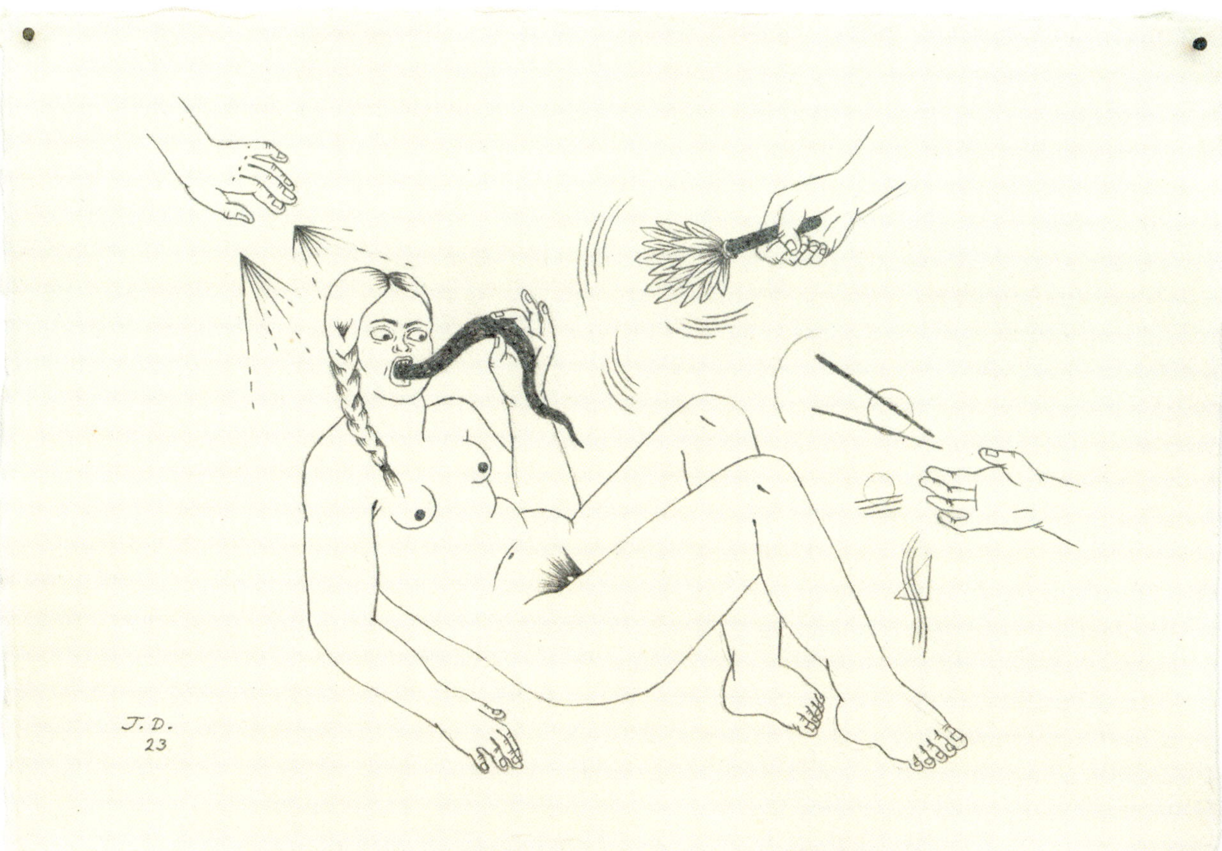
J.D.
23

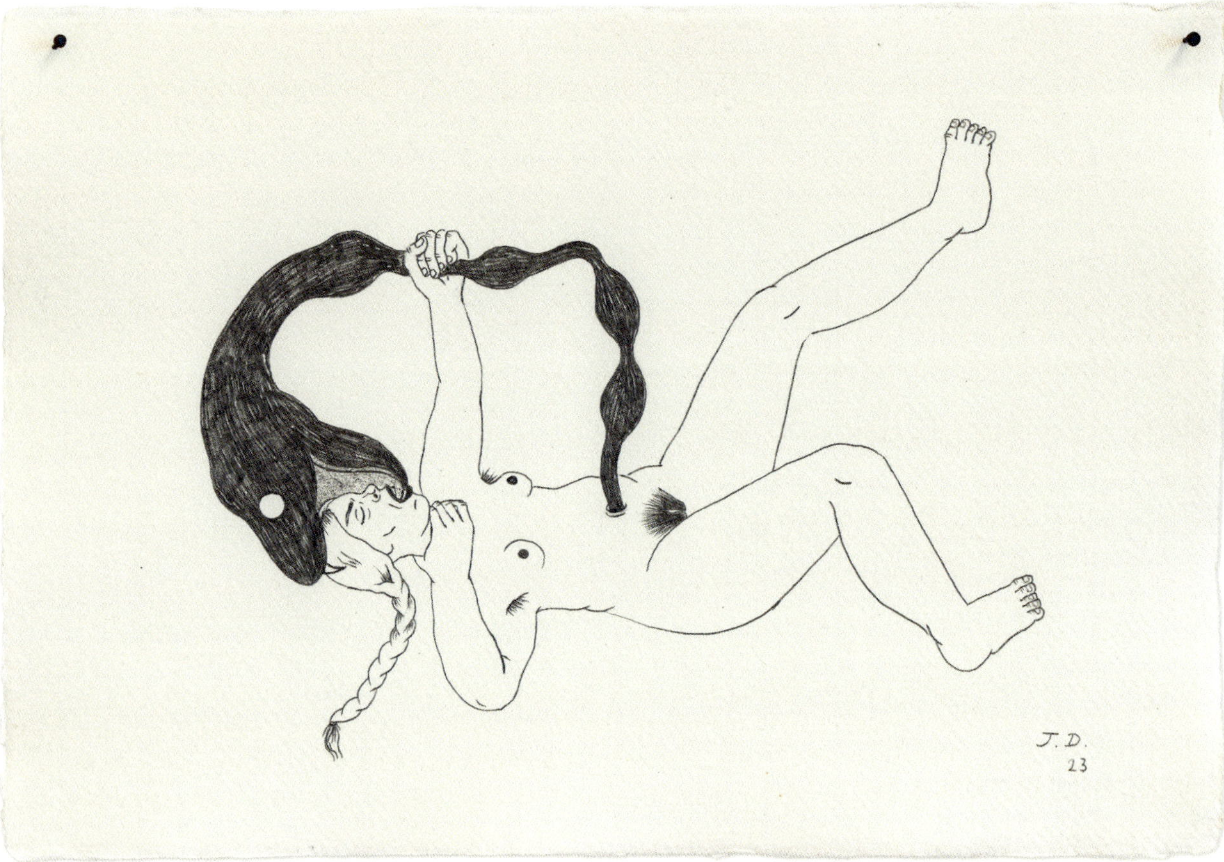
J.D.
23

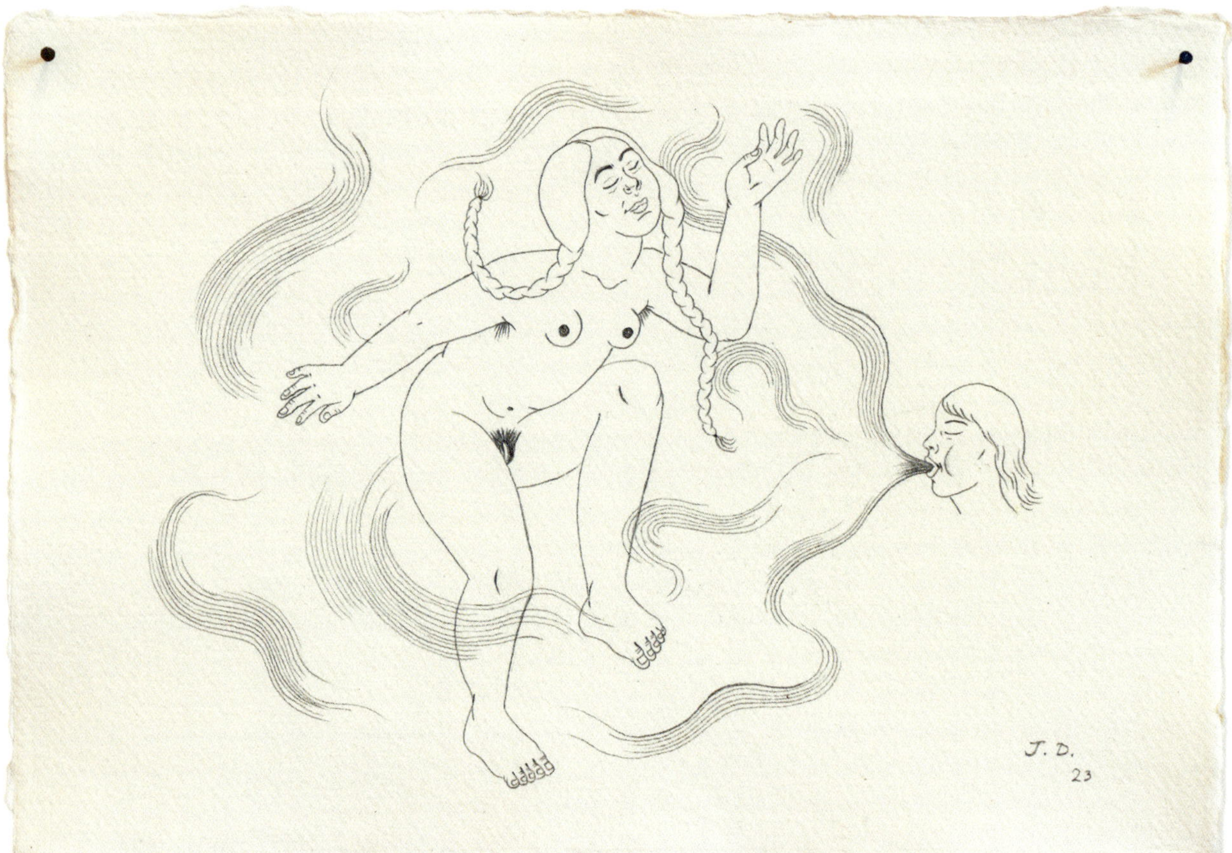
J.D.
23

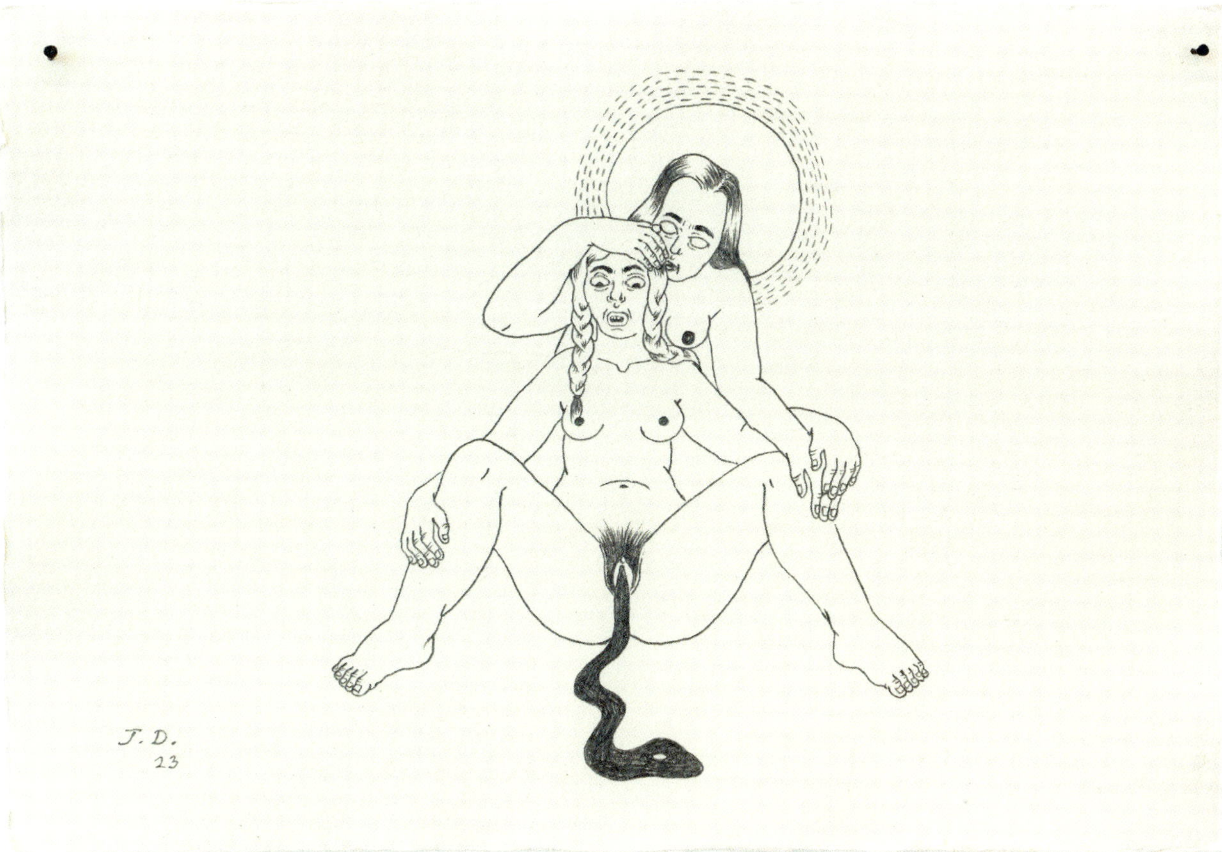
J.D.
23

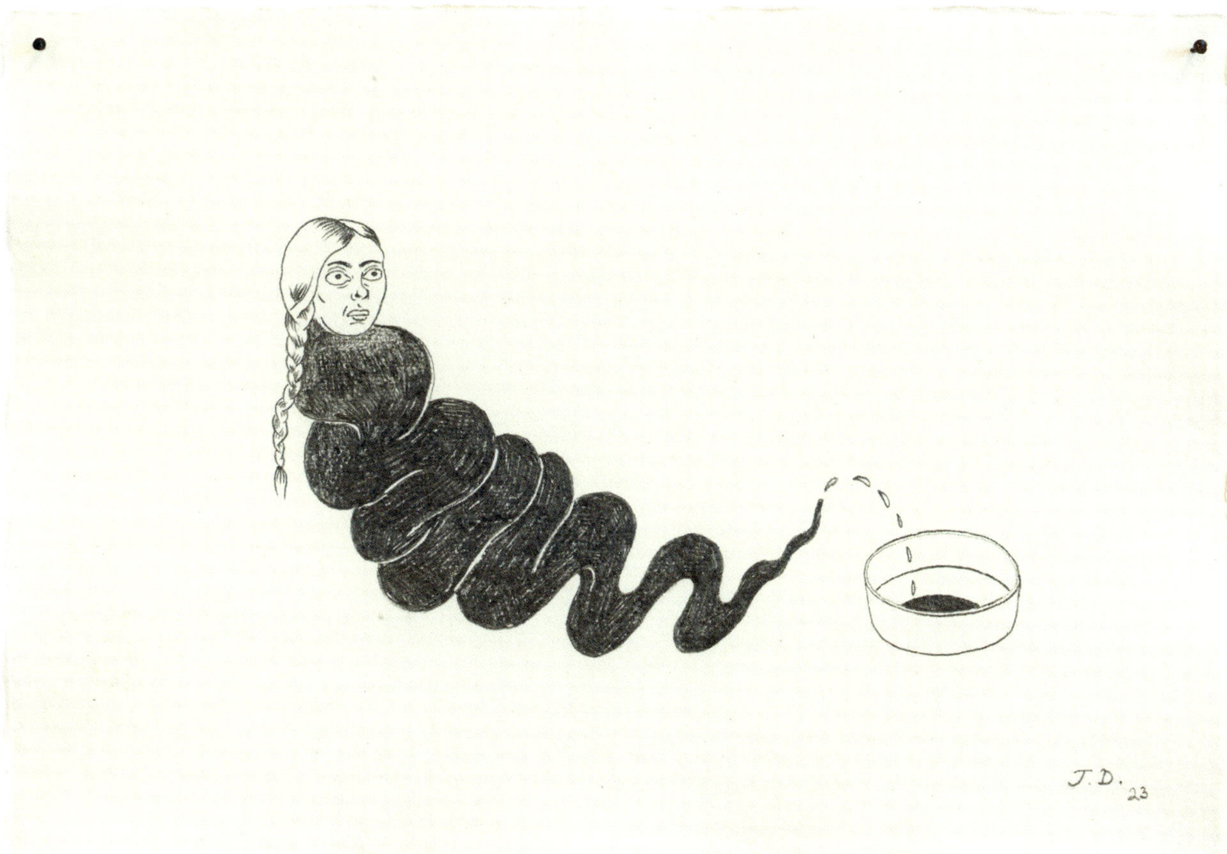
J.D.
23

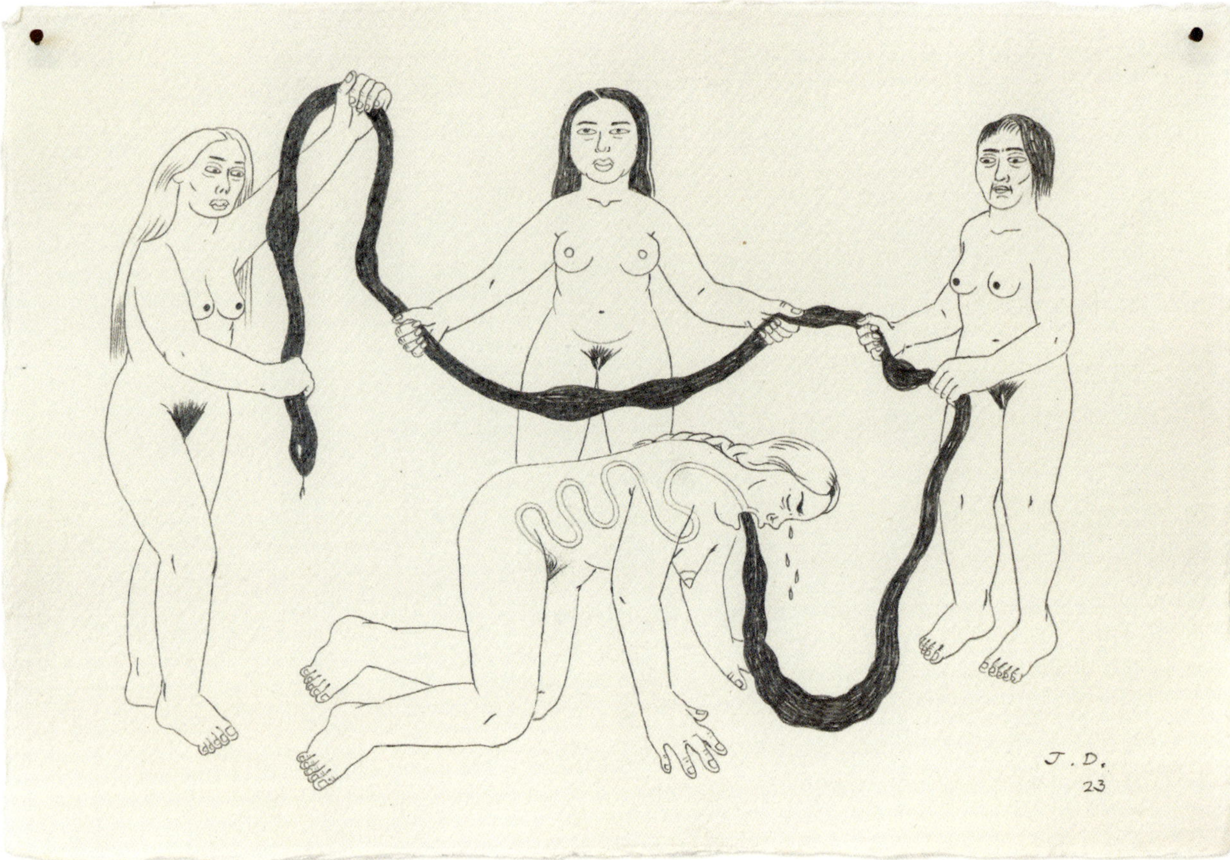
J. D.
23

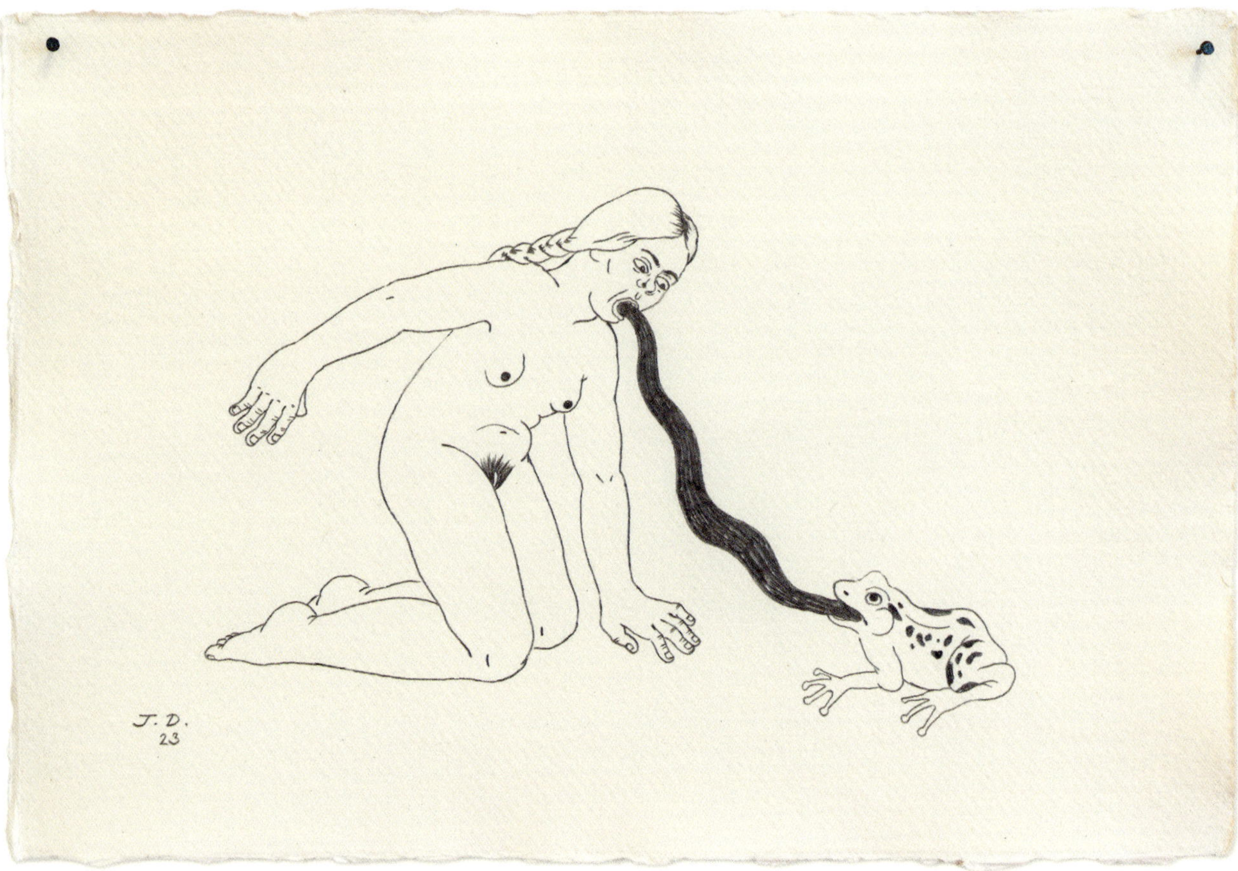
J. D.
23

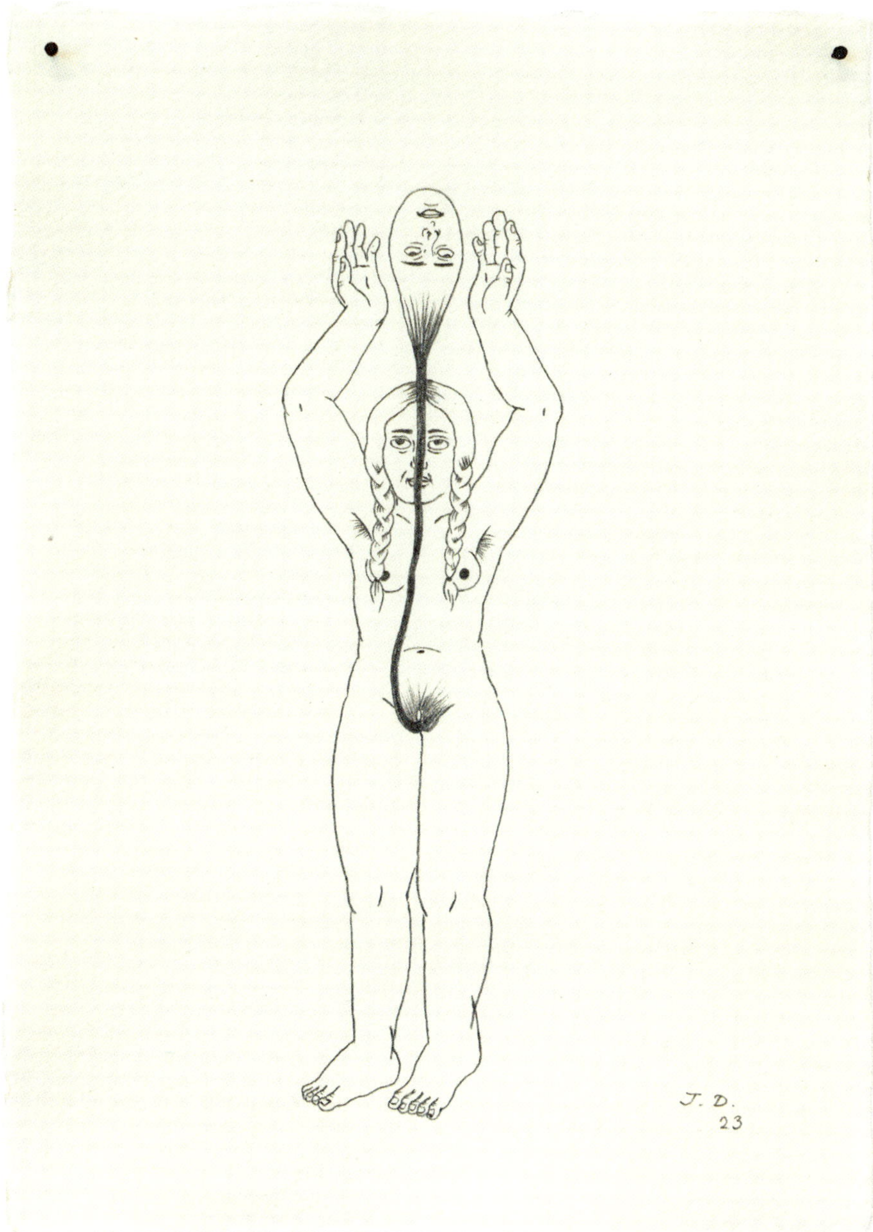
J. D.
23

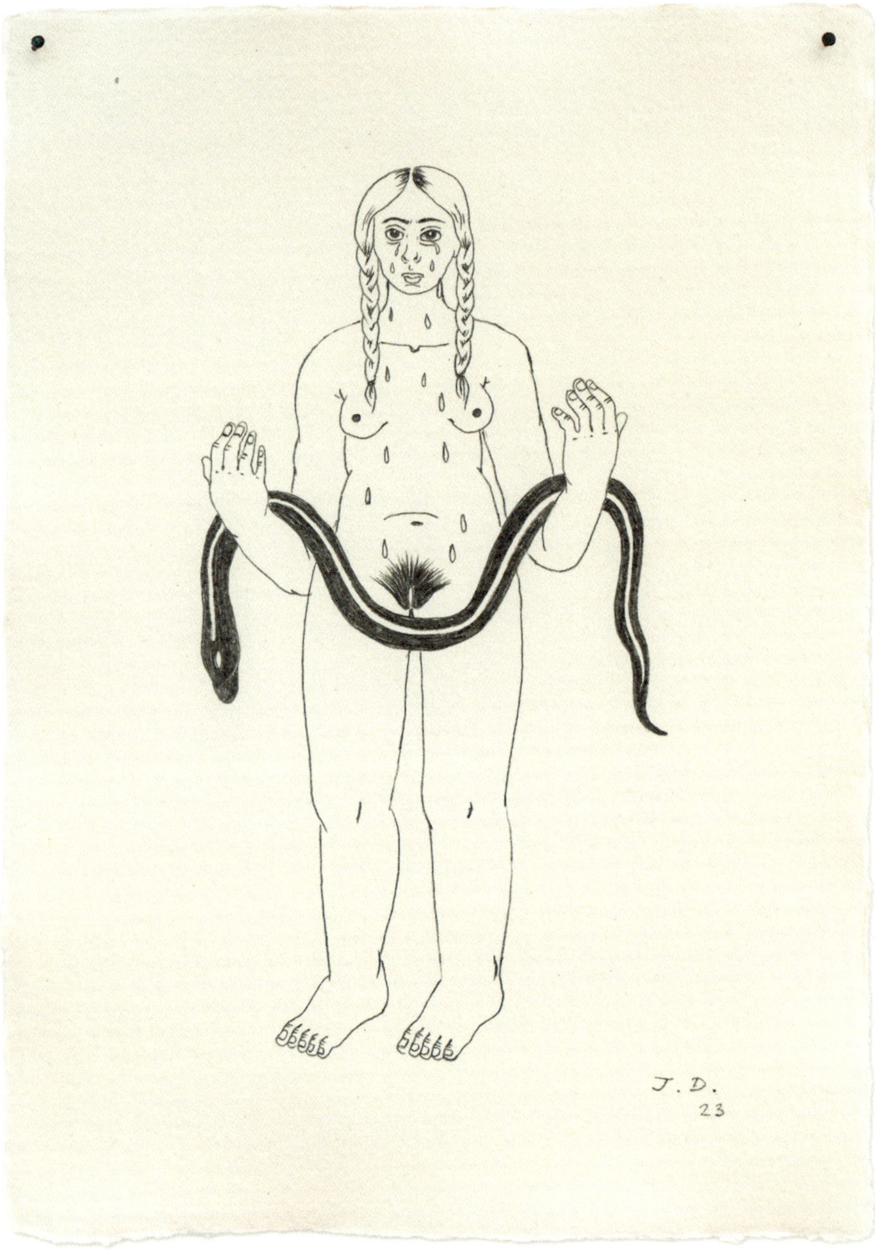
J.D.
23

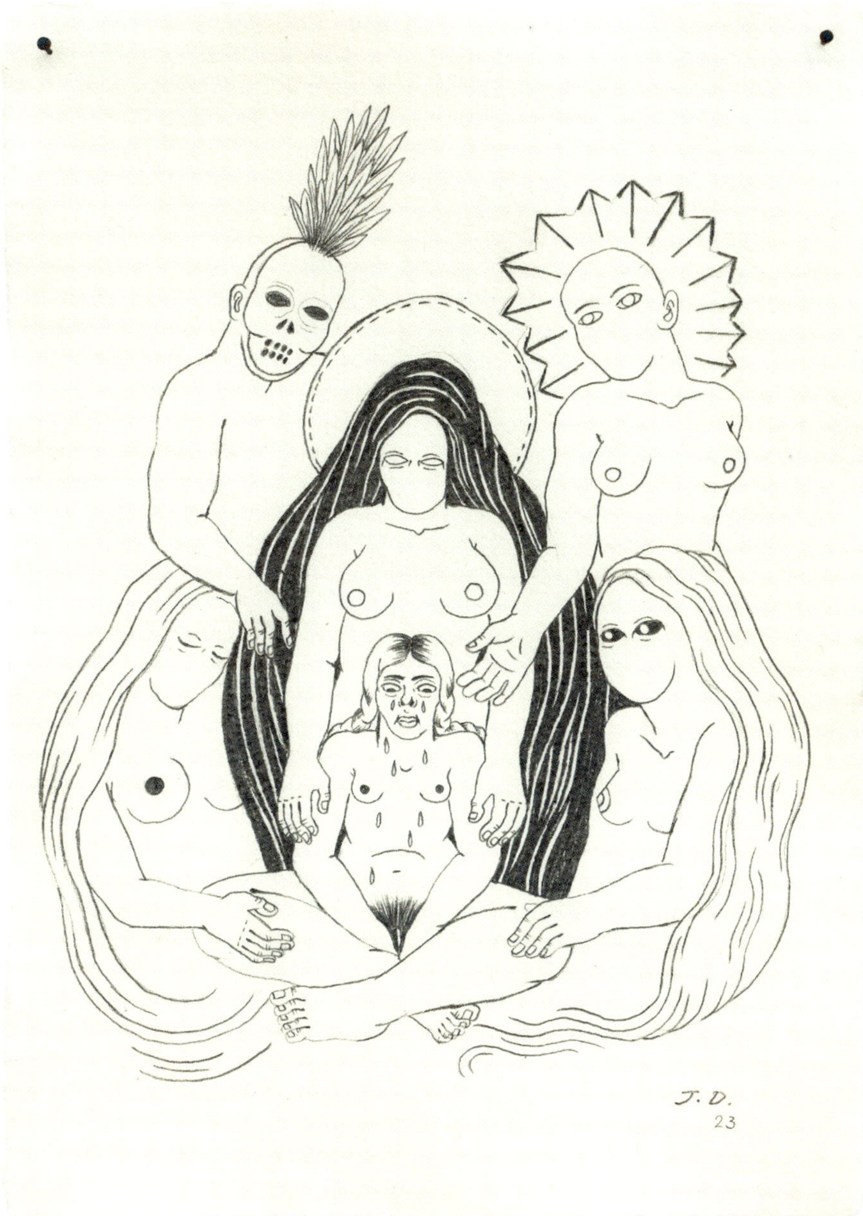
J.D.
23

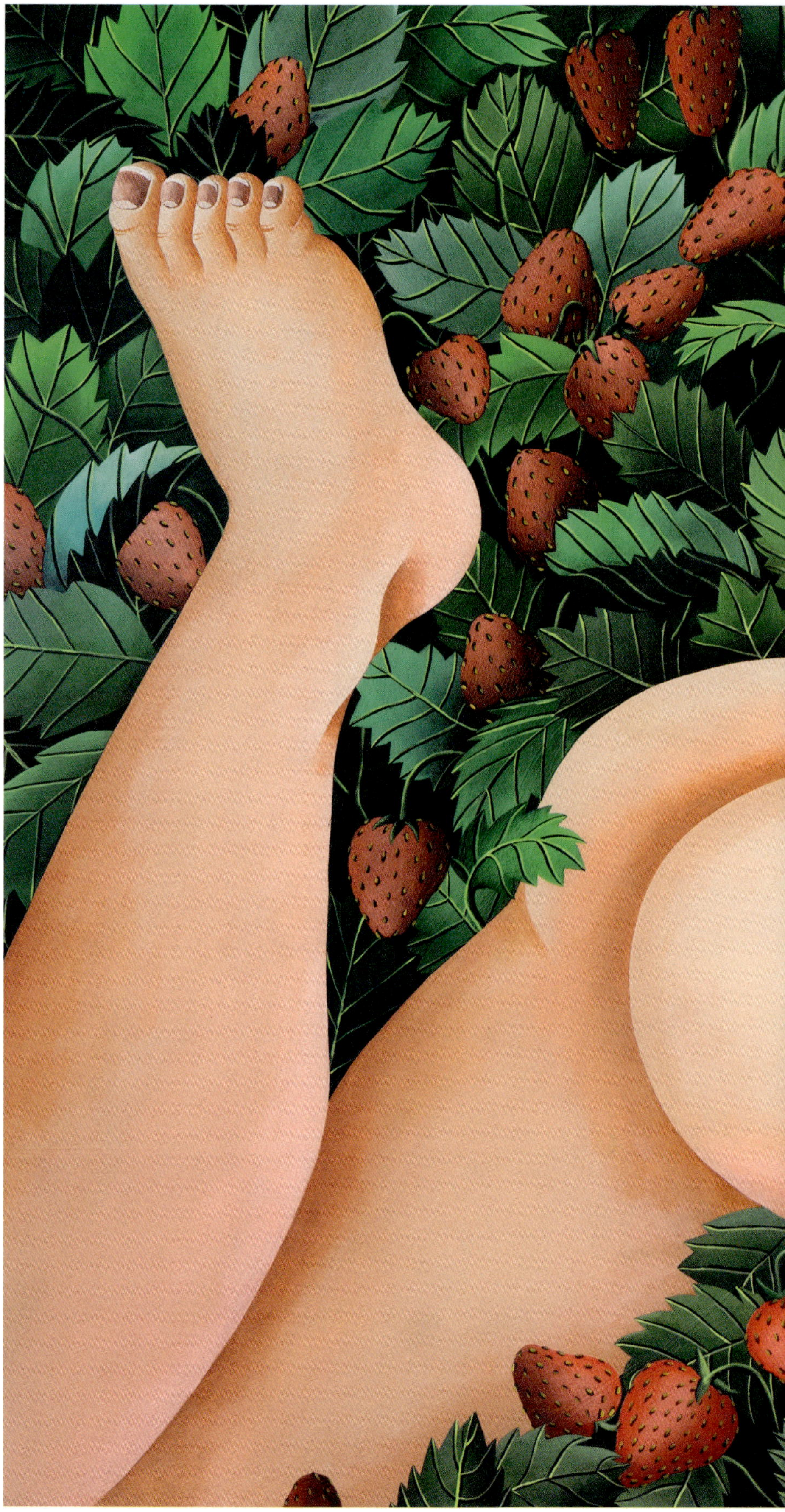

One Summer Day when I Went into My Garden

2023

56 × 76 cm

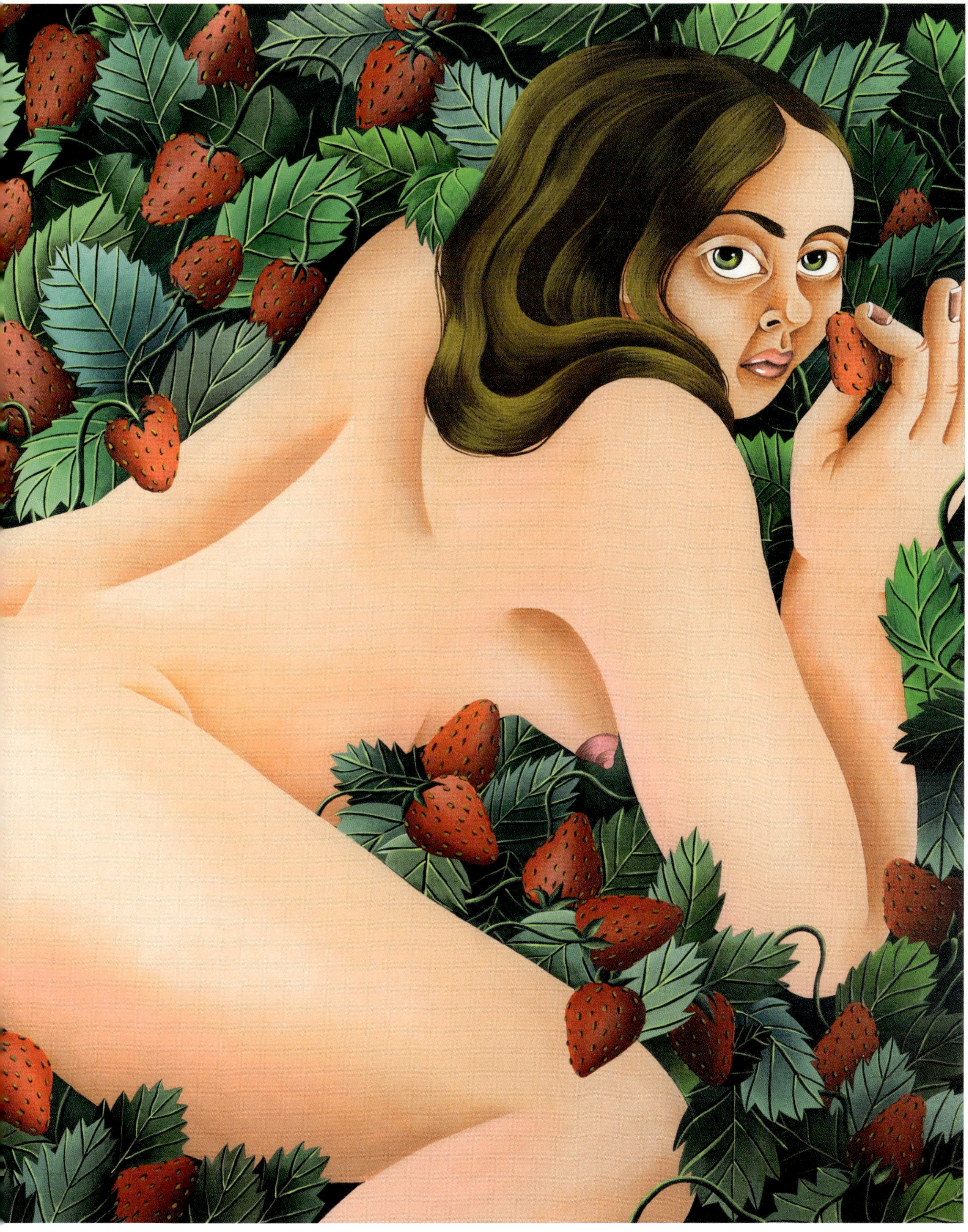

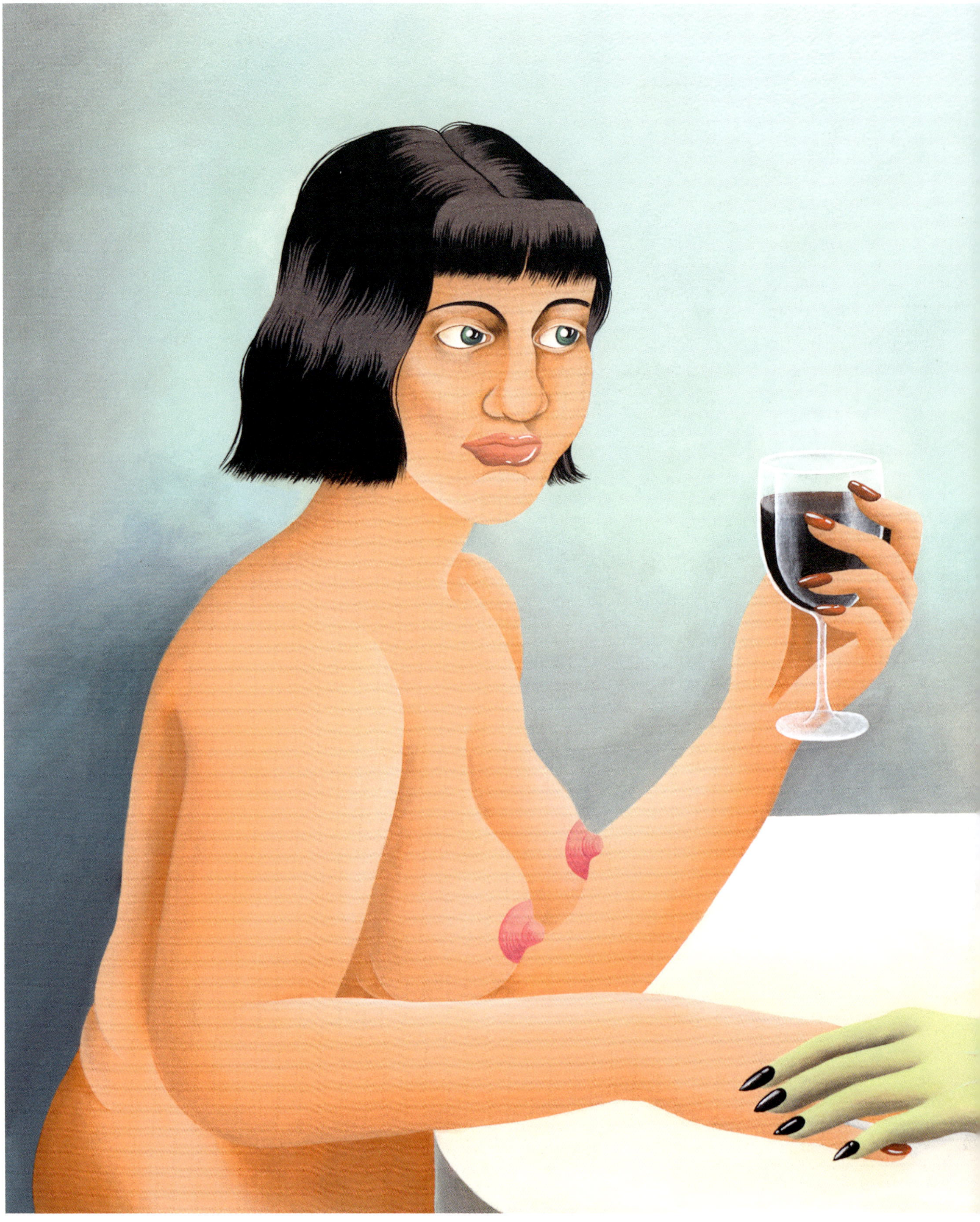

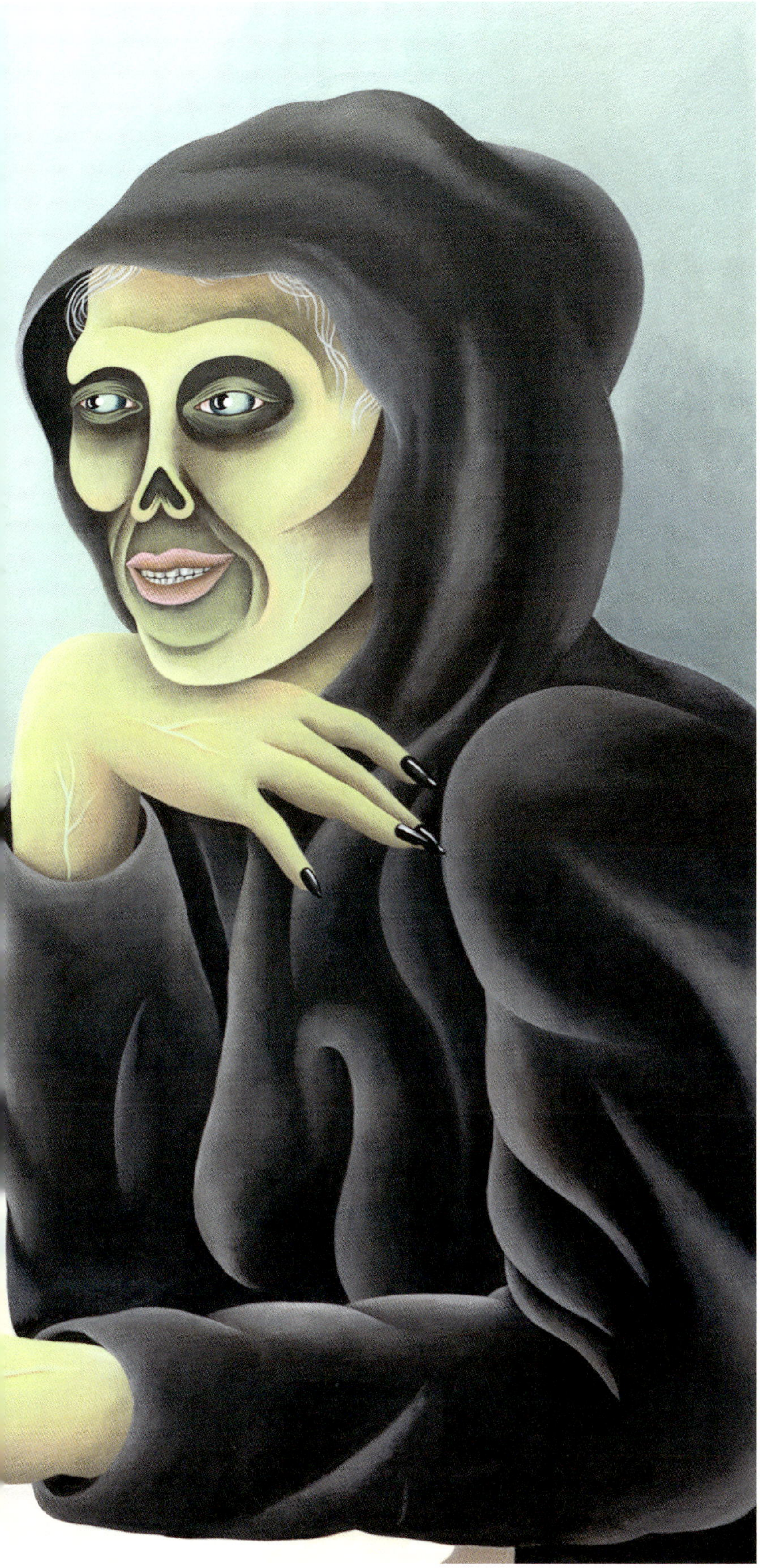

2022

Let Me Finish My Drink First (Homage to Nicole Eisenman)

60 × 80 cm

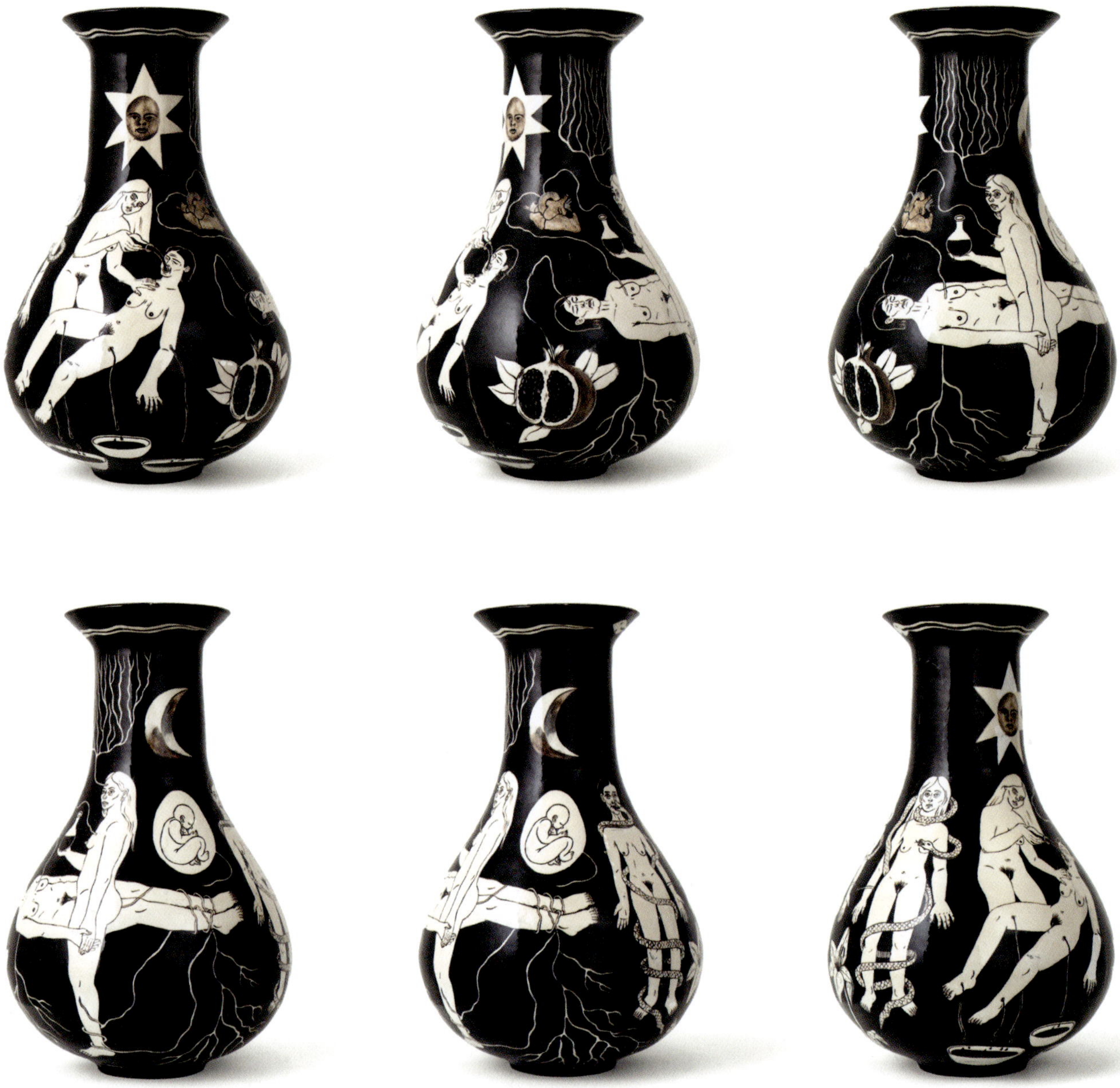

Elixir of Life

2022

38 × 25 × 25 cm

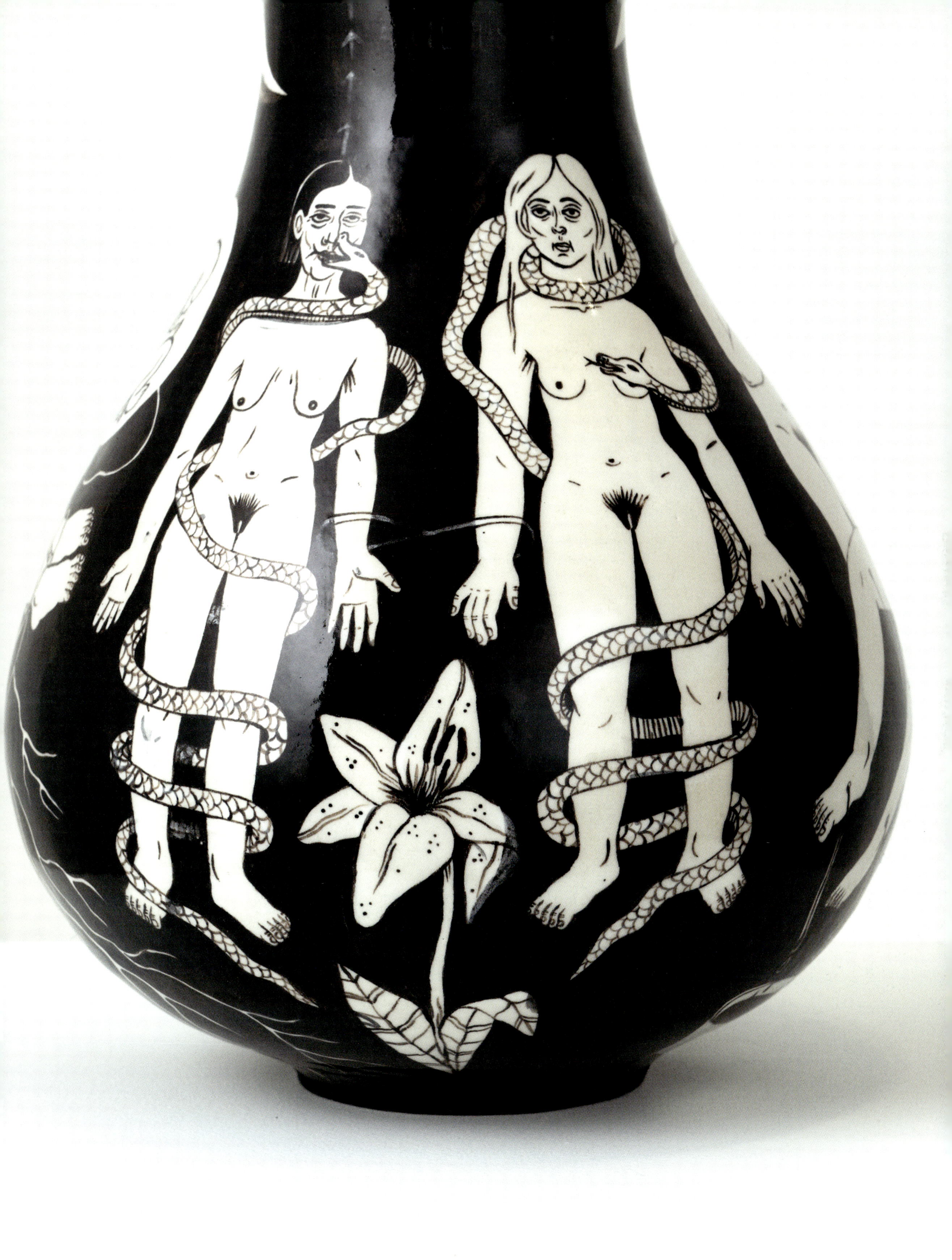

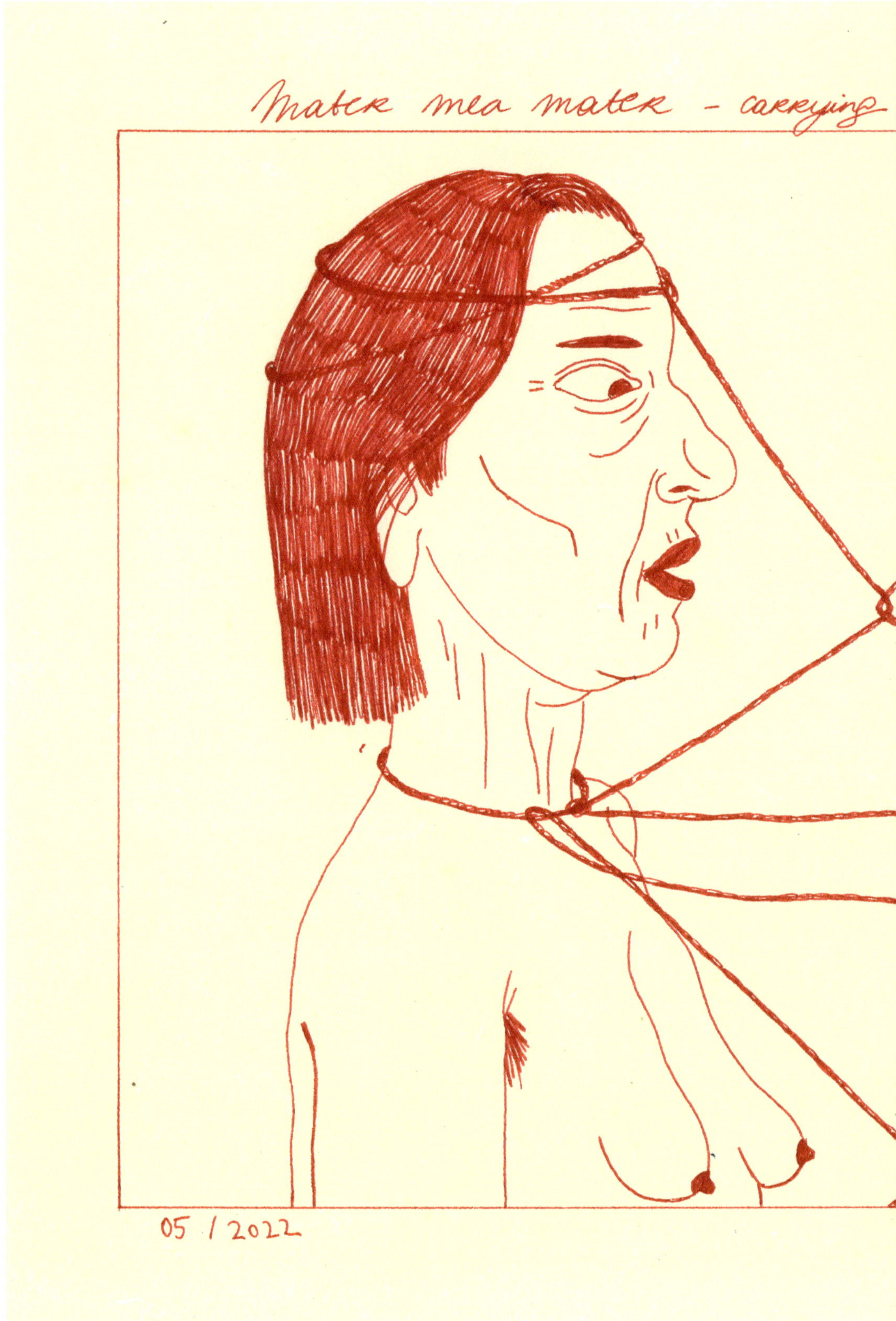

Mater Mea Mater, Carrying On Mother's Wisdom

2022

21.4 × 31.5 cm

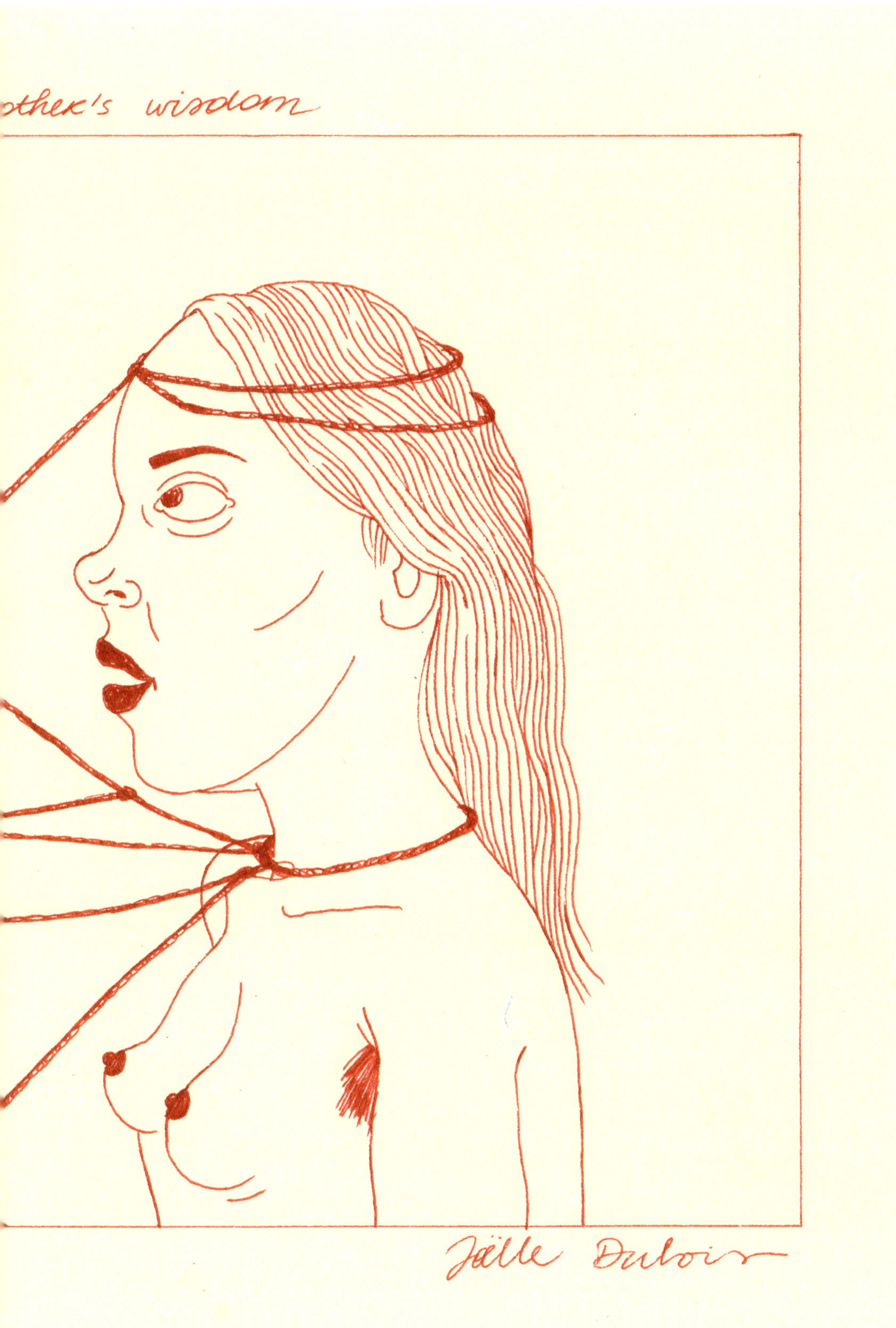
other's wisdom

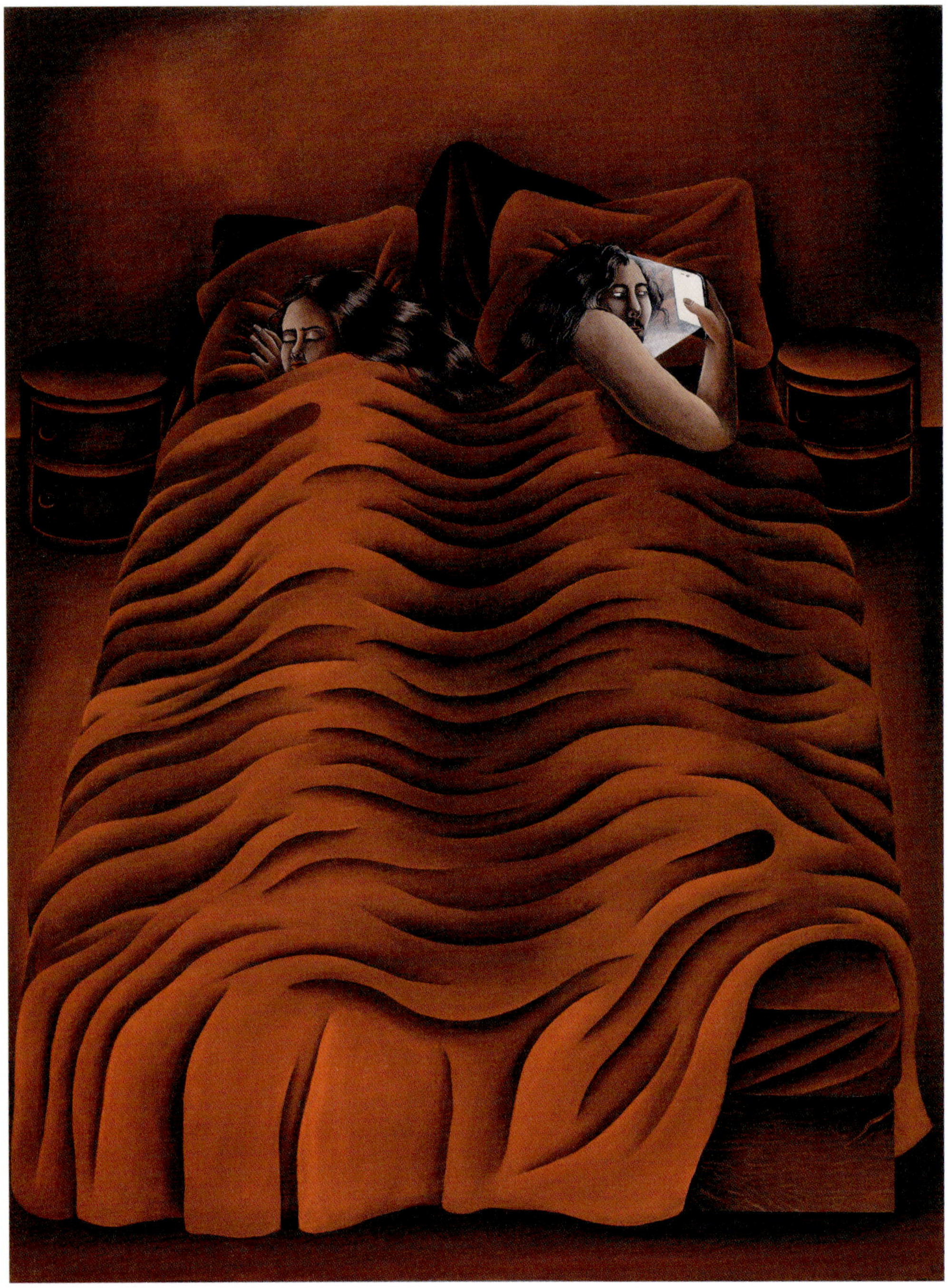

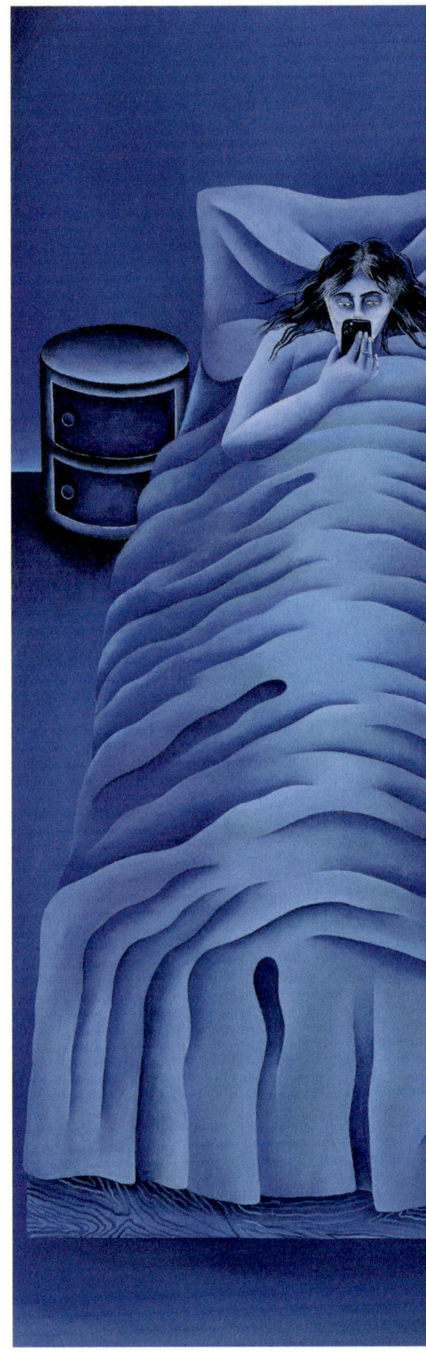

Dark Was the Night

2023

75 × 55 cm

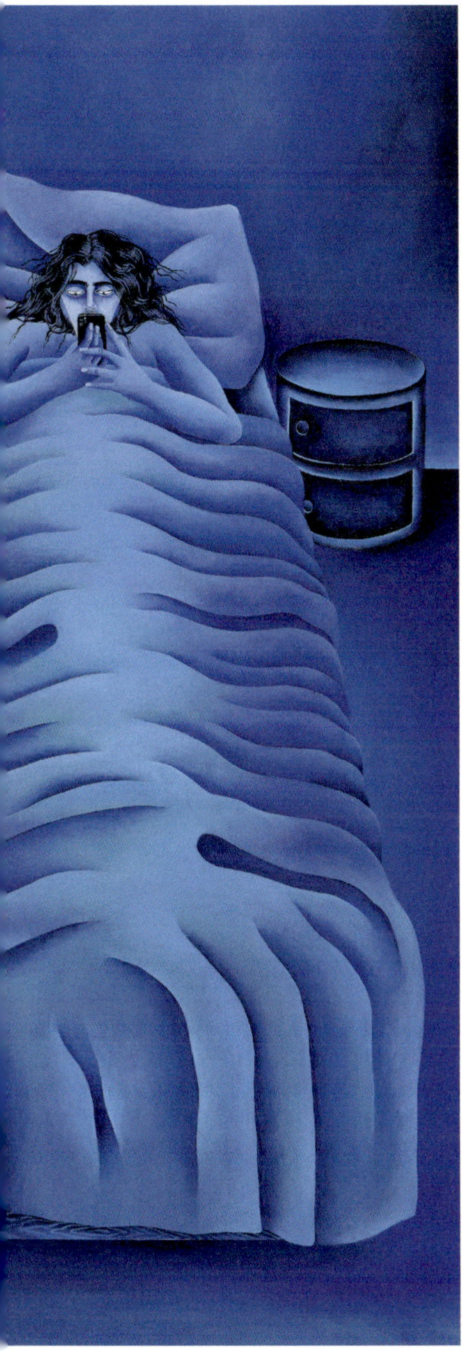

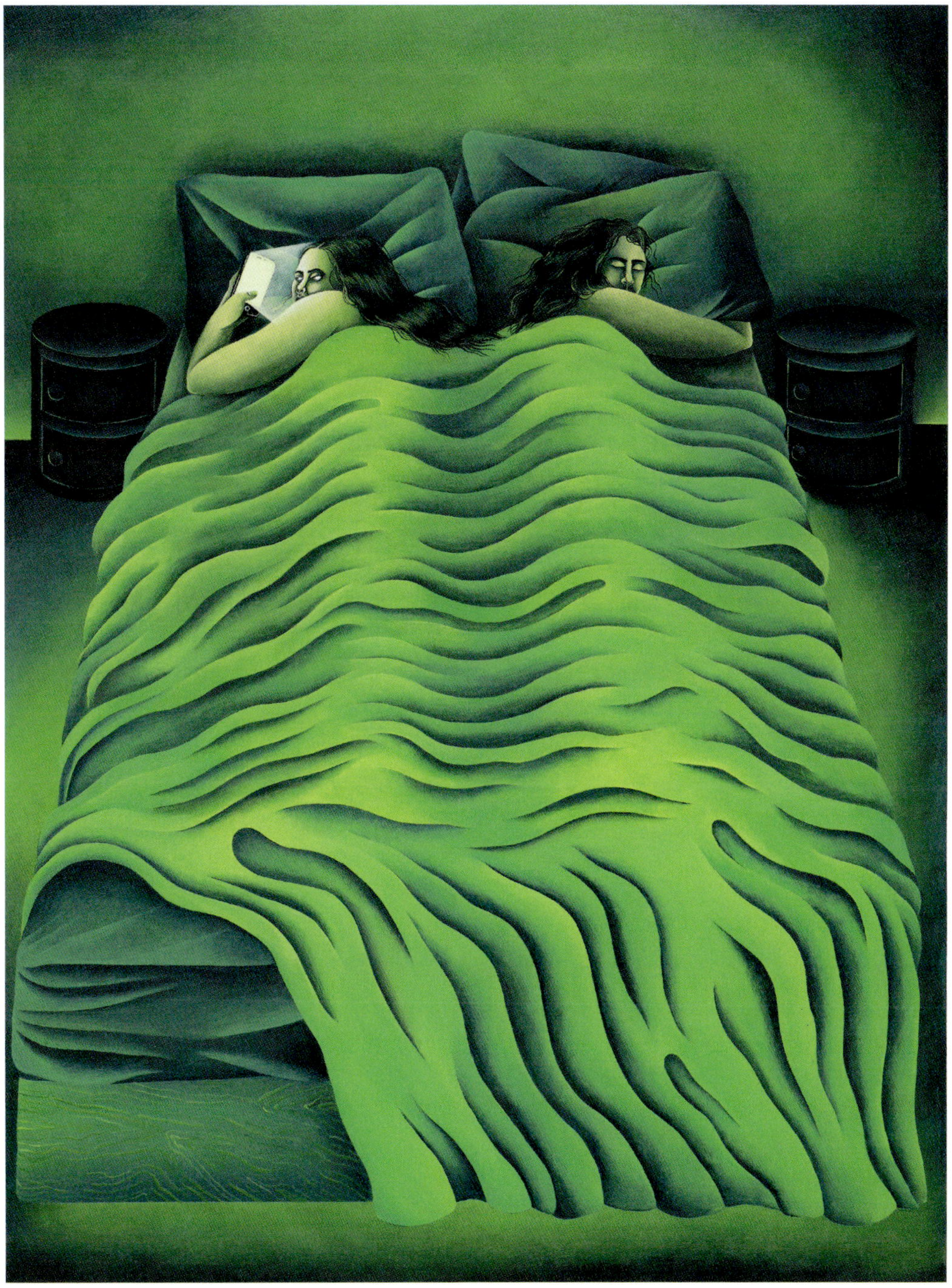

76 × 55 cm

Quickly in Between

2023

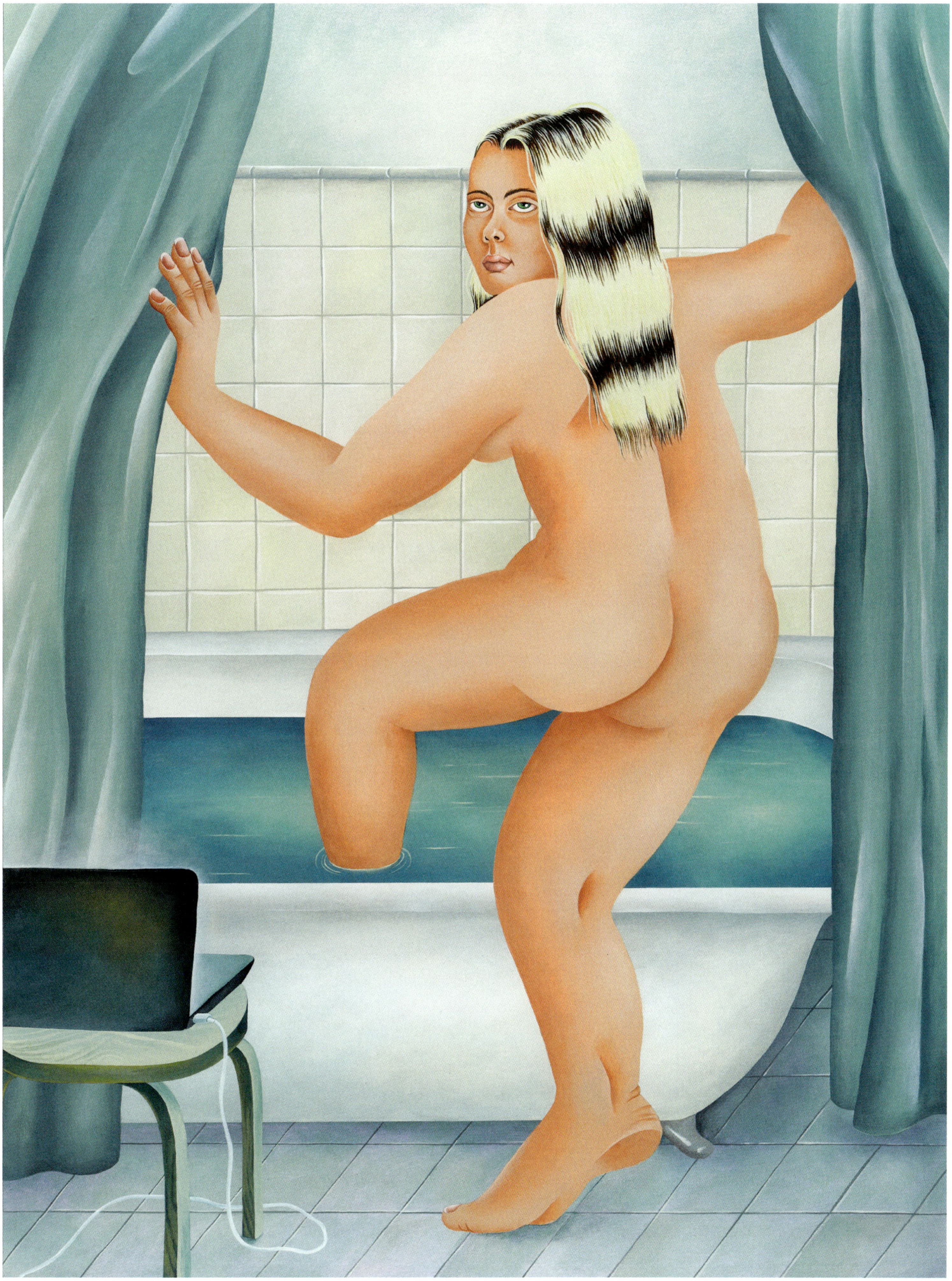

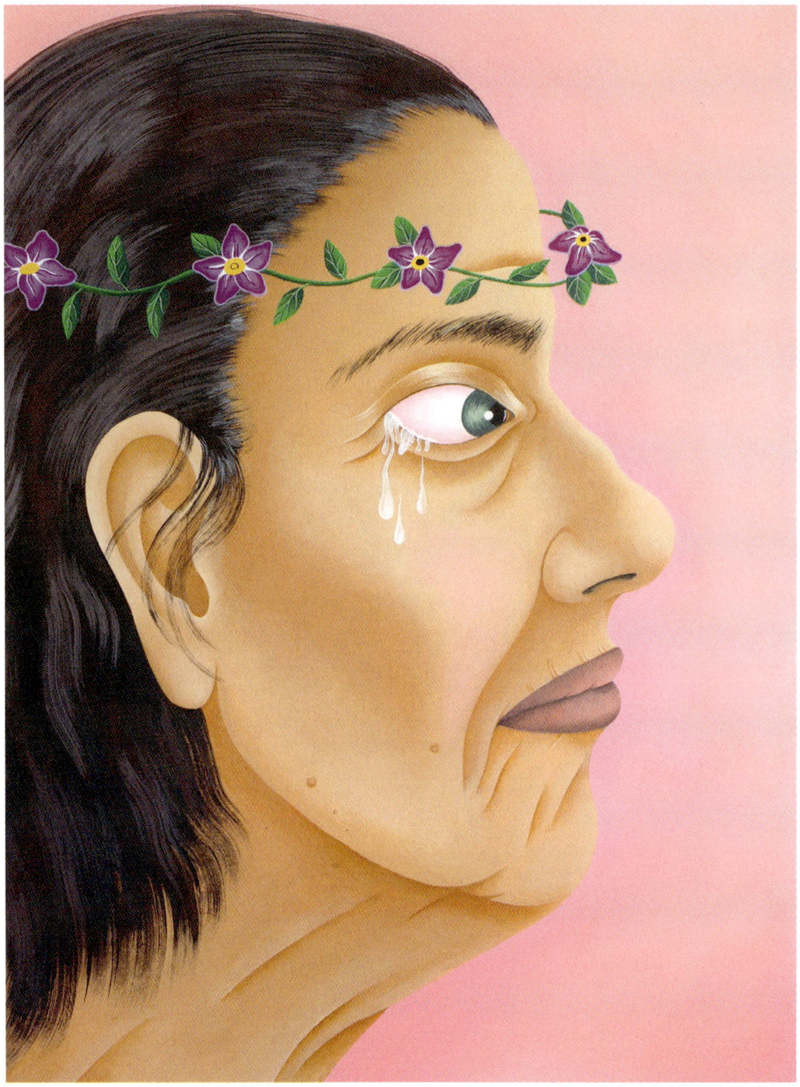

Looking at Me

2022

75 × 56 cm

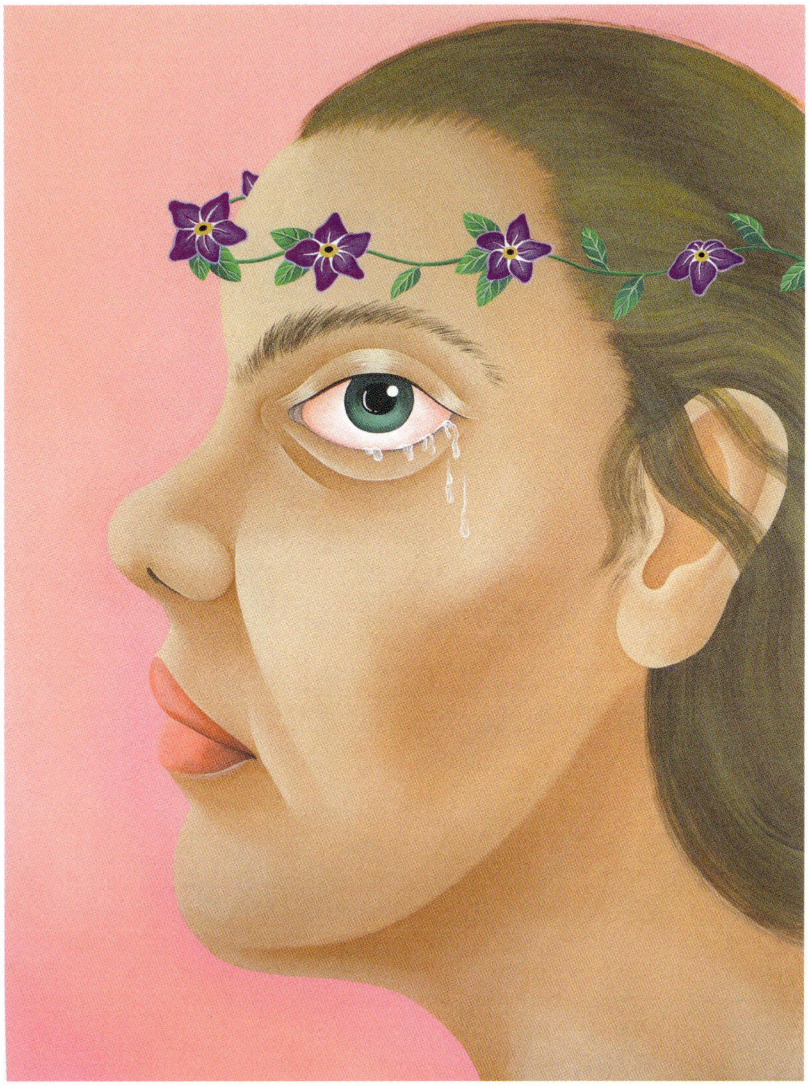

Looking at You
2022
75 × 56 cm

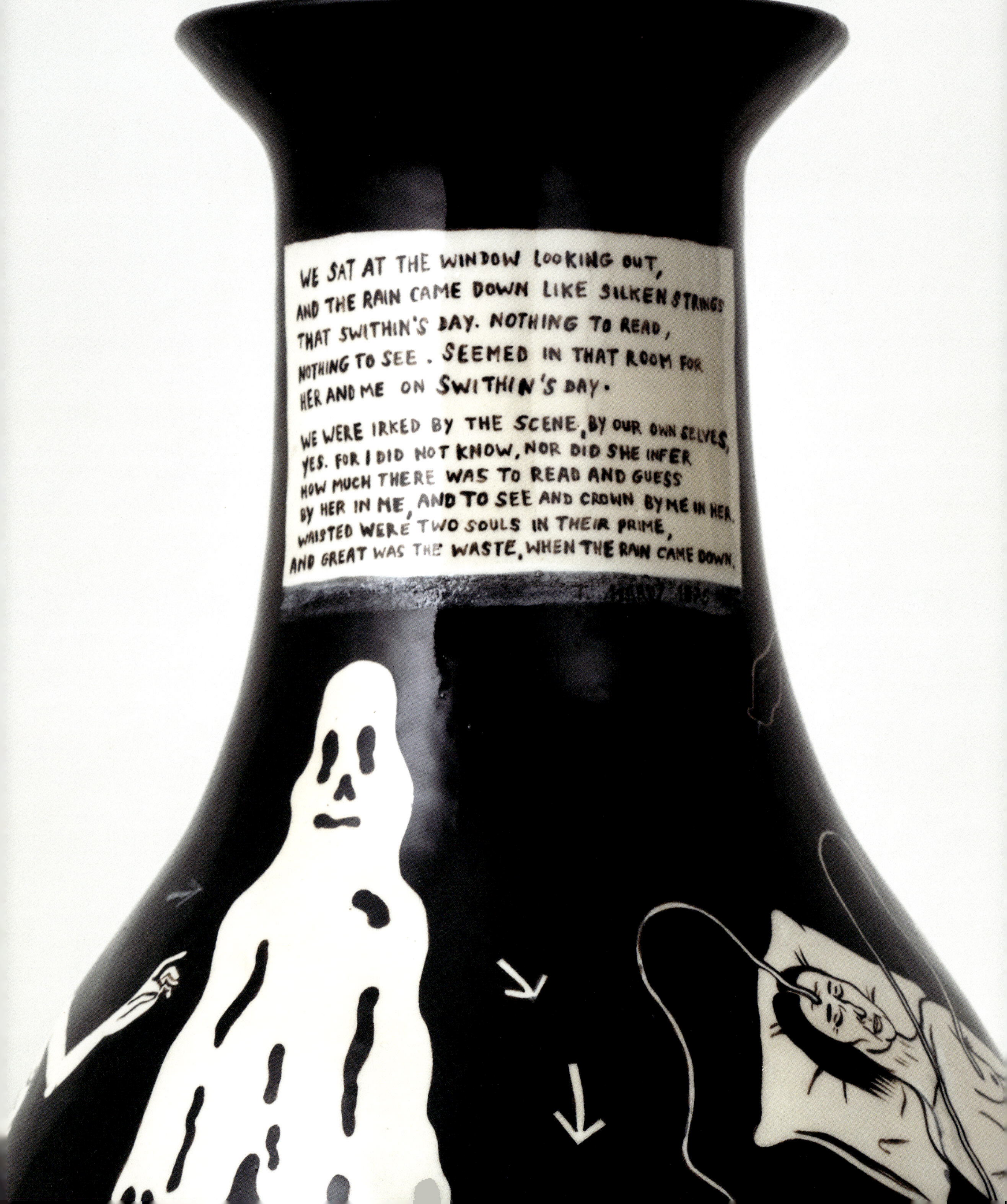
WE SAT AT THE WINDOW LOOKING OUT,
AND THE RAIN CAME DOWN LIKE SILKEN STRINGS
THAT SWITHIN'S DAY. NOTHING TO READ,
NOTHING TO SEE. SEEMED IN THAT ROOM FOR
HER AND ME ON SWITHIN'S DAY.
WE WERE IRKED BY THE SCENE, BY OUR OWN SELVES,
YES. FOR I DID NOT KNOW, NOR DID SHE INFER
HOW MUCH THERE WAS TO READ AND GUESS
BY HER IN ME, AND TO SEE AND CROWN BY ME IN HER.
WAISTED WERE TWO SOULS IN THEIR PRIME,
AND GREAT WAS THE WASTE, WHEN THE RAIN CAME DOWN.

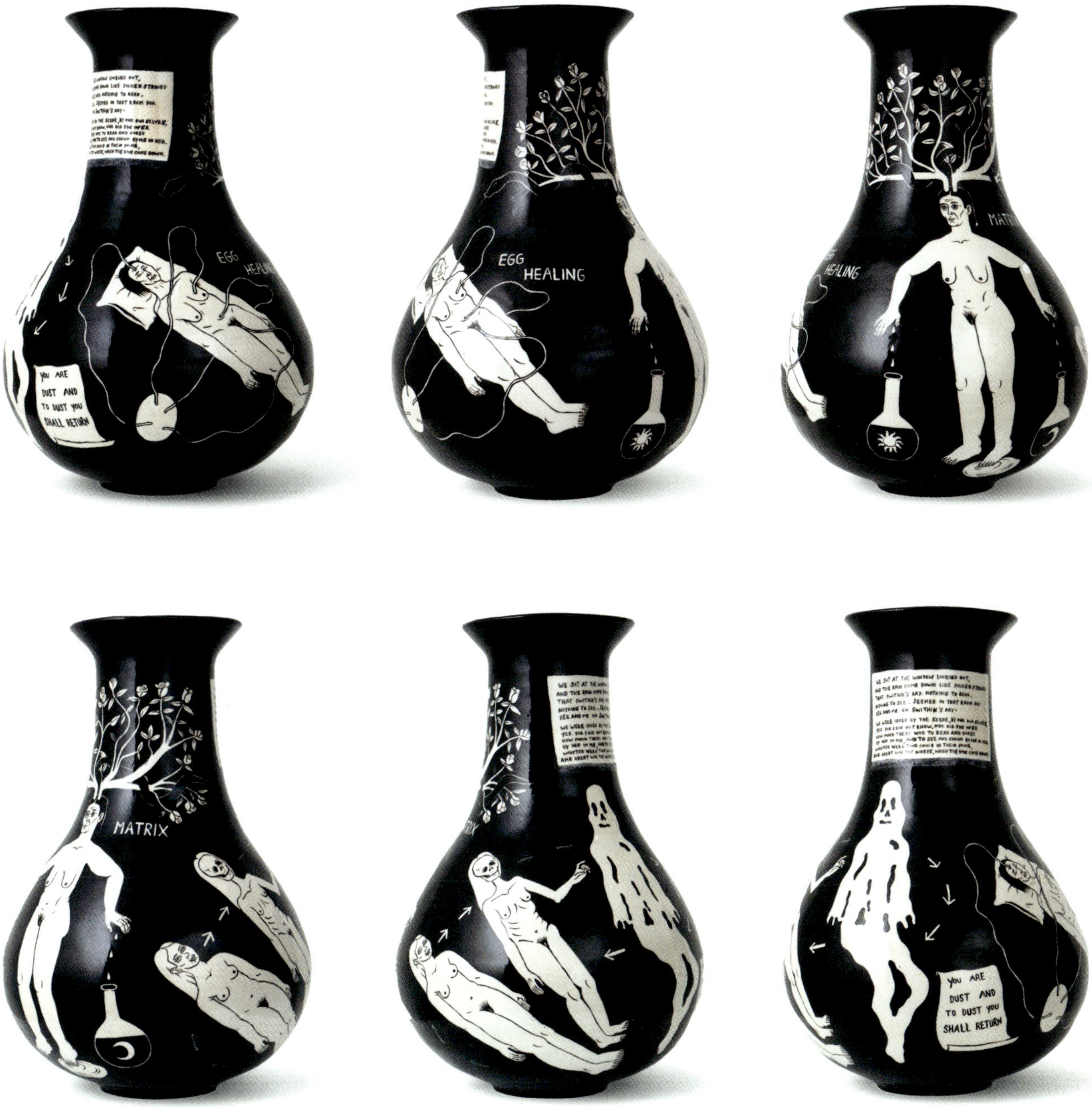

Elixir of Life

2022

38 × 25 × 25 cm

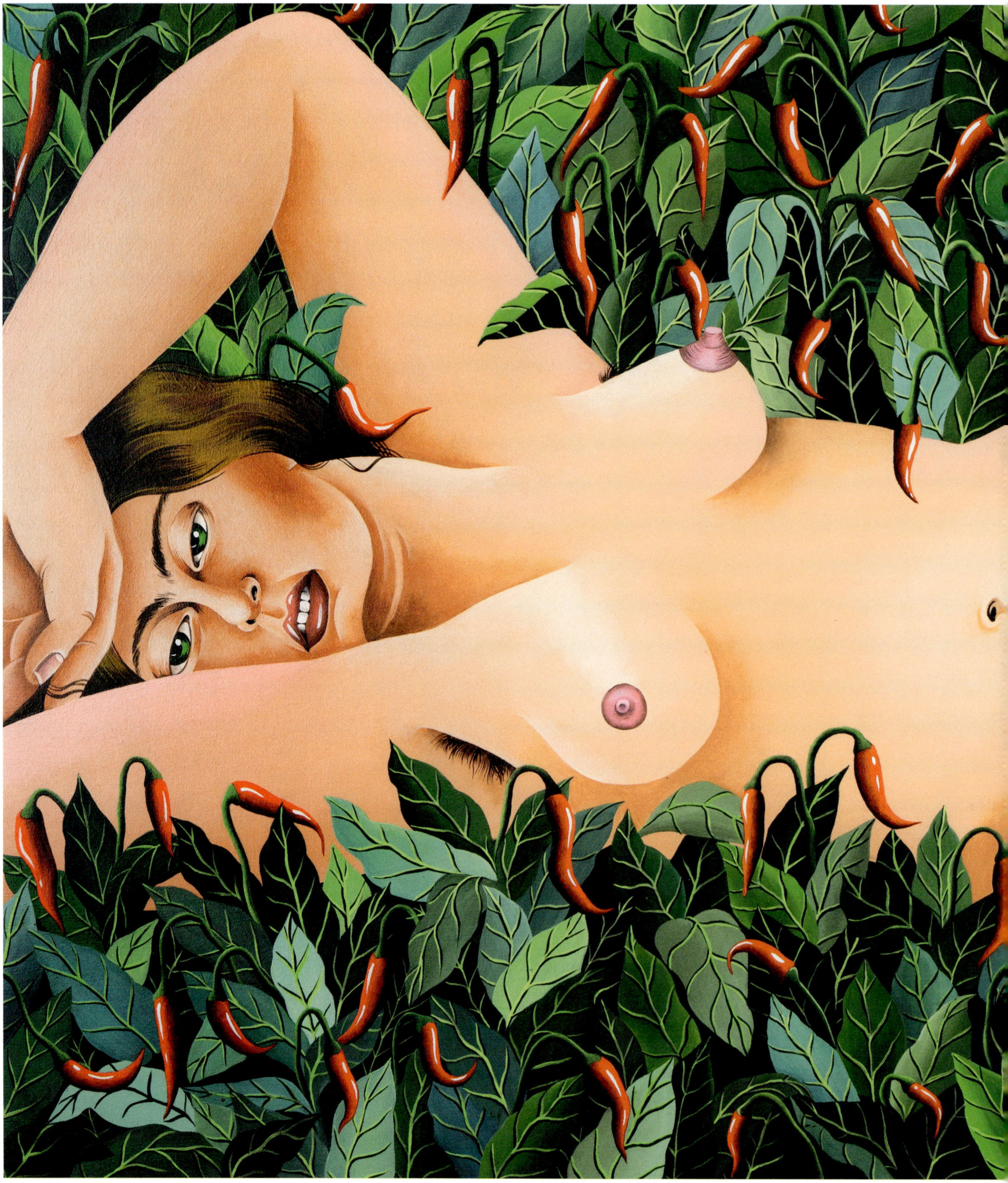

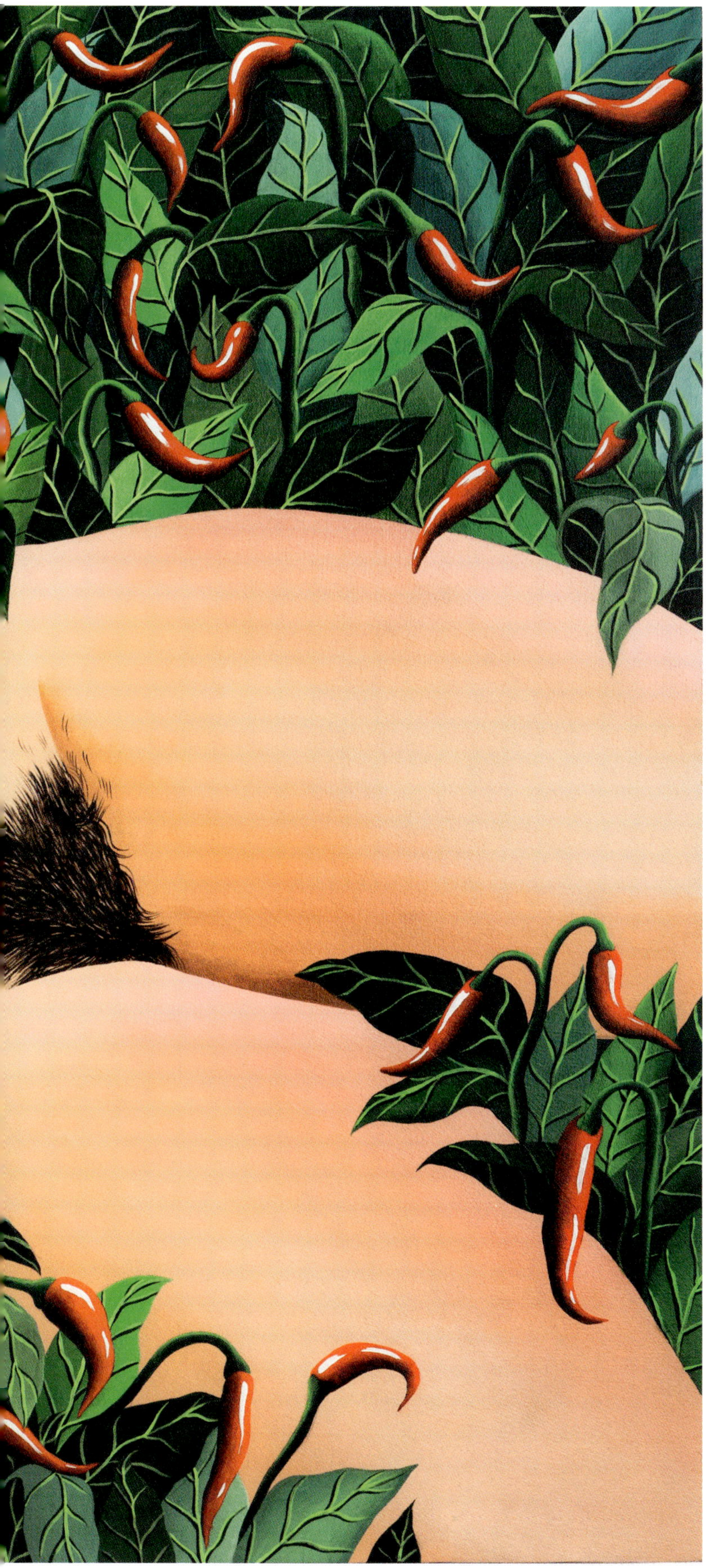

2023

In this Garden I Felt Safe and Protected

56 × 76 cm

ABOUT

TRANSFORMATION,

THE ARTIST'S GAZE

AND

ALL THINGS SHINY

Joëlle Dubois in conversation
with **Katrina Schwarz**
in Whitechapel, London

Katrina Schwarz: You've said that this is the third chapter of your work – the final part of a kind of triptych. Can you tell me more about that?

Joëlle Dubois: A few weeks ago, I realised this exhibition is actually the third chapter in a trilogy – a [p. 8] → triptych of solo shows. The first was *Forget Me Not* and explored the theme of forgetting. It was about my mother, who had Alzheimer's. The show in 2022 reflected on how to cope with her condition – how our relationship changed. She had always been the caregiver – the mother who raised me. But then, suddenly, I became her mother. In a way, it felt like everything had come full circle.

And the second exhibition followed soon after, shaped by this relationship as well?

[p. 88] → Yes, *From Here On Out* in 2024 continued to explore these ideas, but it was created under very different circumstances. My mother passed away while I was preparing this exhibition. Her passing was so sudden that it changed the vibe of the show mid-production. The strange thing is, I don't even remember making them. It was as though I was painting in a trance. Grief does strange things to people.

At the exhibition opening, I stood there looking at all these works on the wall – and felt like an [p. 136] → outsider. They were mine, but they felt distant. *Rekindling* is the third part of this story – a post-mortem. It's really all about transformation.

You've spoken about even forgetting the technical process. Was this 'amnesia' specific to this period of grieving?

I often forget how to do anything when I start painting. Every time I paint, let's say, a hand or an eye, I feel like it's a new experience all over again. I'm like, 'Wait, how did I do this last time?' It's ridiculous. But the knowledge is still there, somewhere in my unconscious mind, and it always comes back again. With this trilogy, though, it was a different kind of forgetting. It was about the whole painting – not just the technique.

I often don't like my paintings while I'm making them. It's like a battle. I love the quote by Philip Guston, because it's so recognisable: 'Frustration is an important, almost crucial, ingredient. I think that the best painting involves frustration.' I share a studio with my best friend Nina Van denbempt, and she laughs when I make these guttural noises of unease while I'm painting. She then says, 'Keep going baby! You can do it!' Sometimes I just want to cover the whole thing up, or repaint it, or bin it – but I never do.

What stops you from doing that? How do you know a painting is done and ready to share?

Deadlines! [laughs] I'm not sure if it's ever really done. I need to walk away and abandon it for a while. I guess it's finished when I feel the image starts to come to life, that's usually how I can tell... I can't stop until something unexpected happens, and everything suddenly fits. All of a sudden, there is a certain unity – then it's done.

Do you ever come to appreciate the work later?

Yes, once it has left the studio. Sometimes when I see a piece again, I think, 'It's not *that* bad.' Especially when people tell me they're touched by it – that's when I realise, okay, maybe it does work. But I don't know, it always remains the most puzzling thing to me. I often work around the clock whenever a deadline is creeping up. I have to keep going until it's done – that's what works for me, really. And then I think, 'Wait, what did I make?'

Let's talk about this new chapter and the new exhibition. I know it features both new work and selected pieces from private collections. In the second show, you shifted to a mostly monochrome palette – is that something you've continued here?

That's right. Yes. After my mother died, everything became very loud – my memories, emotions, thoughts ... I felt the need to silence the noise in my head, so I started using just one colour, to bring everything back to its essence. I try not to think about it too much.

Does the subject determine the materials you prefer using?

Ideas often come to me when I am in my bed, and I kept having flashes of objects and scenes from the house I grew up in. For example, we had many doors and windows with stained glass, so I've designed [pp. 149, 185] → two stained-glass pieces in honour of that past. After my show *Forget Me Not*, I became fascinated by alchemy and its historical obsession with immortality and the mystical quest for the 'elixir of life'. It was believed that alchemy could cure all diseases and even defy death, and that fascination with this ancient desire is present in my recent work. In 2022, I [pp. 24–5, 64–5, 74–5] → painted three ceramic vases titled *Elixir of Life*. And now, for *Rekindling*, I made three bronze sculptures – [pp. 140–1, 156–7, 180–1] → *Catharsis* – each in an edition of eight, all influenced by these ideas.

What draws you to move away from the walls and work with sculpture?

I always feel like I need to shake things up from time to time, and how that manifests itself – well, nobody knows. It comes naturally – the subject determines the material. It's honestly more about feeling and enjoying the process, transforming raw substances into form, almost like channelling a process of transmutation. It begins with this desire – a powerful urge to see what you've imagined. I might think, 'Wouldn't it be fantastic to... ' And then I simply have to go for it. There's no such thing as an idea that's 'too crazy'. The wildest ones are often the most important to pursue.

This isn't your first time bringing installation into your shows. Can you tell me about the tent or 'fort' you built for your solo exhibition in 2022?

[pp. 42–5] → That's right, *Moon Cave* was inspired by the universal act of children building makeshift shelters with sticks, sofas, blankets... I believe it's about safety, and I connect the image of the womb or a cave to it. I made a fort that was inspired by K'NEX [a toy construction system that consists of interlocking plastic rods, connectors, gears, wheels, etc.]. I covered the house-like form with a white sheet overlayed with lace. In Belgium, and Flanders in particular, lace is a traditional craft passed from grandmother to mother to daughter, but it also has a sexual connotation and highlights the combination of fragility and strength. This tension continuously runs throughout my work.

Inside the installation were silk forget-me-not flowers – like the kind you'd put on a grave – and a pink UV light, the type used to help flowers grow. But of course, these flowers are artificial, so they will never grow.

And they will never die?

Exactly. You could also hear my mum's voice, talking about how she felt after receiving her diagnosis – but her answers were muffled, like the sound of a mother's voice in the womb. Visitors had to come close to hear. When I create installations, I like to play with all the senses.

Why is it important to engage all the senses?

Because it allows the work to become an experience rather than just an image to look at. It allows people to fully immerse. I like to believe it goes straight to the nervous system.

The way you have described your mother, and painted her, makes it clear she had tremendous energy. Did that make her illness – her retreat from life – especially painful?

Yes, my mother was very proud, outspoken, and rock 'n' roll. My parents always hosted dinners and parties for their friends, and this energy was present in the interior of our home as well. Every wall was painted a different colour – pink, lilac, blue. I was also allowed to paint on the walls. That past is visible in my work. I guess it's where the bright colours come from. Colours and music were always very present and important. It was chaotic and free. But I liked it. It shaped who I am.

You also grew up surrounded by esoteric influences – your father practised Buddhism, you've spoken about tarot and symbolism, and also the influence of comic books. Does that run through your work as well?

Yes, definitely. My mum taught me everything about astrology, palmistry, and tarot, which I often incorporate in my work. And I've been into comics since I was a kid. My dad has a whole collection of Belgian comics like *Nero*, *Asterix & Obelix*, and *Gaston*. When I was about nine, I discovered his collection of [Milo] Manara comics, and it blew my mind – even though I was obviously too young to see this kind of erotic imagery. Not long after, my obsession with manga and anime kicked off. Katsuhiro Otomo's *Akira* and Hayao Miyazaki's films will always have a special place in my heart.

That instinct for looking – for scrutiny and voyeurism – seems to echo in your paintings. I'm thinking of works like *The Watcher* from 2016.

I'm fascinated by watching and being watched. I think all artists are. The first thing you learn at art school is to look, to gaze, to stare during life drawing classes, for example. As a visual artist, you are a constant observer of things you later appropriate. The artist's gaze is fundamental in the search for subject matter, and for me, technology offers a new way of seeing and being seen. So yes, I guess I see myself as some kind of voyeur. But the creative process is not necessarily a voyeuristic experience, if voyeurism is defined as gaining sexual pleasure from watching others. I zoom in on specific aspects. I even created a 'secret detective agency' when I was little with the kids who lived next door. We would watch the street with binoculars, writing notes like, 'Black cat moving at 4 p.m.'

Your works often contain specific symbolic motifs – eggs, fruit, insects, flowers... Are you deliberately researching their meanings? Or are they intuitive?

Both. When I paint, I often ask myself, 'What do I want to tell? What is the feeling I'm aiming for? What is behind it?' I then add elements that can strengthen the effect I want to establish, and that can reinforce the emotion or the intention I'm looking for. Sometimes, I'll feel the urge to include a particular object – a broken bottle, say, a pepper, or a certain type of bird. This then happens intuitively, but it's really satisfying when I later research the symbolism behind these objects and the meaning actually fits. I guess it means my intuition is doing well? Also, themes like forgetting or even love and death are abstract concepts, so it feels natural to lean towards symbolism.

Could you share a specific example of that process?

[pp. 94–5] → I have a blue monochrome painting [*Cut to the Core*, 2024] where I'm cutting my hair. When I had painted this scene, it felt unfinished – something was missing. I then added a centipede, and it changed the painting. I like adding unexpected elements. I try to capture 'weird' and 'messy' human experiences, so that my art can be a representation of life and all the emotions that go with it. In this case, I wanted to evoke discomfort. Later, I looked up the symbolism behind the centipede – turns out it's a symbol of transformation, protection and resilience. It resonated perfectly.

And now you've filmed yourself actually cutting your hair for a new video work. Can you tell me about that performance? ← [pp. 161–73]

Yes. It's the final scene in one of the videos of a new video installation, *The Memory Machine*, I've made with Florinda Ciucio. I braid and then cut my hair. I hadn't really cut my hair since my mum got very sick. It had gotten long and the strands still carried that time of my life. One day I just felt I needed to cut my hair, and I wanted to film it. I considered shaving my head, but that felt like a protest. This was something else – it was about letting go. Across many cultures, the cutting or shaving of hair is a ritual tied to mourning and transformation. In Indigenous American traditions, as well as in Buddhism, hair is believed to carry memory. Cutting it becomes an act of release – letting go of pain, of attachment, of the past. It was very emotional – a real release.

Could you describe the collaboration behind your video work?

I had been filming my mother with my smartphone since 2018, the year she was diagnosed with Alzheimer's. I did this instinctively, as a way of holding on to her as she started to change. Later, I felt I wanted to make this into a full audiovisual installation. So I got in touch with audiovisual artist Florinda Ciucio. She was deeply moved by my story, and our collaboration flowed easily right from the start. She really gets what's going on in my mind and what I am trying to say. She is amazing at translating all of it into audiovisual art.

And what you have created together is very ambitious.

We created a two-screen video installation – an immersive, contemplative space where the screens function as sculptural objects, almost as two entities in the room. Each one loops a video projection, pulling the viewer into a tension between external action and internal thought. As you enter, both videos act as a guide to the subconscious. The first one draws you into a cycle of relentless, almost Sisyphean actions

– an almost desperate attempt to connect with something or someone beyond. The second screen shifts inwards, into the mind itself. Images appear and dissolve like memories trying to come to the surface.

What do you want the viewer to experience?

The images pull you in as you're watching. The rhythm hits something deep – it maybe stirs up old memories you didn't even know you had. The whole setup isn't really meant to be watched linearly either. You sort of float between the two screens, caught in this liminal space where past and present, doing and thinking, all blur together. It's less about overthinking and more about just feeling.

And the second screen?

While the first video connects to memory through physical action, the second one mirrors how our minds reconstruct and reshape memories. It's fluid, it shifts, it's almost hypnotic. It's fragmented with fast-moving images that come and go, similar to one's thoughts. This video is a mix of found footage, shots we filmed ourselves, and parts of my smartphone recordings. I also had some old VHS tapes digitised, so there are glimpses from my childhood mixed in as well.

Could you elaborate on the cycle of actions you perform in the first video?

The first action involves ringing a bell, the second action takes place in water. It symbolises a transitional space. The third action only exists as sound. The final scene is where I cut my hair.

The bell feels like a powerful symbol. Can you tell me more about it?

Ringing a bell is often associated with rituals surrounding death. Here, the ringing symbolises both a call and a release. A desperate call to be heard.

And the bell is incorporated into a form of costume?

Florinda and I first talked about a costume with bells, but after a while, we decided to refine it and just keep one single bell – that's where the headpiece I created with a goat's bell came in. I wanted to add an absurd quality to the performance, which is absolutely there and is present throughout most of my work. I became some sort of walking church bell. Not religiously, but rather symbolically.

Were the movements in the video choreographed or improvised?

Both. The general choreography was already laid out. But since we filmed everything in nature, we also let the environment decide the end result. The act of ringing the bell shifted from slow and gentle to fast and loud. It was physically painful, but it became cathartic.

Do you see these filmed actions as more vulnerable than your paintings or self-portraits?

In a way it absolutely is. With painting, there's some sort of distance – a filter. Even when the work is personal, there is still space to step back, to reflect. But making this video, especially with actions where you only have one take, is very raw. The tears, my pain, the sense of loss, the transformation that comes with grief – it's all exposed.

And you've also created another action for video, reading from a visitors' book that you set up for your mother...

When she was still able to speak, my mother often believed she never had anyone coming over, even though people visited almost every day. But because of her condition, she couldn't remember. I couldn't tell her, 'That's not true, I was here yesterday.' Because it would've only confused her even more. So I made a visitors' book. I asked everyone to write something after they had visited – a sentence, the date, their name ... It helped her, for a while. That's the book that's used. Throughout the entire video, you can hear me read diary entries of moments with my mum. They are just simple, banal details, but when read like a mantra, they become powerful. At a certain point, the entries come to an end – and the silence after that is very loud.

Thinking about how photographs and memories are preserved and revisited in and through technology, I am curious about the proliferation of phones in your work. Are these phones a source of comfort and connection, like we're discussing, or are

the phones a symbol of the fact that we are alienated and separated from each other?

Both. It's not a critique, but rather an observation. I struggle with my phone. I sometimes disappear into it and it often fries my brain. And then there is the idea that we live in two realities. We can be sitting here, talking physically, but at the same time, I can text and be in touch with many people all over the world all at once. A lot of people say these devices have made us anti-social, but I think we're hyper-social. We're constantly online. It's interesting, but also overwhelming and scary.

On the subject of intimacy, there is a rawness to your work – not only in how you depict bodies, intimacy and emotion, but also in how much of yourself you reveal. What role does vulnerability play?

That's the word – vulnerability. Sometimes I think: 'What am I doing?' This is so personal. But I have to make these works. It's a necessity – for myself, and maybe for others too, I hope. So many people who came to the first two shows cried. They then told me their own stories. These connections are deeply human. They matter.

Sexual connection and identity are important too...

For me, nudity is about more than sexuality. Yes, women *are* sexual beings, but the nudity is about our shared vulnerability. There's so much erotic and nude imagery within fine arts. And I think that's where these images stem from. But my imagery is also a critique, in a sense, of what's considered decent or indecent. I try to normalise the natural body – something that's been lacking in our culture for decades already. I remember that when I was growing up, the women around me always seemed unhappy with their bodies, always trying to achieve an unattainable standard. As a woman myself, I absorbed that behaviour too. So in a way, it's an attempt to accept my own body.

And yet, there's also strength in that vulnerability.

Yes. And even the other figures I paint, the ones who aren't me, are still me in a way. They're people I look up to. The people I portray have more to offer than their sex appeal. That's how the cone boobs came to be, for example. I make my characters more chunky, and try to paint people who aren't necessarily traditionally beautiful, because I don't want to perpetuate that hollow ideal of beauty.

I want to depict people who are sexual, free, unapologetic. They are not here for your viewing pleasure. They are free from the male gaze. You can stare at them and they will never acknowledge it. If they are sexual, their sexuality is entirely detached from what the viewer wants, so power is taken away from the viewer and lies within the image itself. Here, power is granted to those who identify with the image: women of all body types, ethnicities and identities. Therefore, the male gaze is transformed, and the subjects become empowering. Through my paintings, I feel free.

You've often used candy colours in your palette – do they play a role in softening or contrasting the strength or intensity of your subject matter?

If I were an animal, I'd be a magpie – attracted to all things shiny. Even my wardrobe is full of glitter and colour. It draws people in. Then, when they come closer, they realise: the subject is actually deeper, darker. It's a contrast I like to play with. I think that a lot of my work is experiential, and a lot of elements come from life experience. So now, in my recent work, there's a lot of darkness, stillness and sadness that stems from losing my mother. I also have this desire to tell a story, to relate to people and tell the stories that I think everyone goes through. But to be honest, I don't really *plan* any of that. It's not strategic. It's intuitive.

In earlier works, your depictions of intimacy recall shunga prints or Japanese manga. Do you draw from life, or are these imagined figures?

It's a mix of things. I have about twenty thoughts merging in my head at once, and combine all of this with references to different masterpieces from classical art, Japanese shunga or even screenshots from films. Then I blend all these sources into something that is mine. I just paint what I like, how I want to paint it. Of course, my early work still looks related to the work I do now, but it has become much softer.

As you've said, your work also depicts a wide range of body types and cultural backgrounds. Is that a conscious, political choice, or does it come from personal experience?

I come from a big, multinational family. We have relatives all over the world. I grew up surrounded by people from different cultures. A lot of my best friends have different backgrounds and nationalities. My mother used to say, 'You're always drawn to people who are different.' And I am. I've always loved learning about other cultures and traditions. For me, it's about humanity. These stories are universal. I get why some people see my work as political, but it's mostly personal.

Your work sits in this fascinating space between personal experience and broader cultural storytelling. Does that duality interest you?

It's actually where a lot of my work begins. Personal experience is my point of entry, but the subjects I work with are also collective. When telling a story, I don't want to detach myself from the viewer. I like to leave space where others might recognise parts of their own stories too.

And finally – now that this trilogy of exhibitions is coming to fruition, do you have a sense of, if not closure, then perhaps of healing?

I'm not sure if I'd call it closure. But there is definitely a sense of healing. Making these works has been a way to stay close to what was slipping away, to hold on and to let go at the same time. It gave shape to something shapeless. I found moments of clarity, even peace. So, yes, a kind of emotional release, a softening, a beginning of healing.

100 × 80 cm *The Expectant Mother* 2022

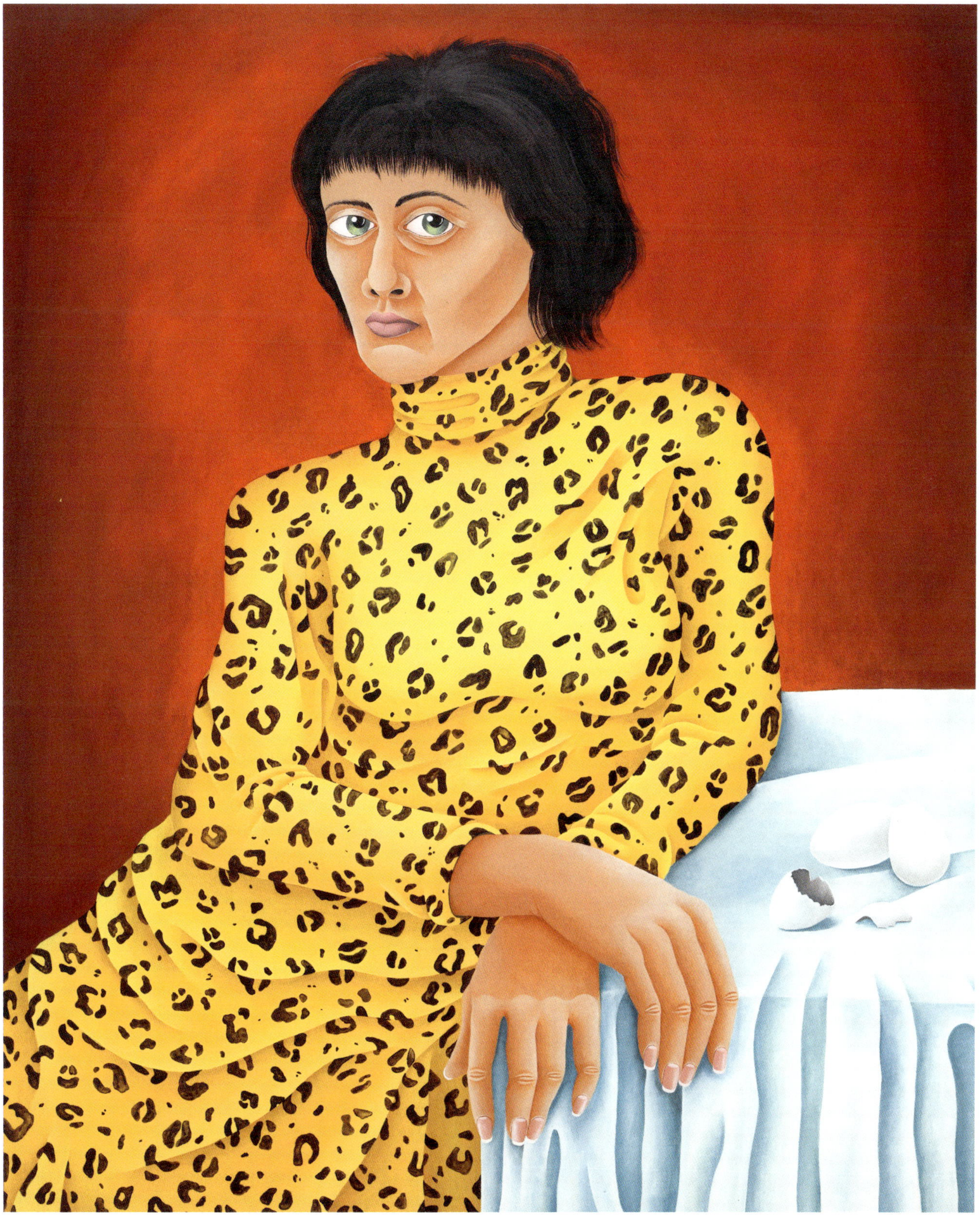

FROM

HERE

ON

OUT

24 × 18 cm *My Mother* 2024

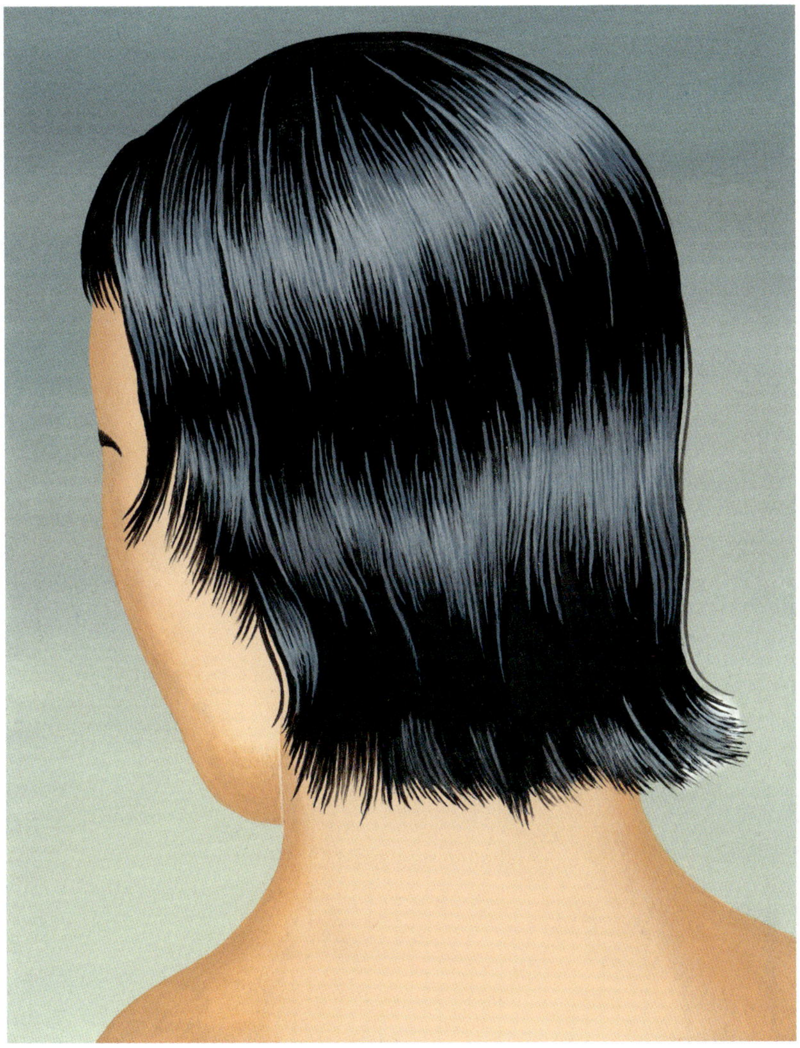

100 × 80 cm *An Omen* 2024

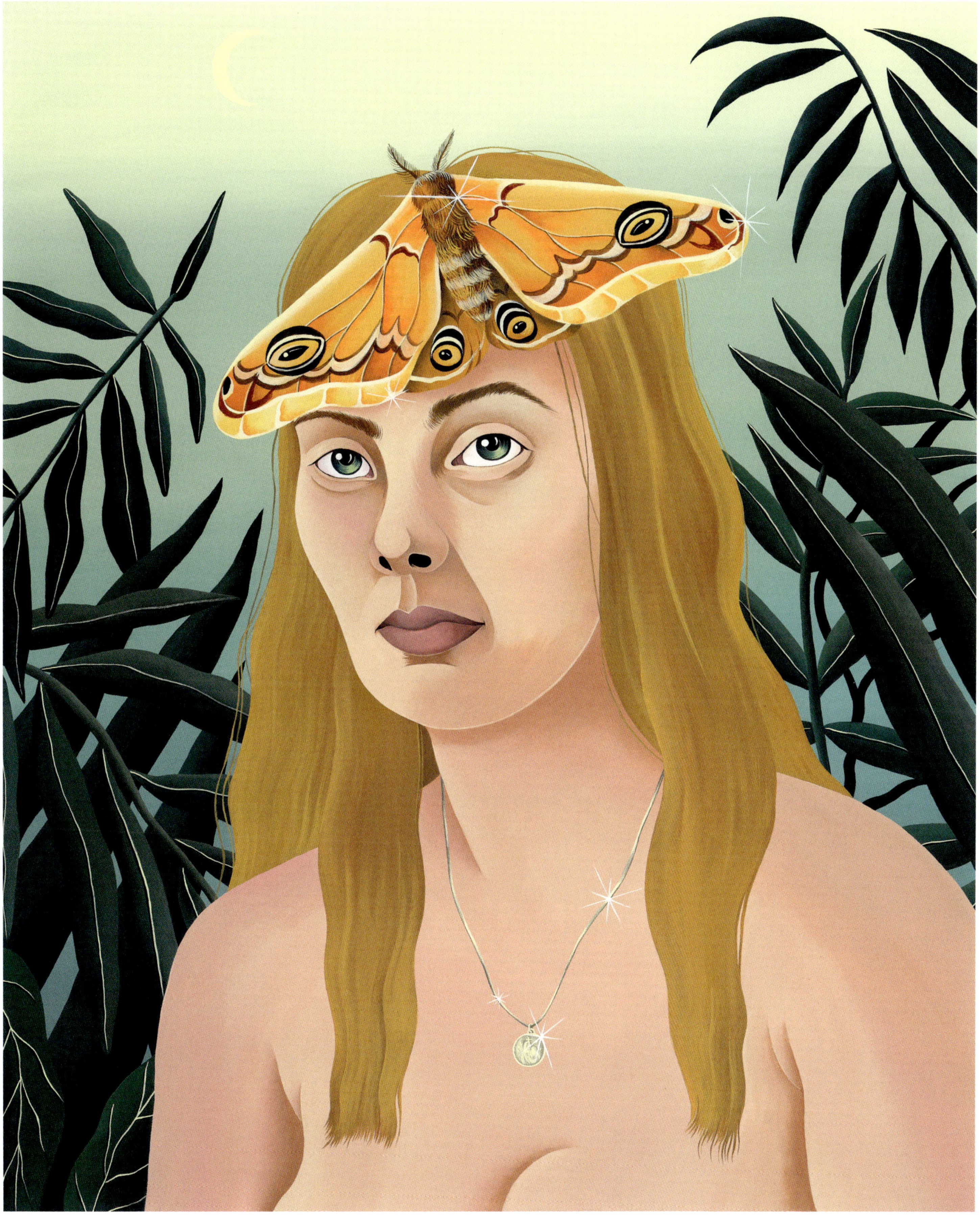

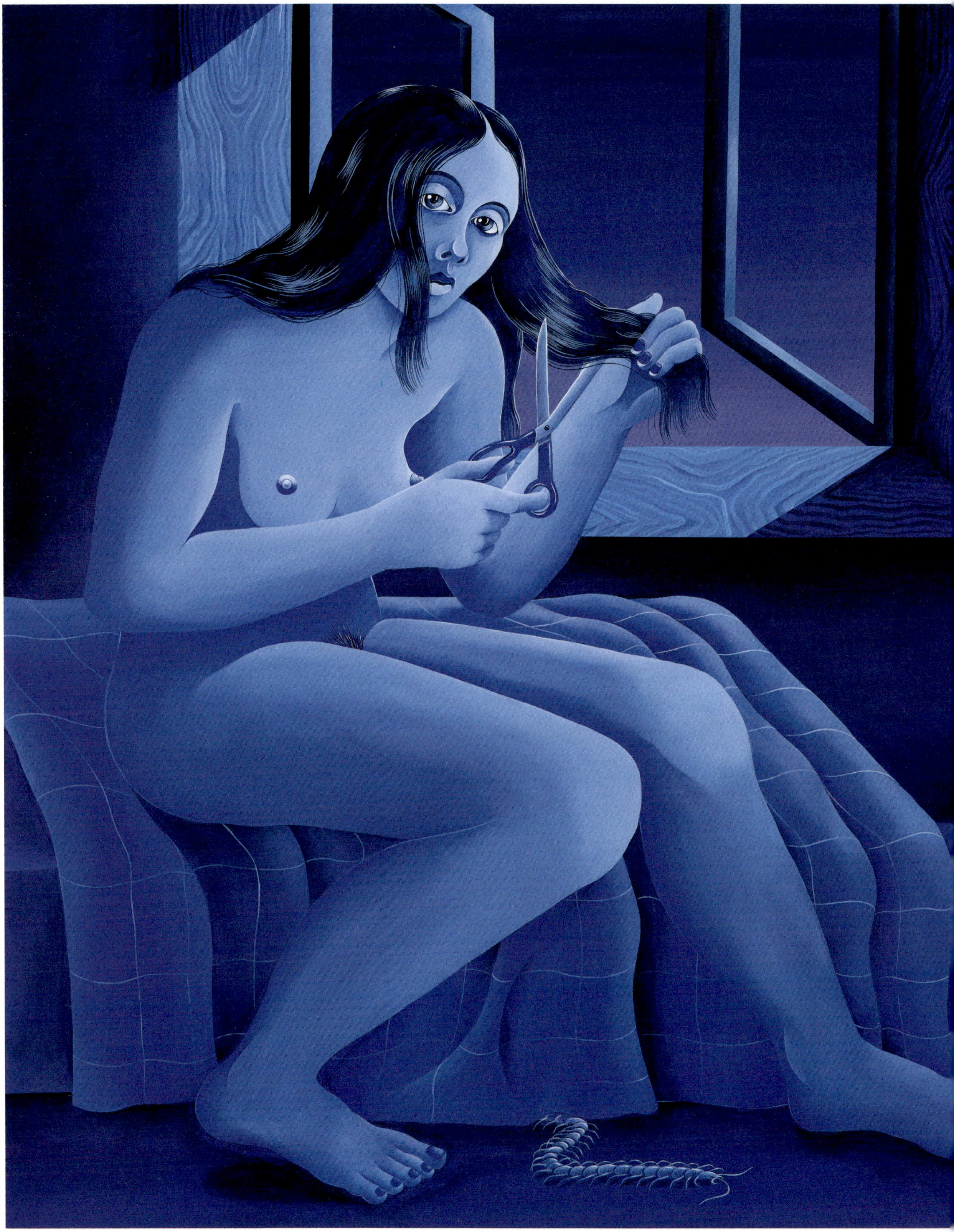

2024 *Cut to the Core* 110 × 97 cm

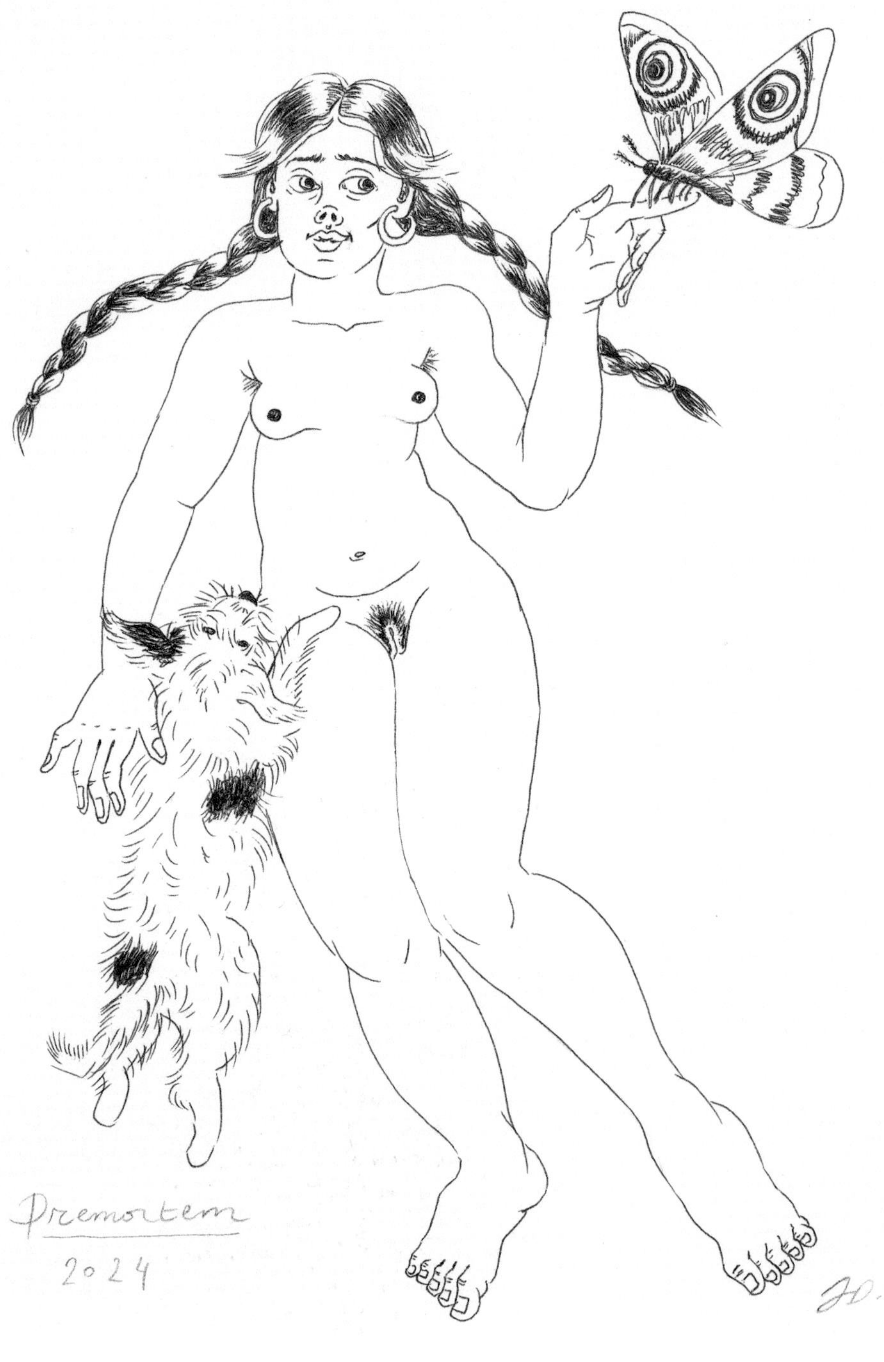

Premortem

2024

21 × 14.5 cm

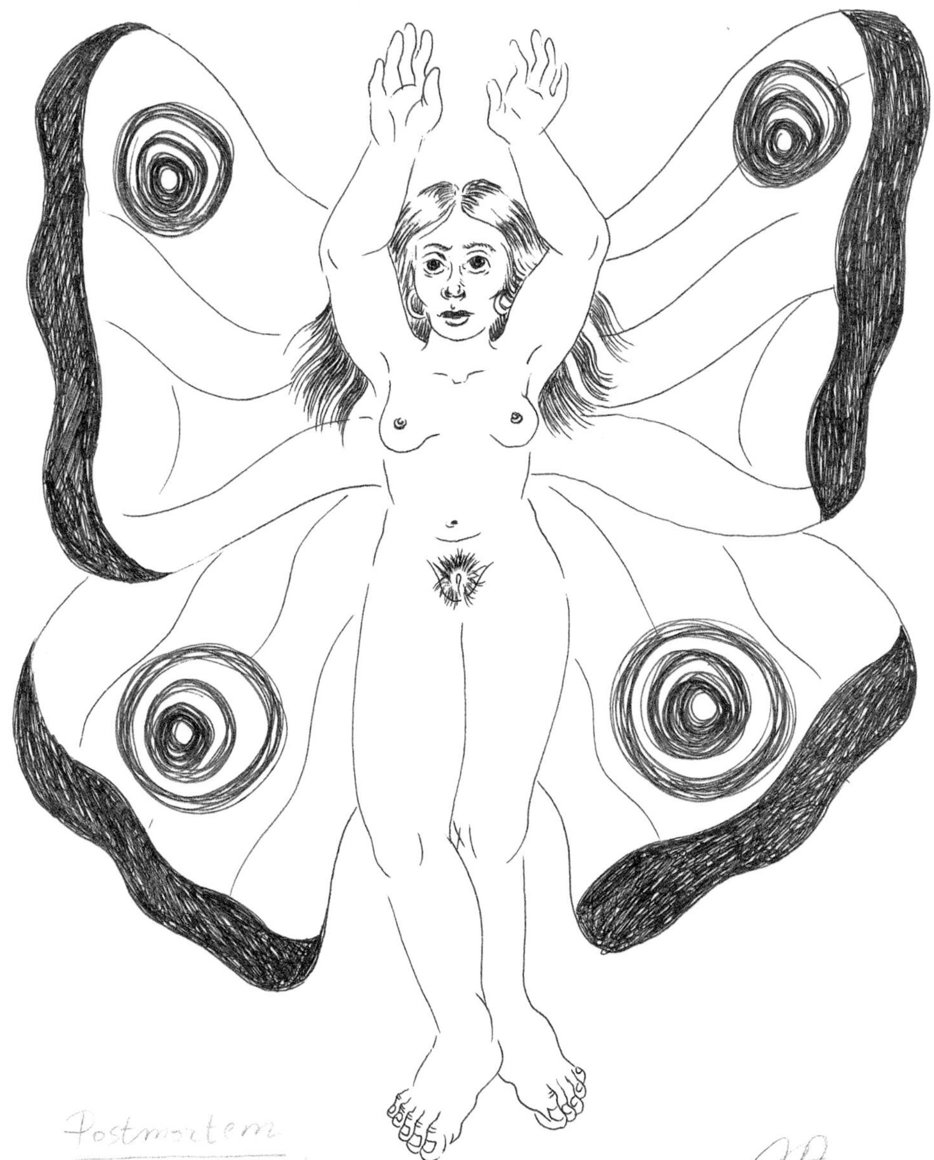

2024

Postmortem

21 × 14.5 cm

100 × 80 cm

Gullible Self-Portrait

2024

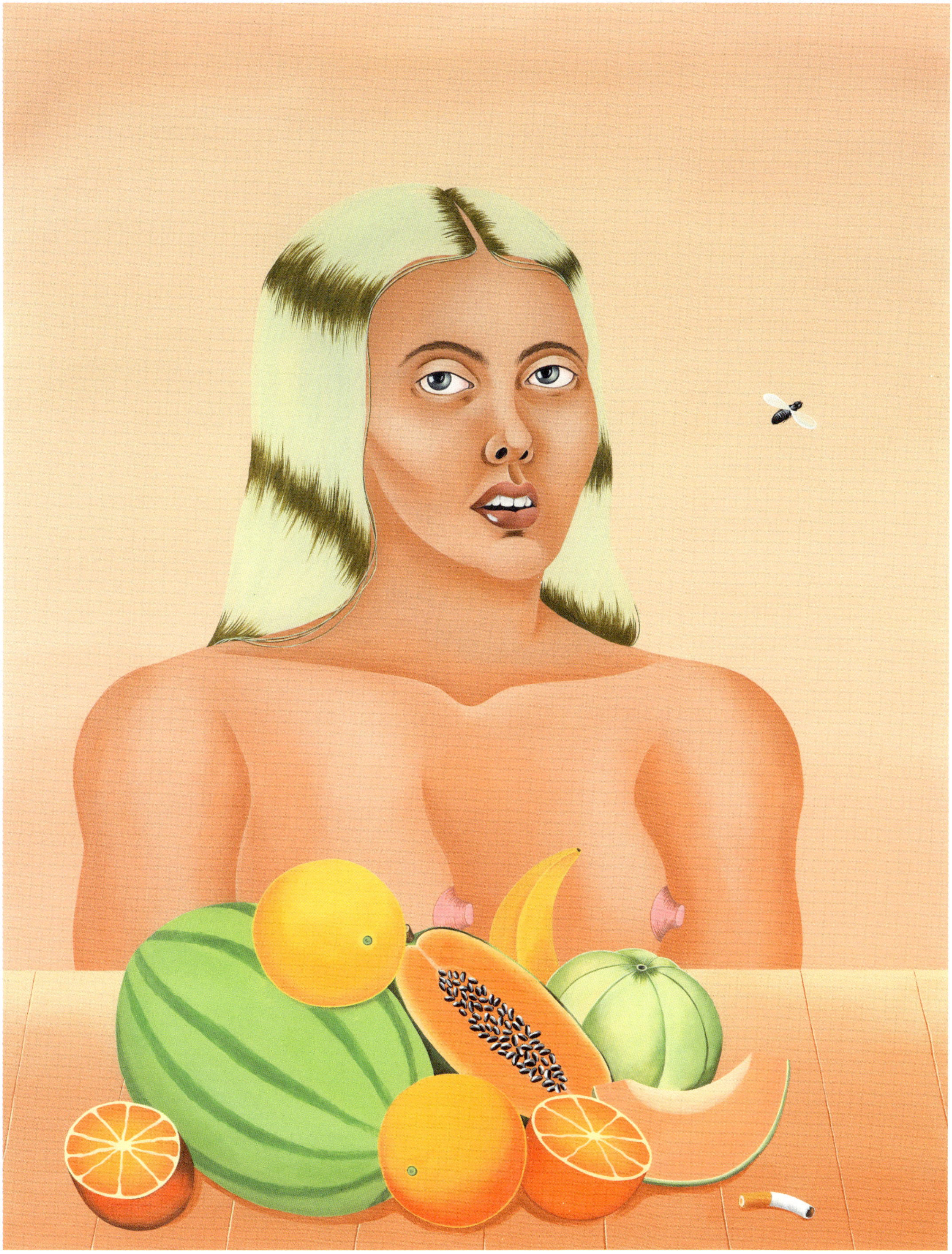

2024

Something's Rotten

40 × 50 cm

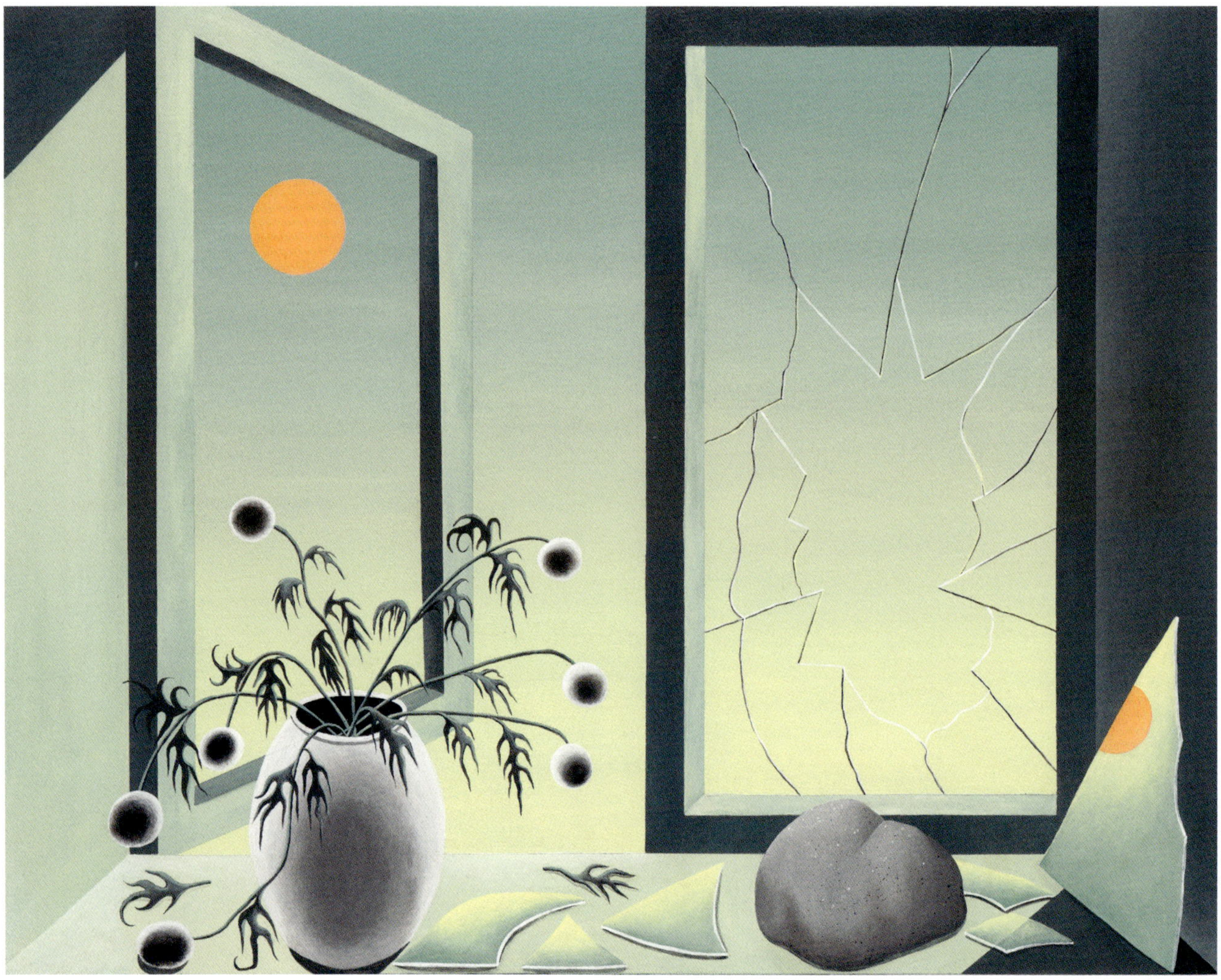

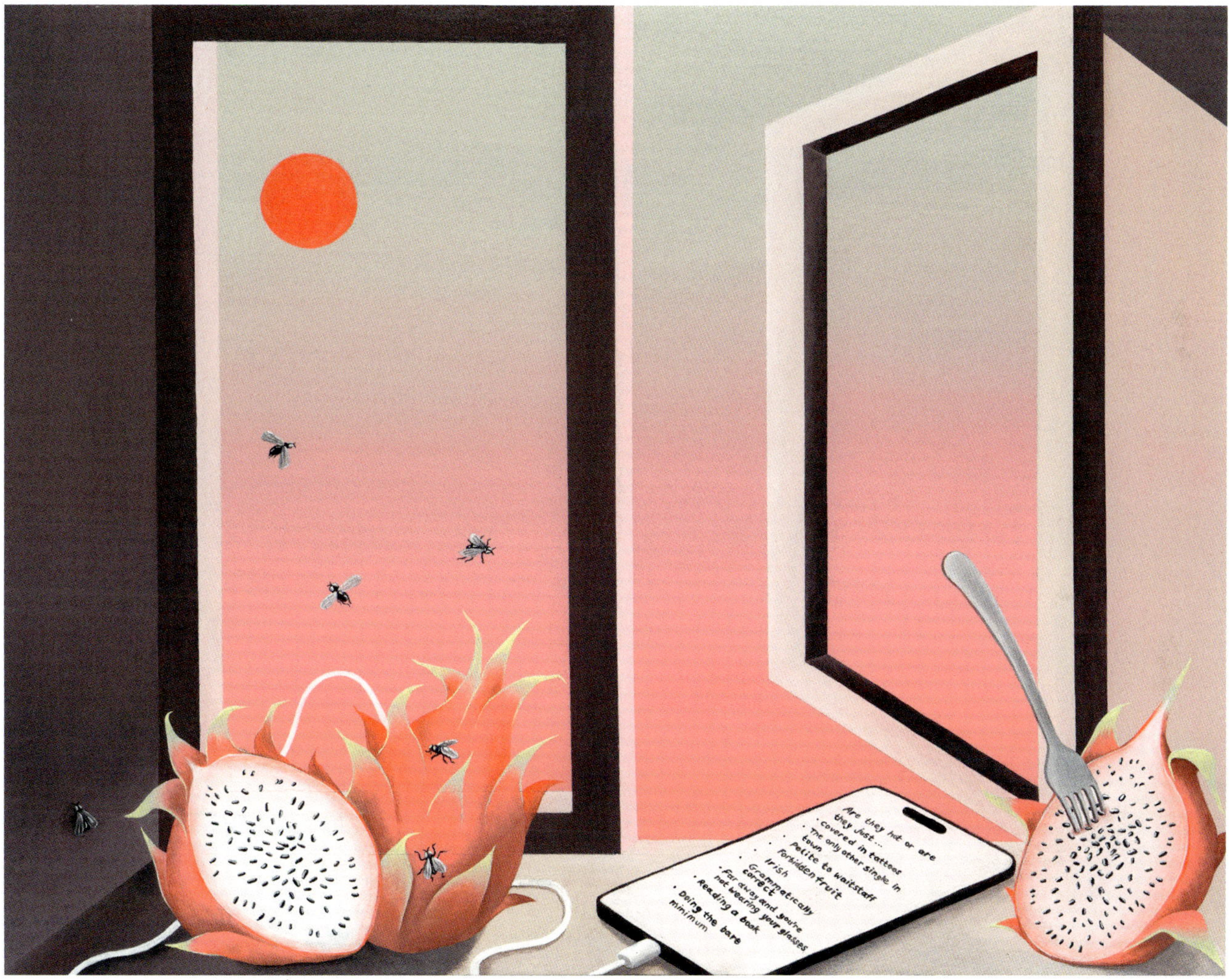

2024

The Day After

40 × 50 cm

110 × 97 cm

From Letter to Memory

2024

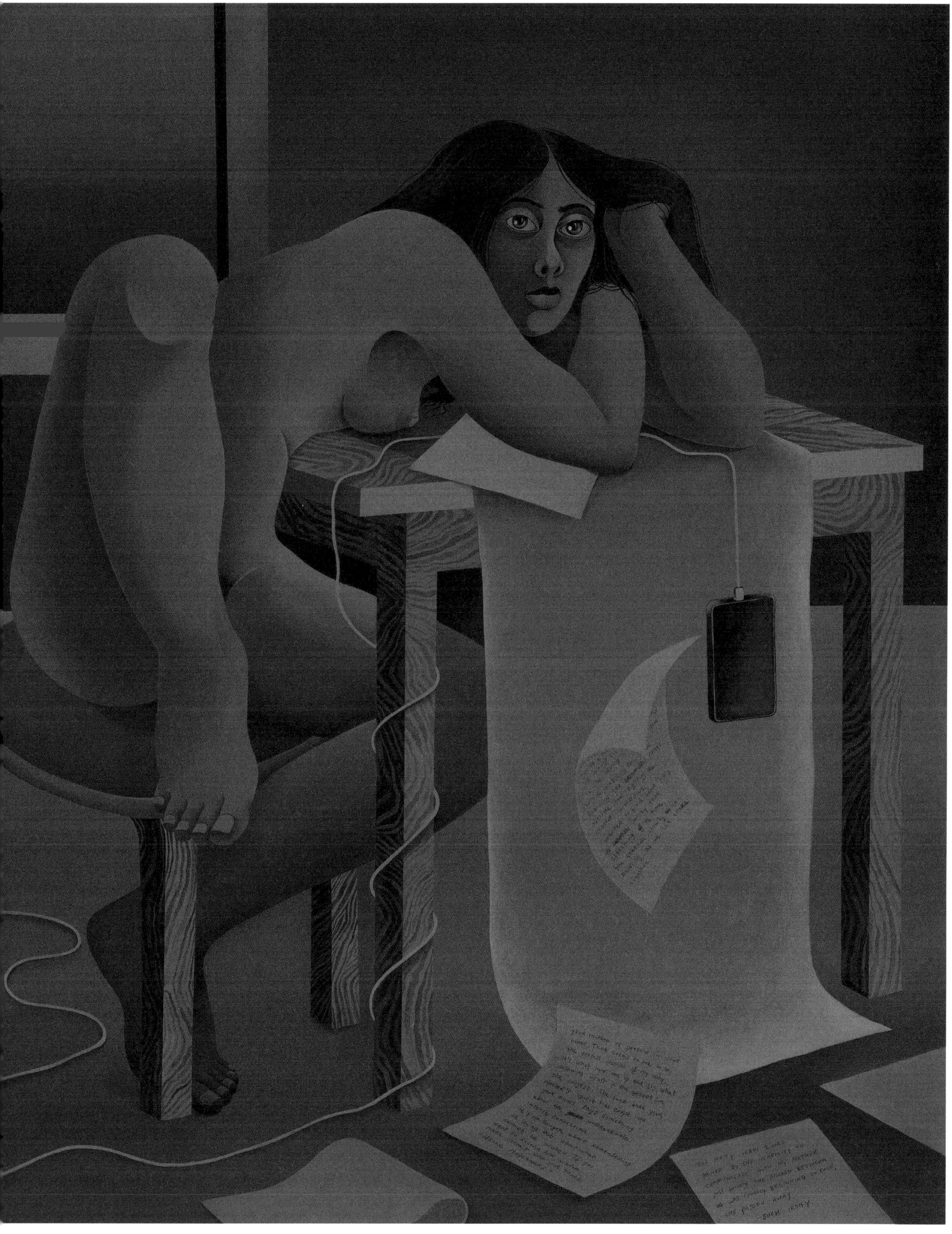
SHE PASSED AWAY
SUCH IRONY.

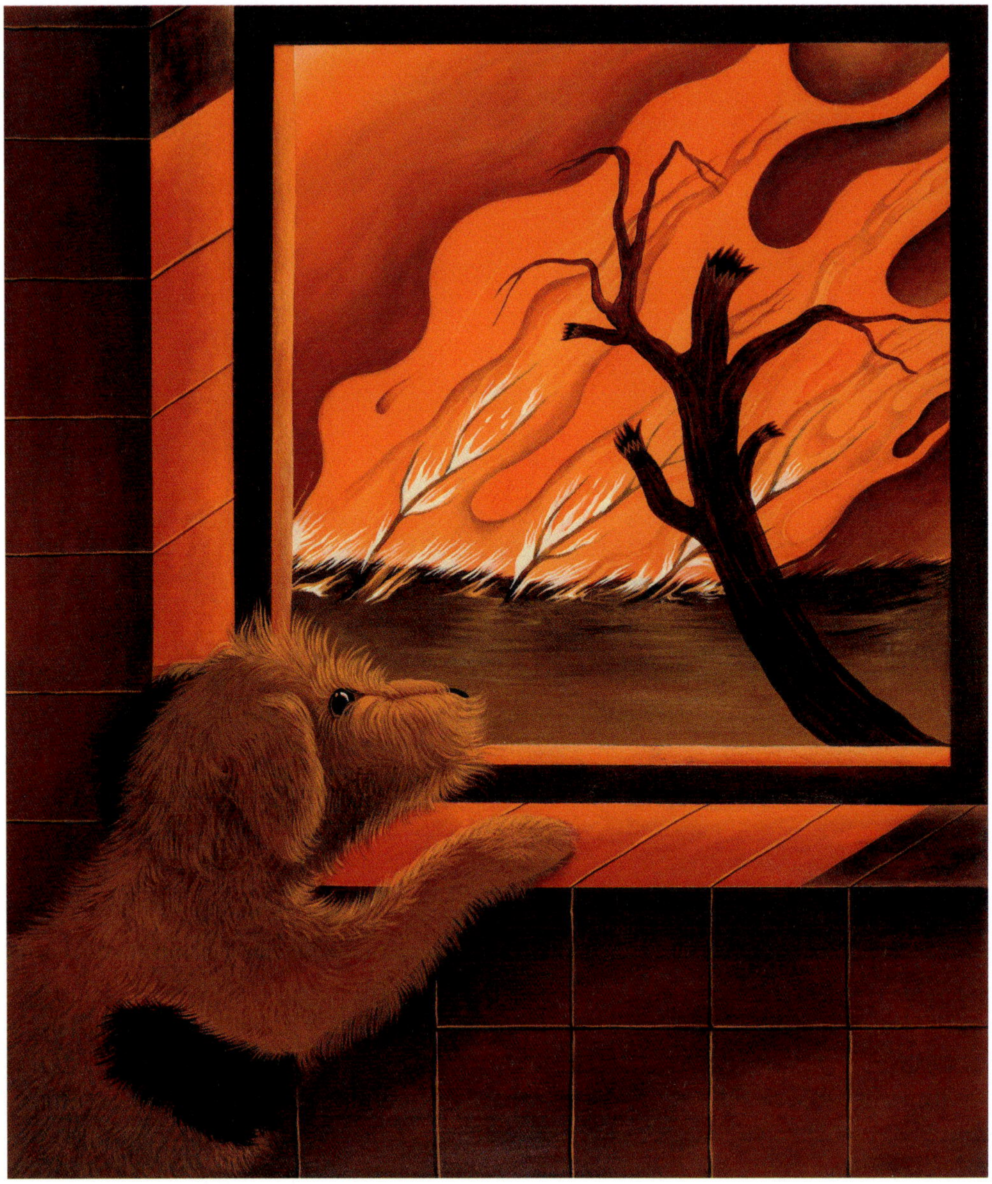

2024

Through the Fire

60 × 50 cm

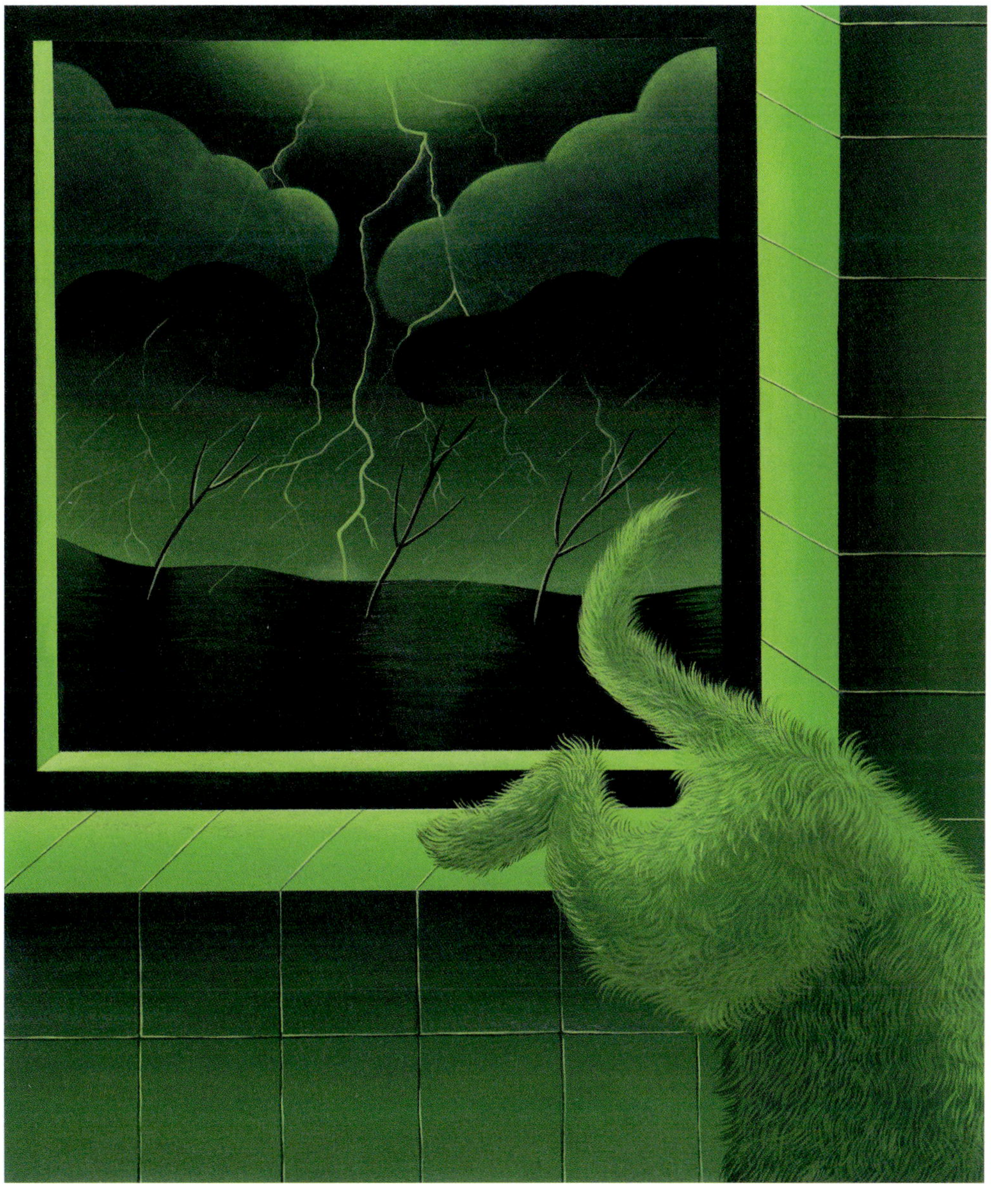

2024

Through the Storm

60 × 50 cm

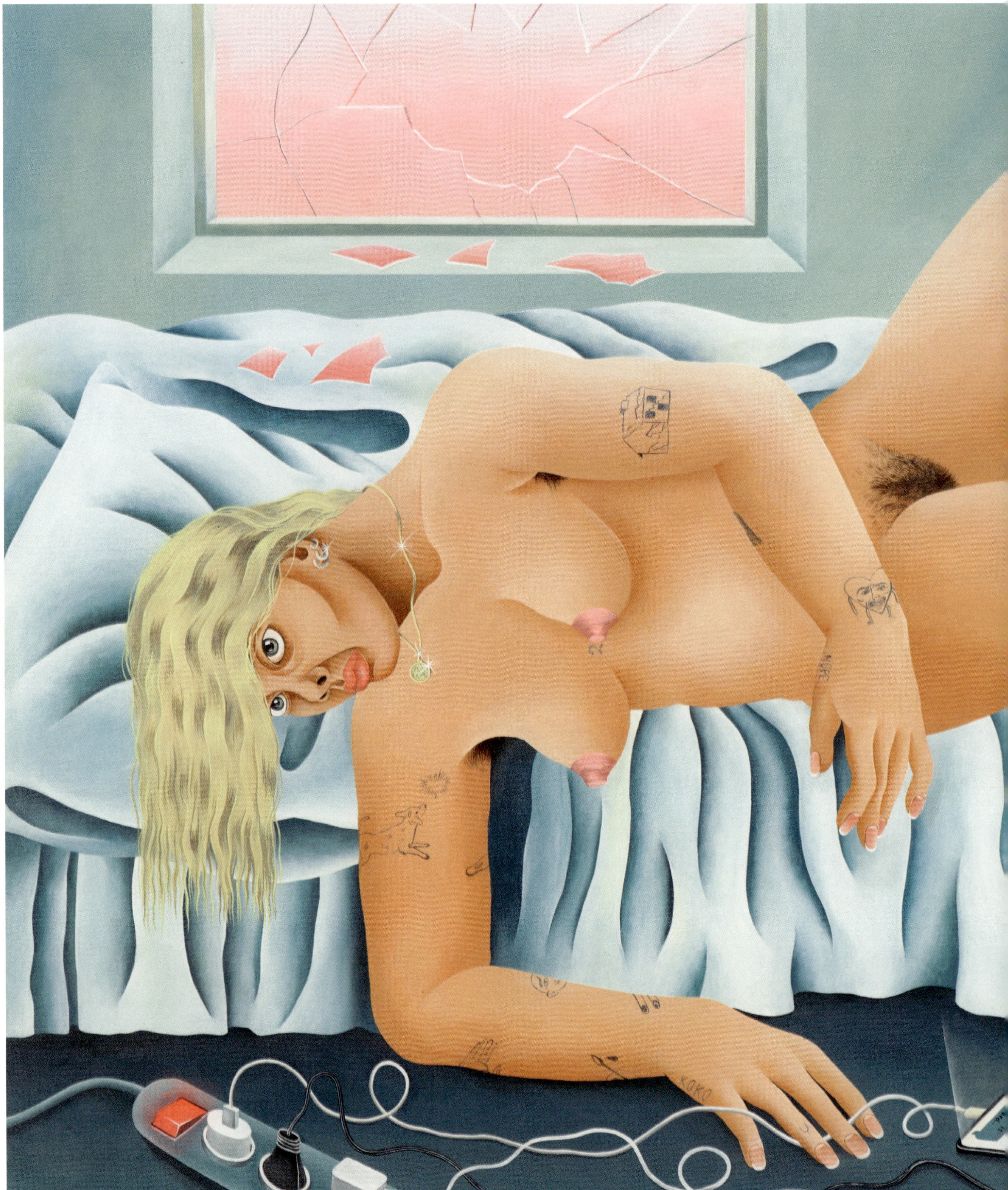

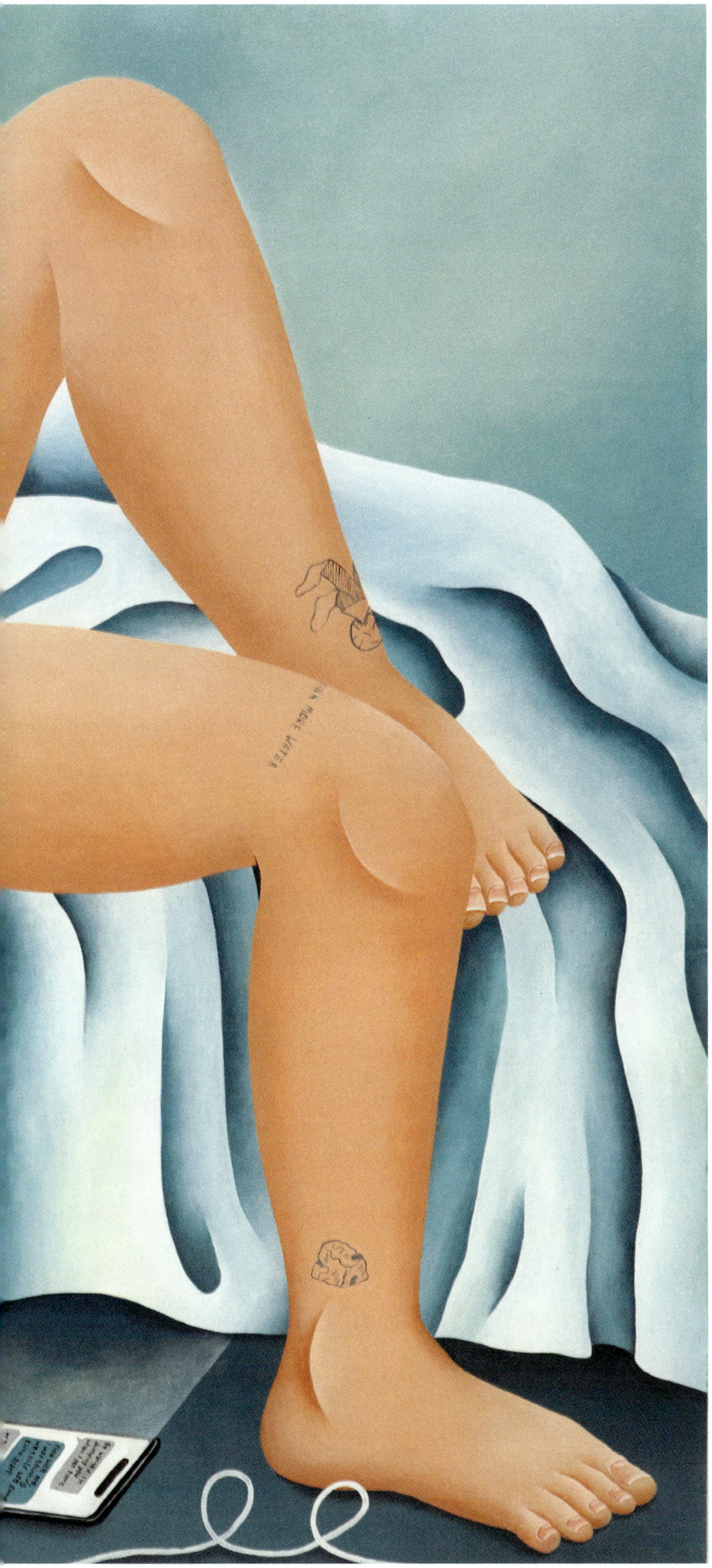

2024

Falling Out of Love

90 × 120 cm

31 × 21 cm (each)

I Am You, You Are Me (series) [pp. 109–11]

2024

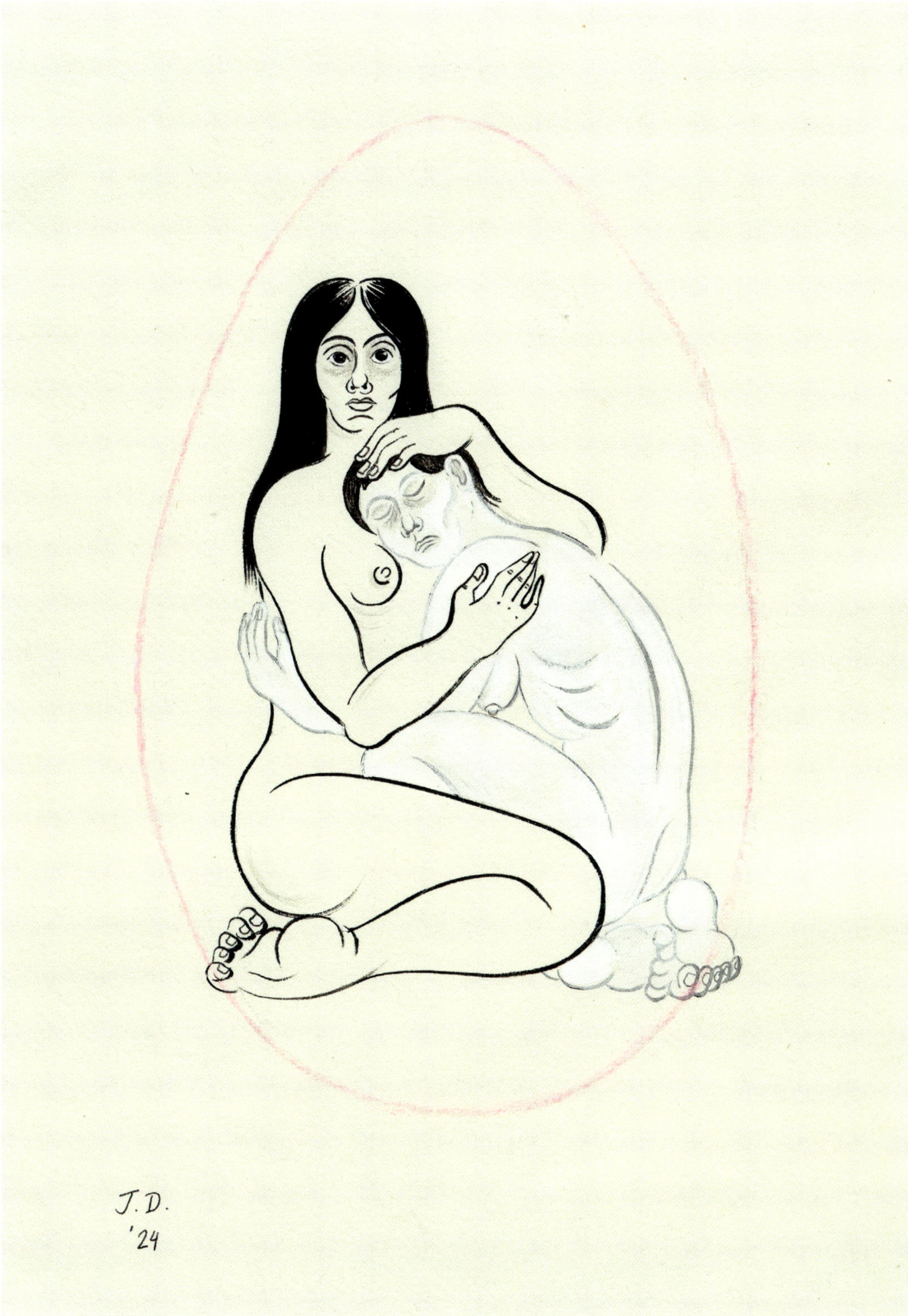
J.D.
'24

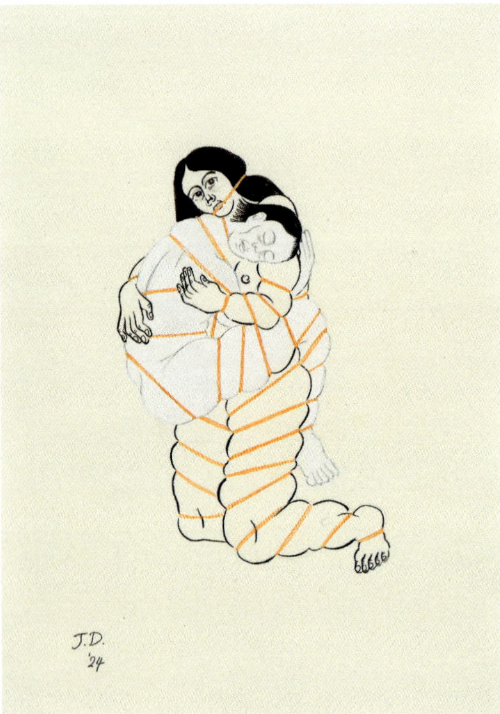
J.D.
'24

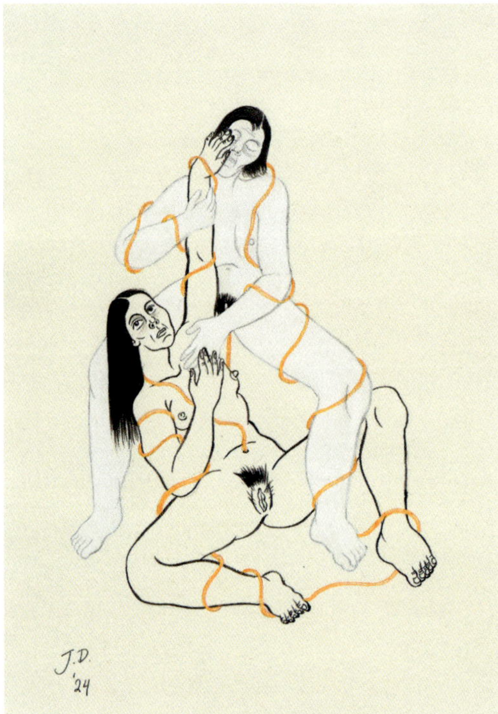
J.D.
'24

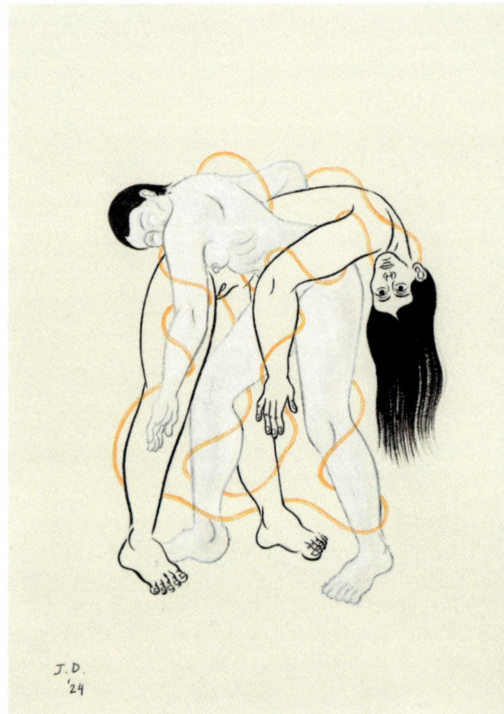
J.D.
'24

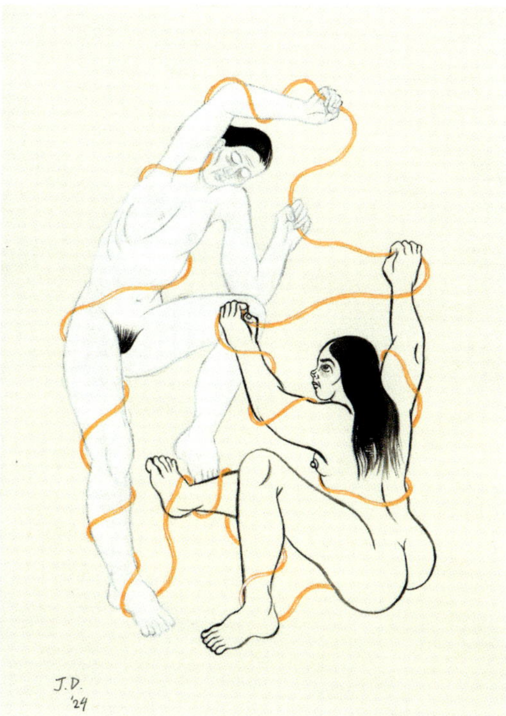
J.D.
'24

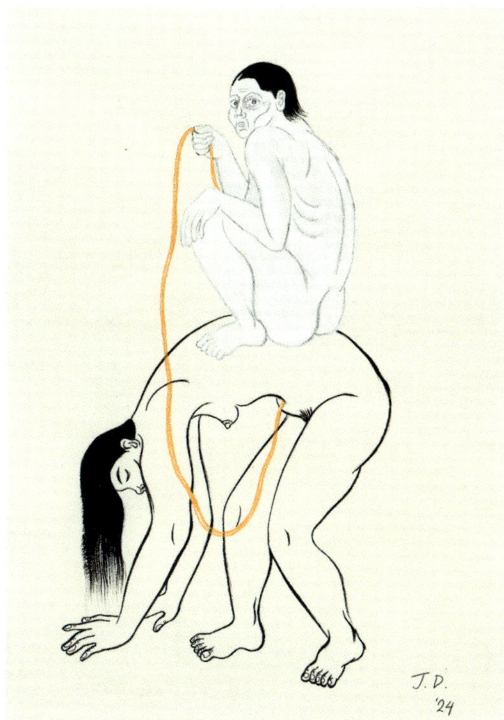
J.D.
'24

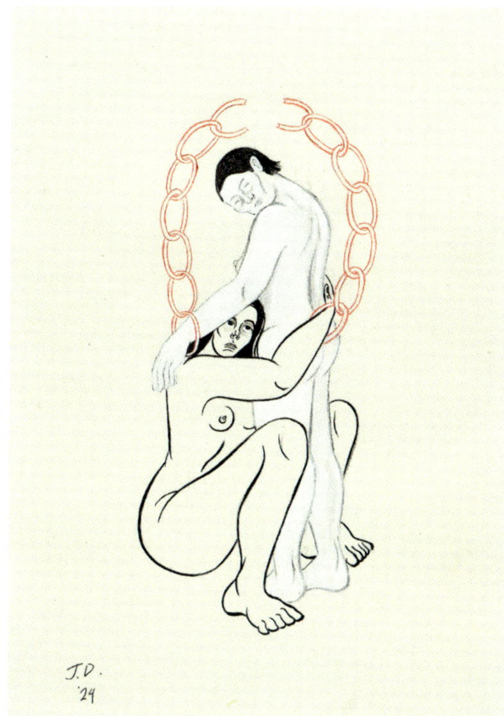
J.D.
'24

Self-Portrait of a Tired Artist

2024

100 × 80 cm

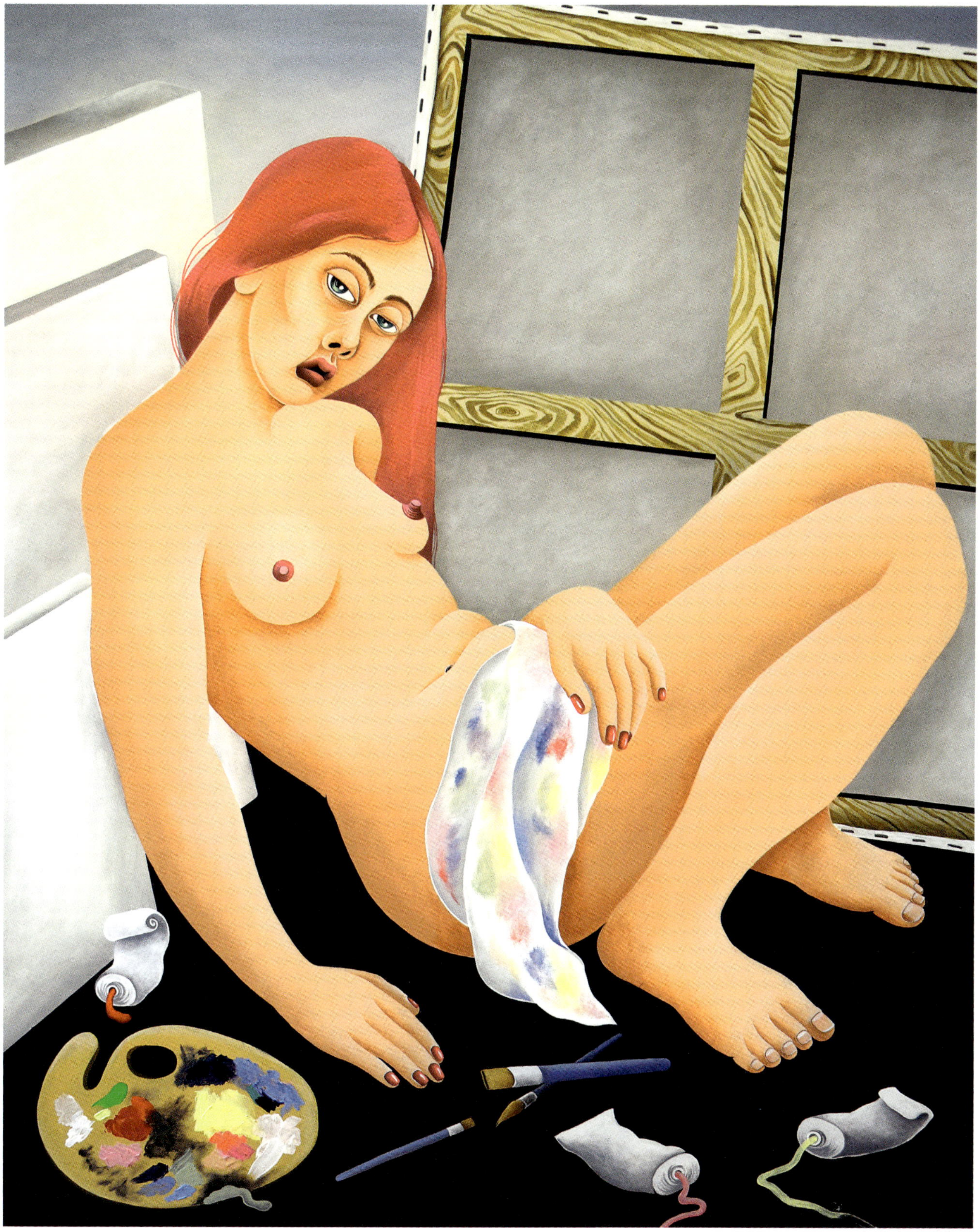

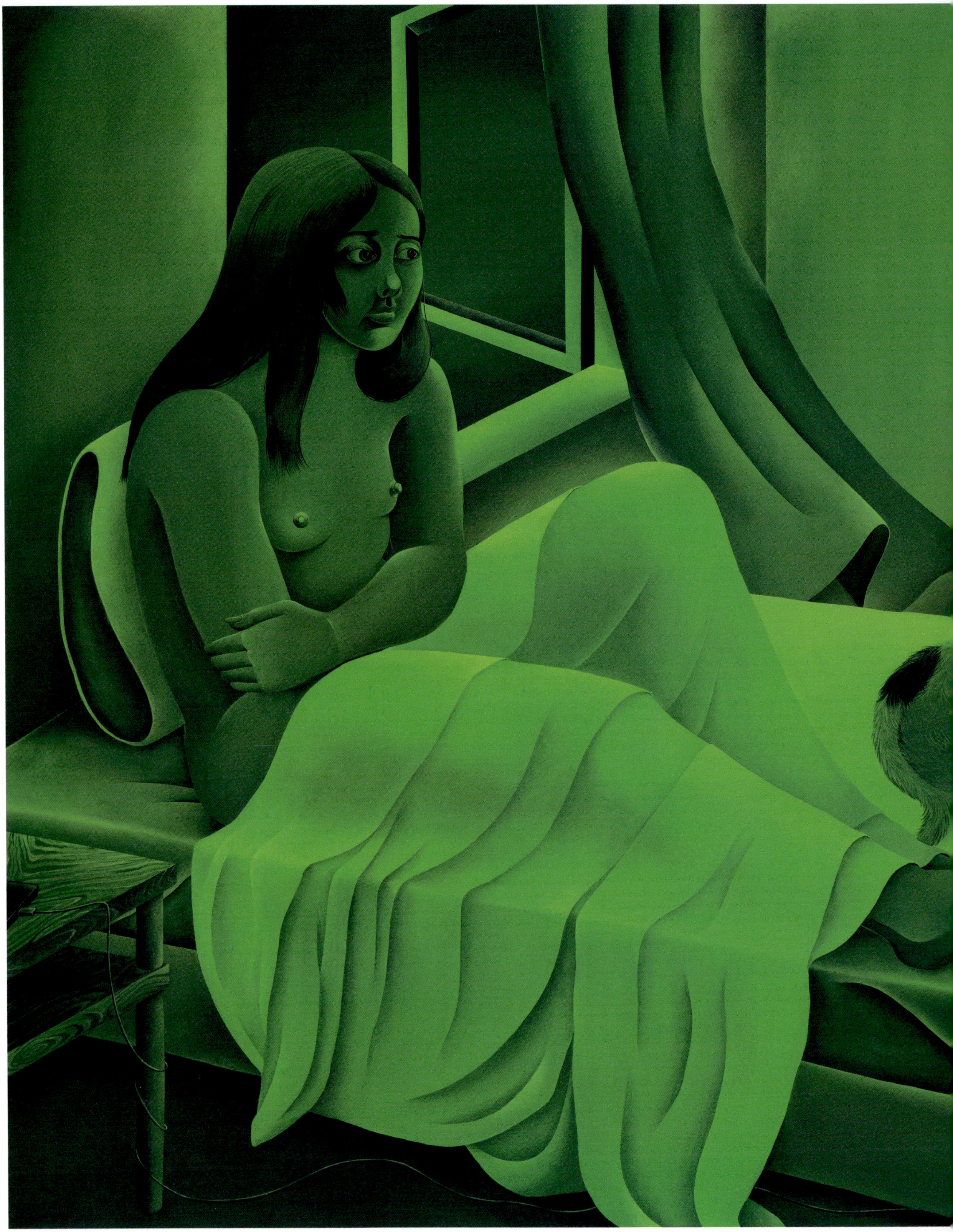

2024 *Awakening* 110 × 97 cm

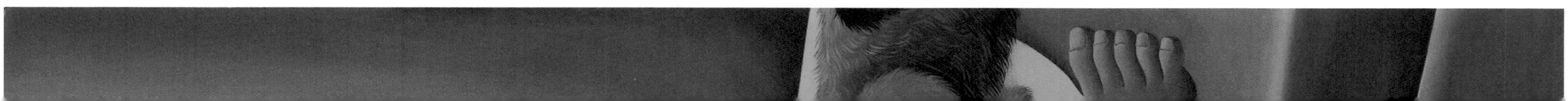

107 × 81 cm

Just the Two of Us

2024

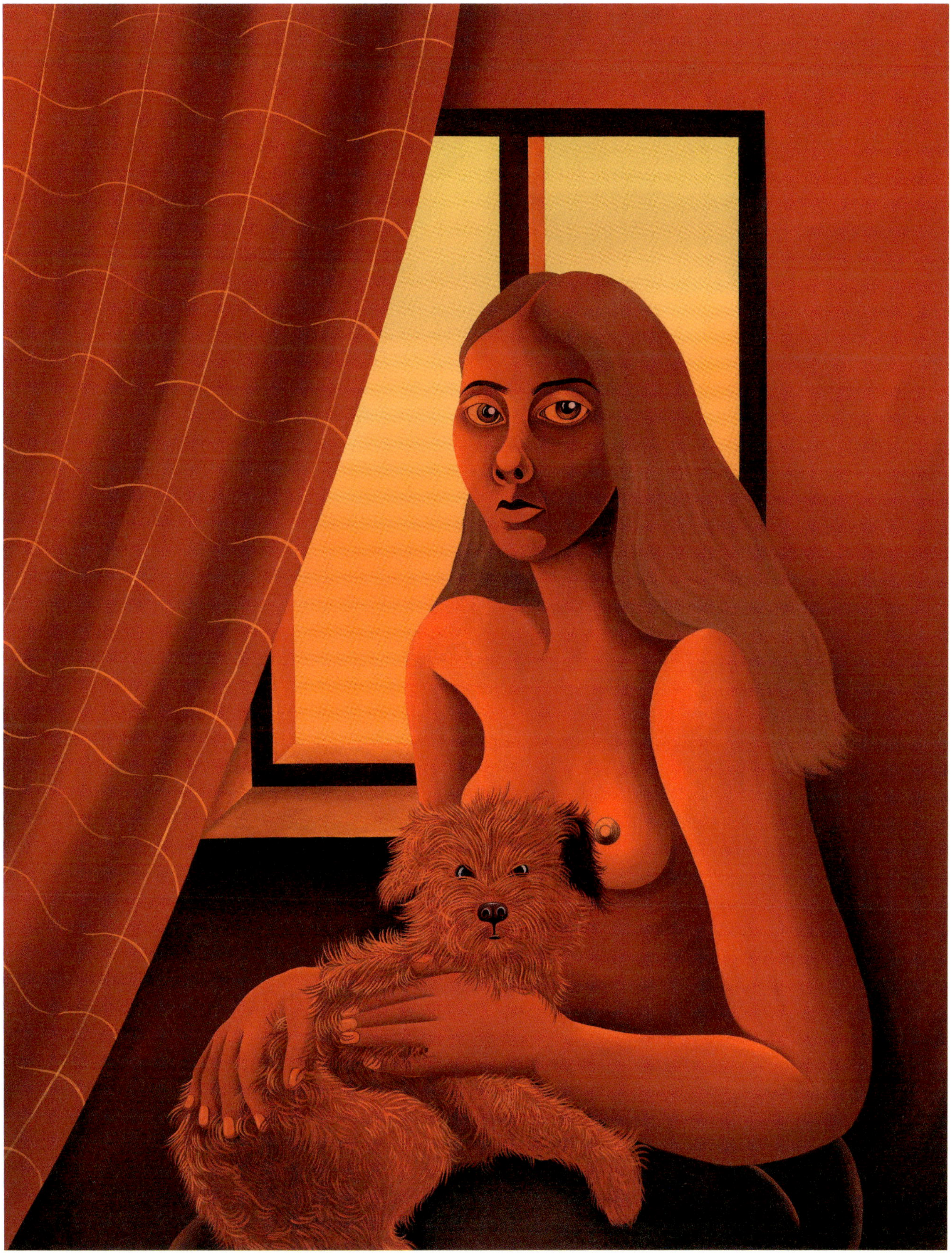

2024

Between Words & Webs

50 × 60 cm

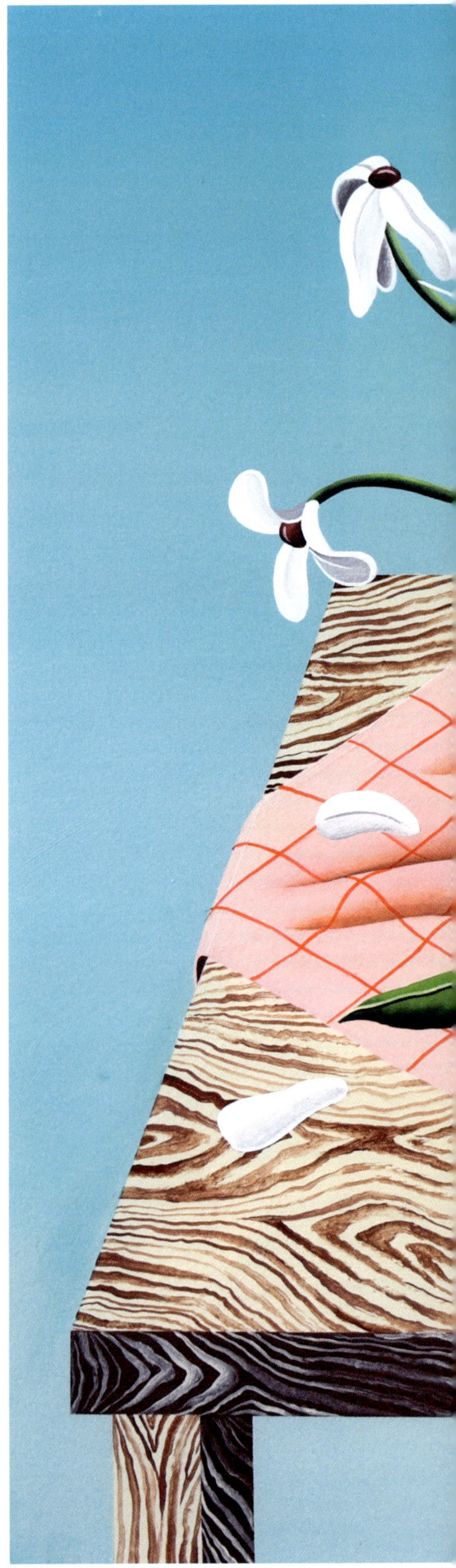

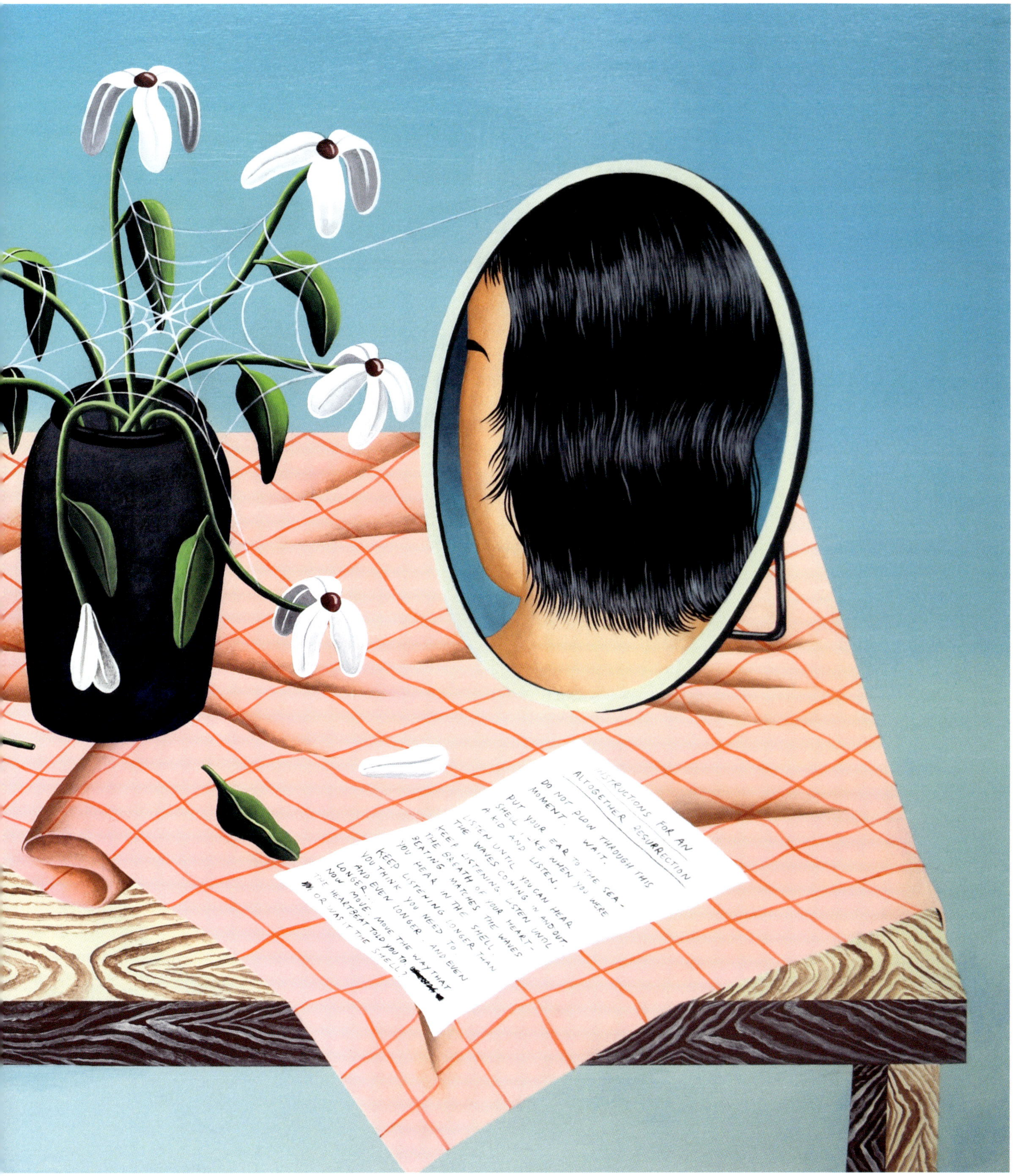
INSTRUCTIONS FOR AN
ALTOGETHER RESURRECTION
DO NOT PLOW THROUGH THIS
MOMENT. WAIT.
PUT YOUR EAR TO THE SEA-
SHELL LIKE WHEN YOU WERE
A KID AND LISTEN.
LISTEN UNTIL YOU CAN HEAR
THE WAVES COMING IN AND OUT.
KEEP LISTENING. LISTEN UNTIL
THE BREATH OF YOUR HEART-
BEATING MATCHES THE WAVES
YOU HEAR IN THE SHELL.
KEEP LISTENING LONGER THAN
YOU THINK YOU NEED TO
AND EVEN LONGER. AND EVEN
LONGER.
NOW MOVE. MOVE THE WAY THAT
THE HEARTBEAT TOLD YOU TO.
OR WAS IT THE SHELL?

Metamorphosis

2024

107 × 81 cm

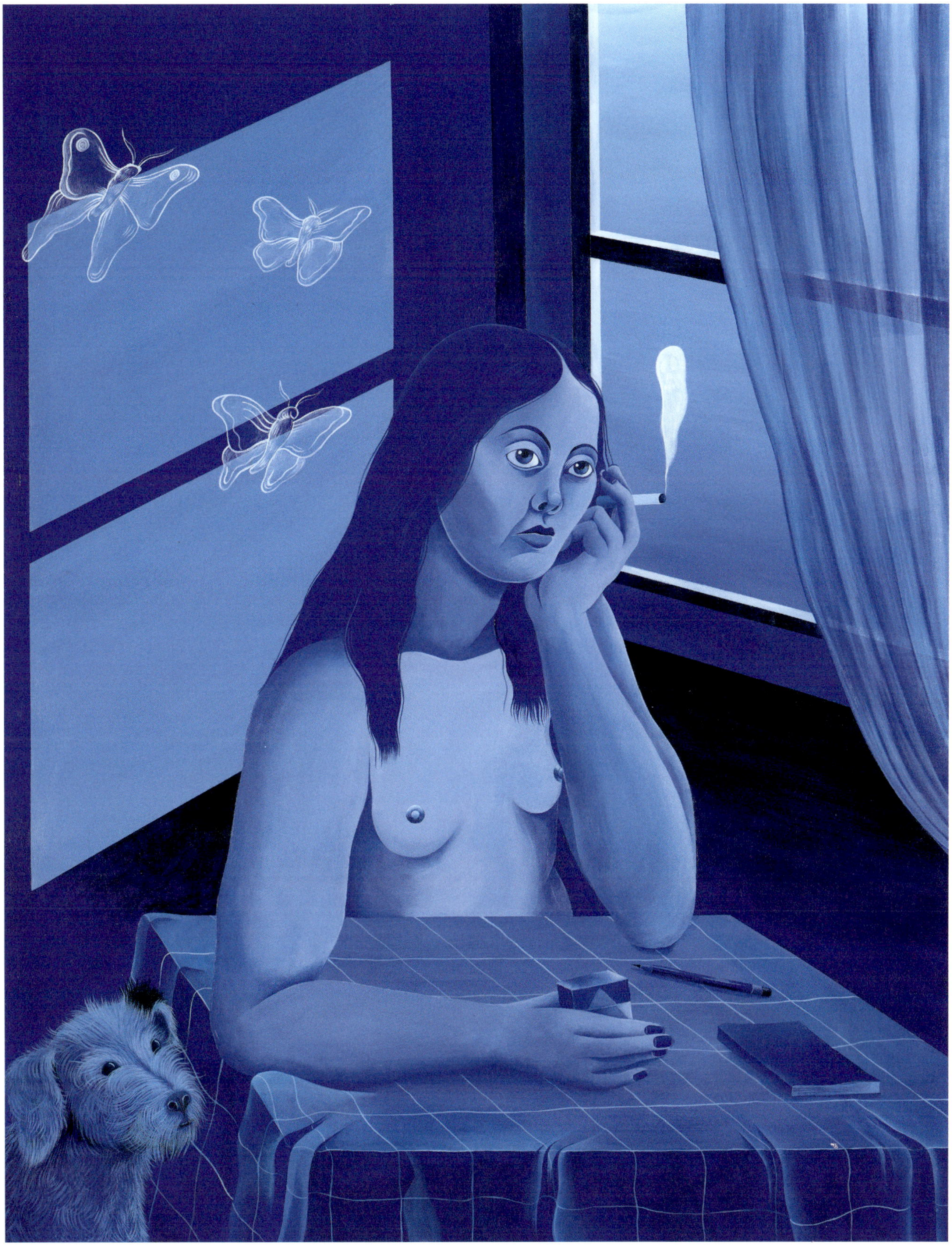

31 × 21 cm (each) *(In)dependency* [pp. 123–5] 2024

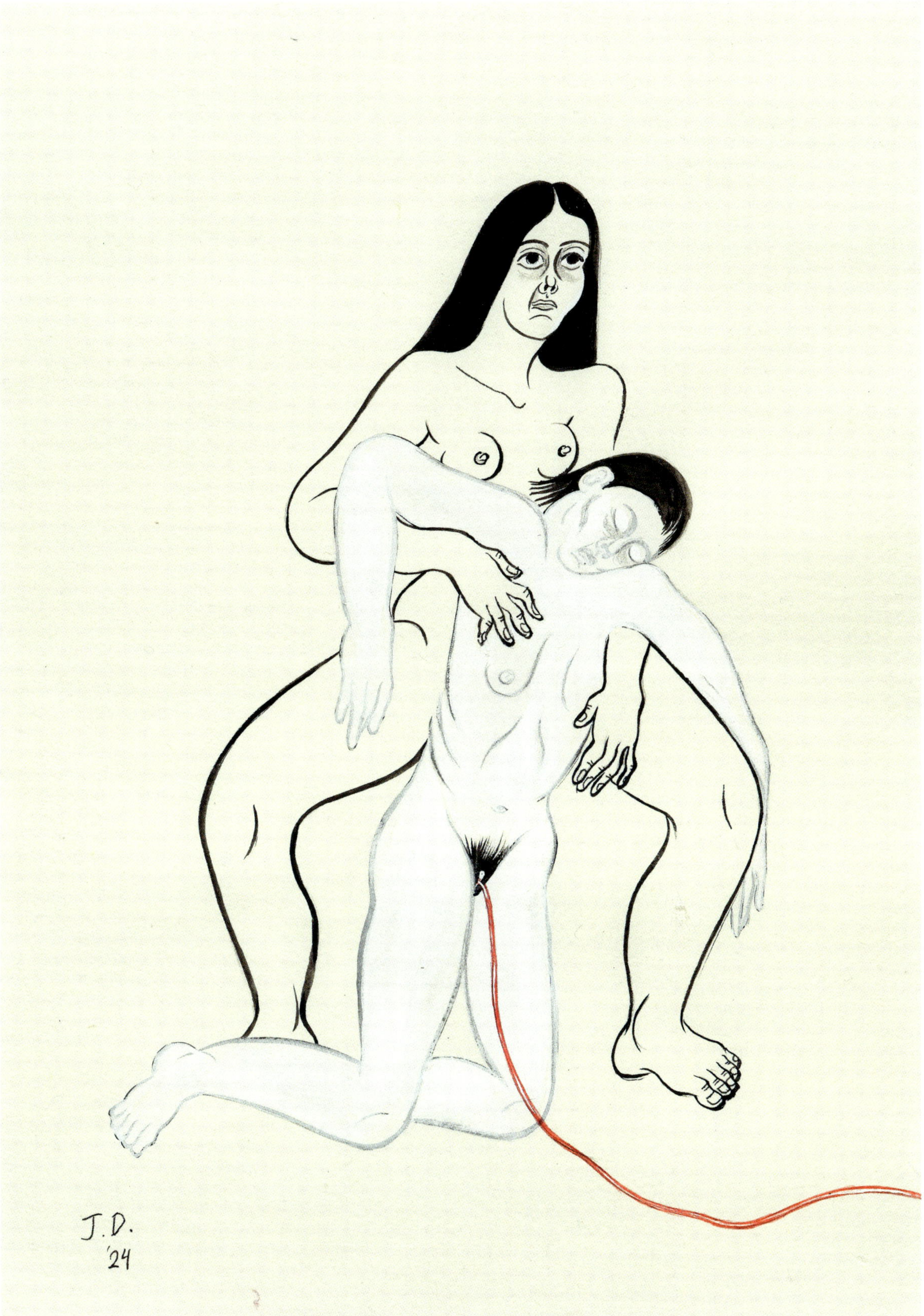
J.D.
'24

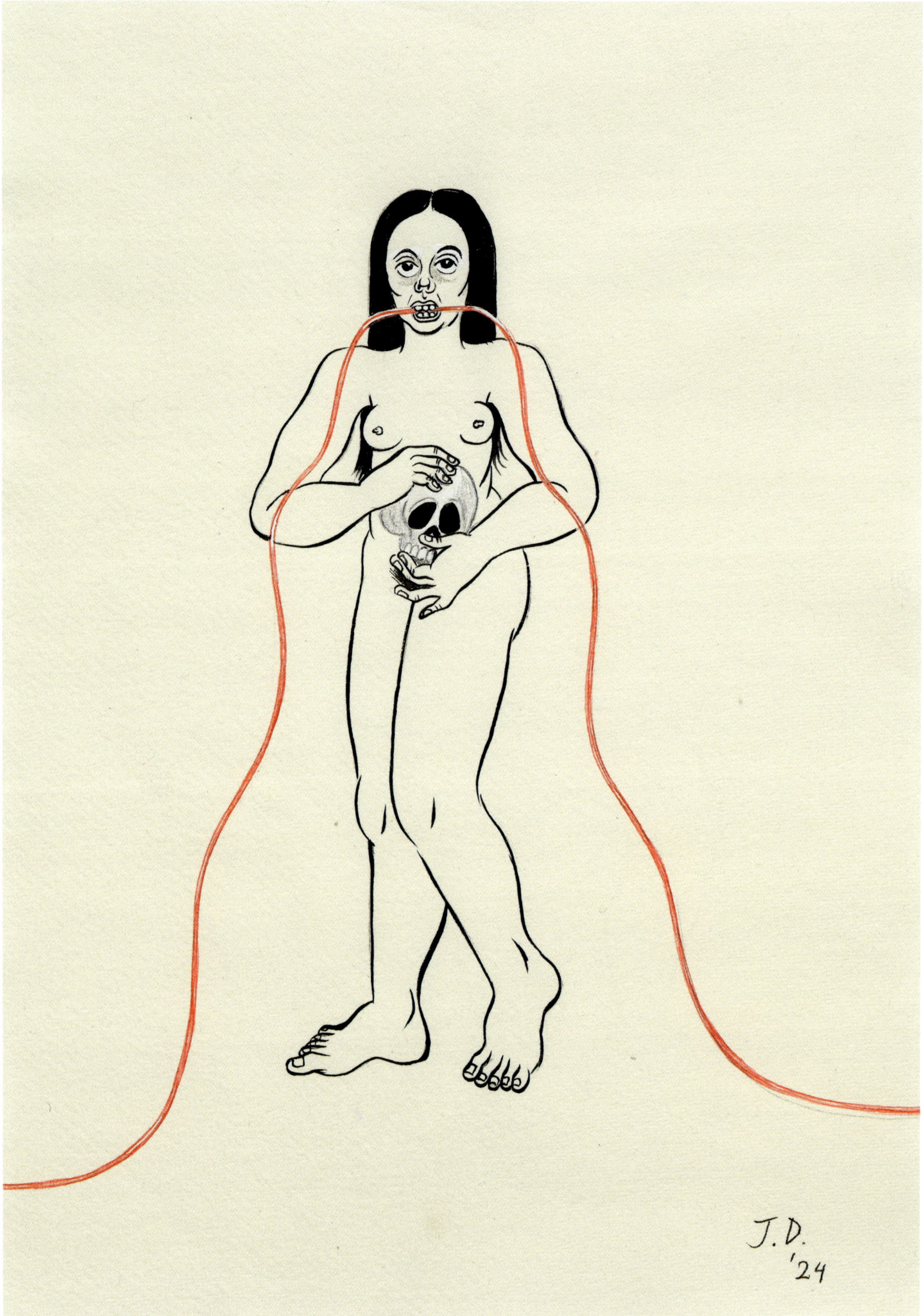
J.D.
'24

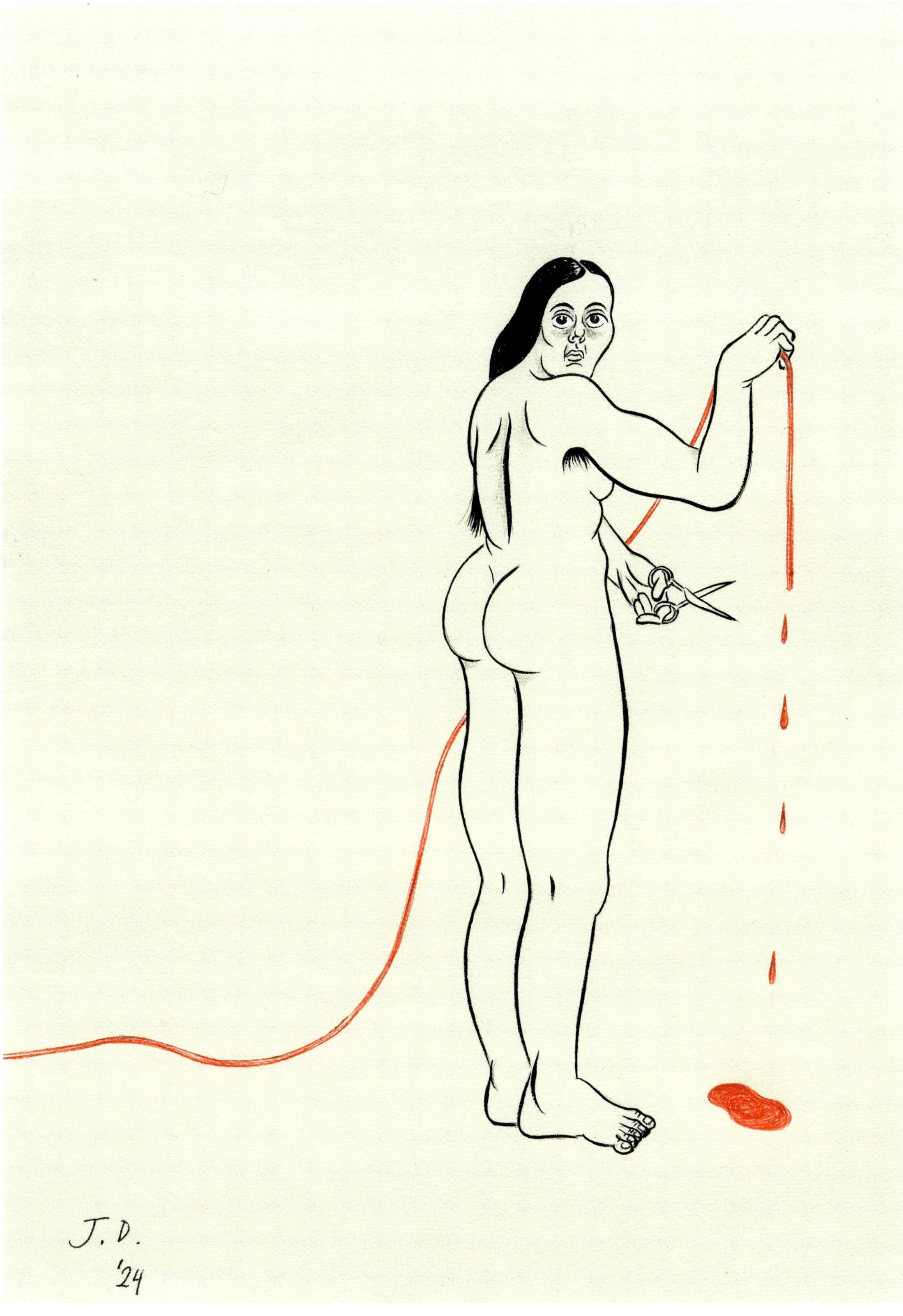
J. D.
'24

Self-Portrait in the Studio

2024

120 × 90 cm

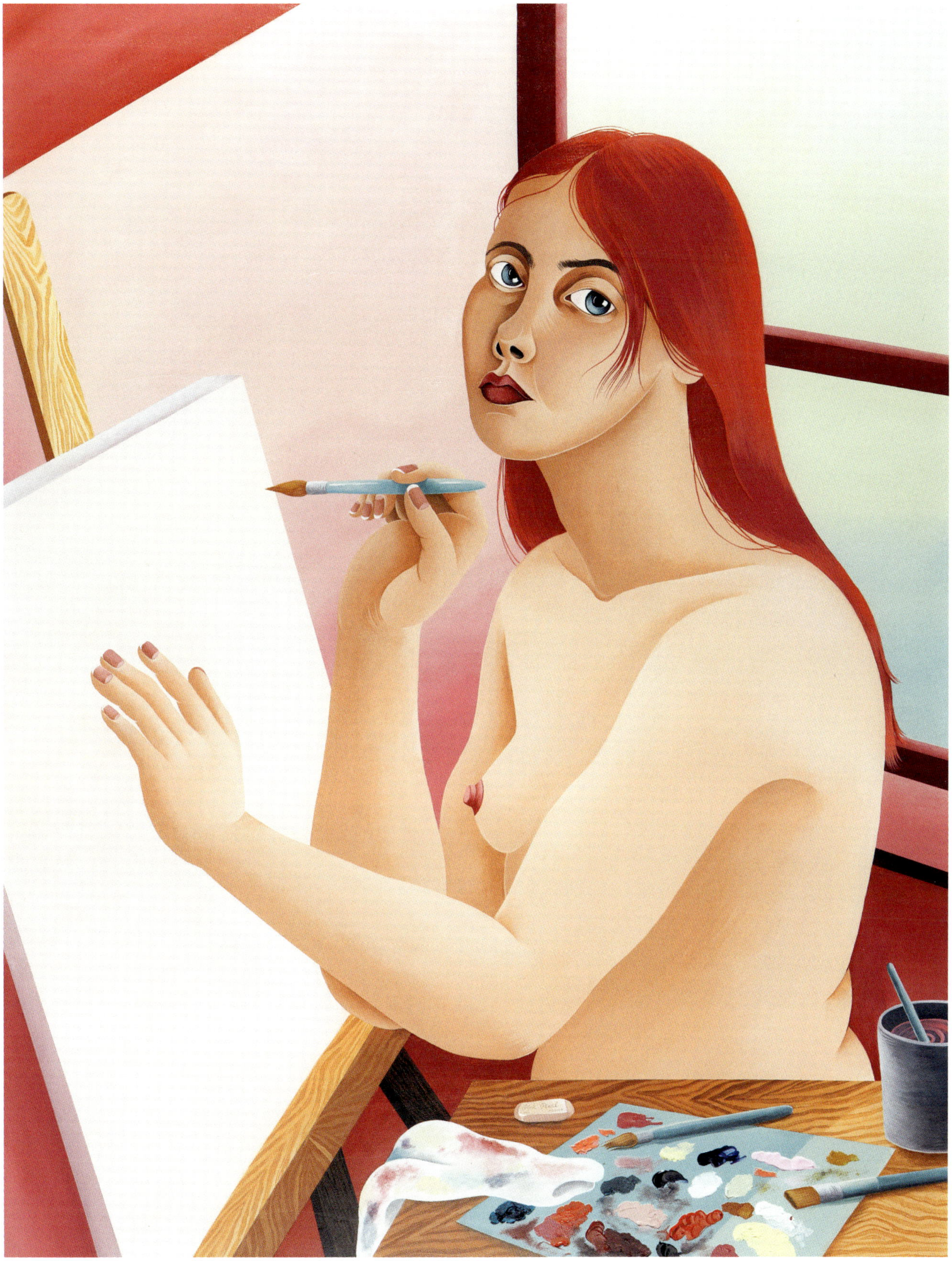

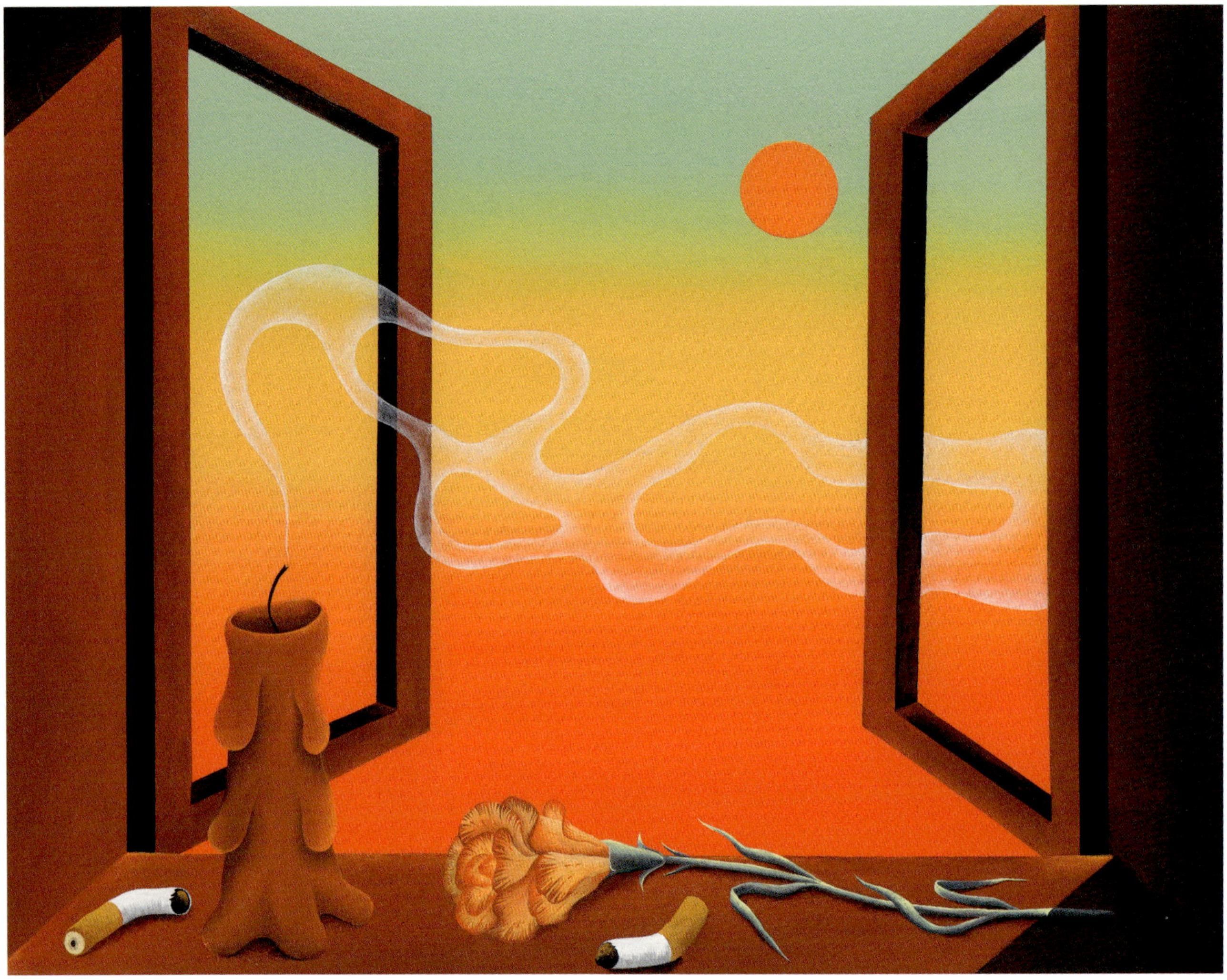

One Summer Evening

2024

40 × 50 cm

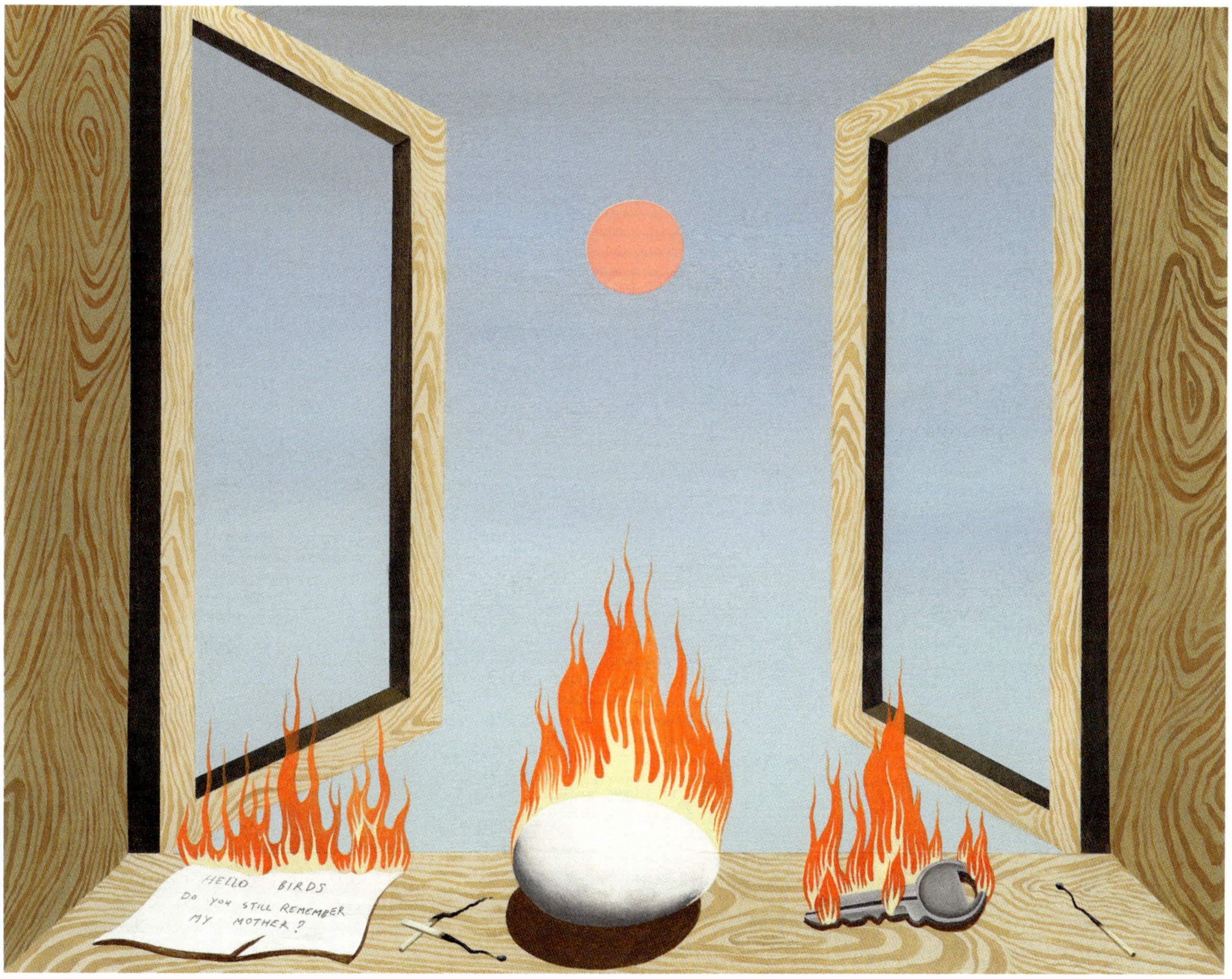

2024

On the Horizon

40 × 50 cm

30 × 30 cm *Milo with Butterflies* 2024

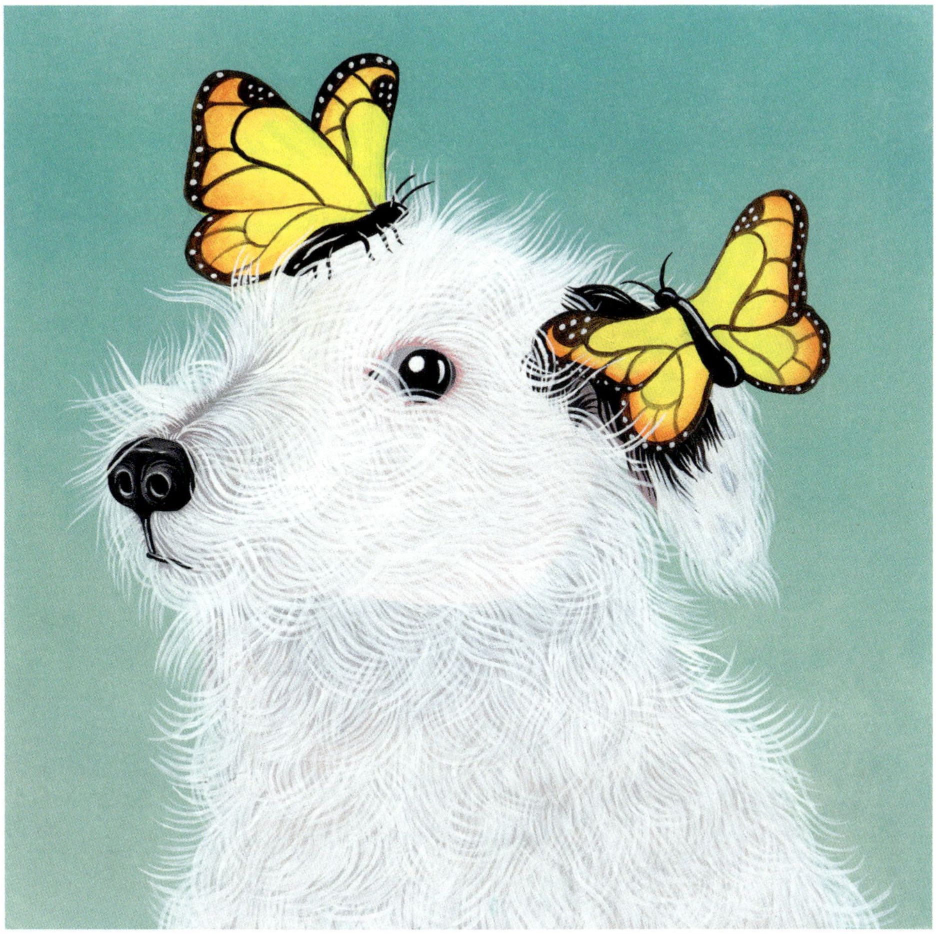

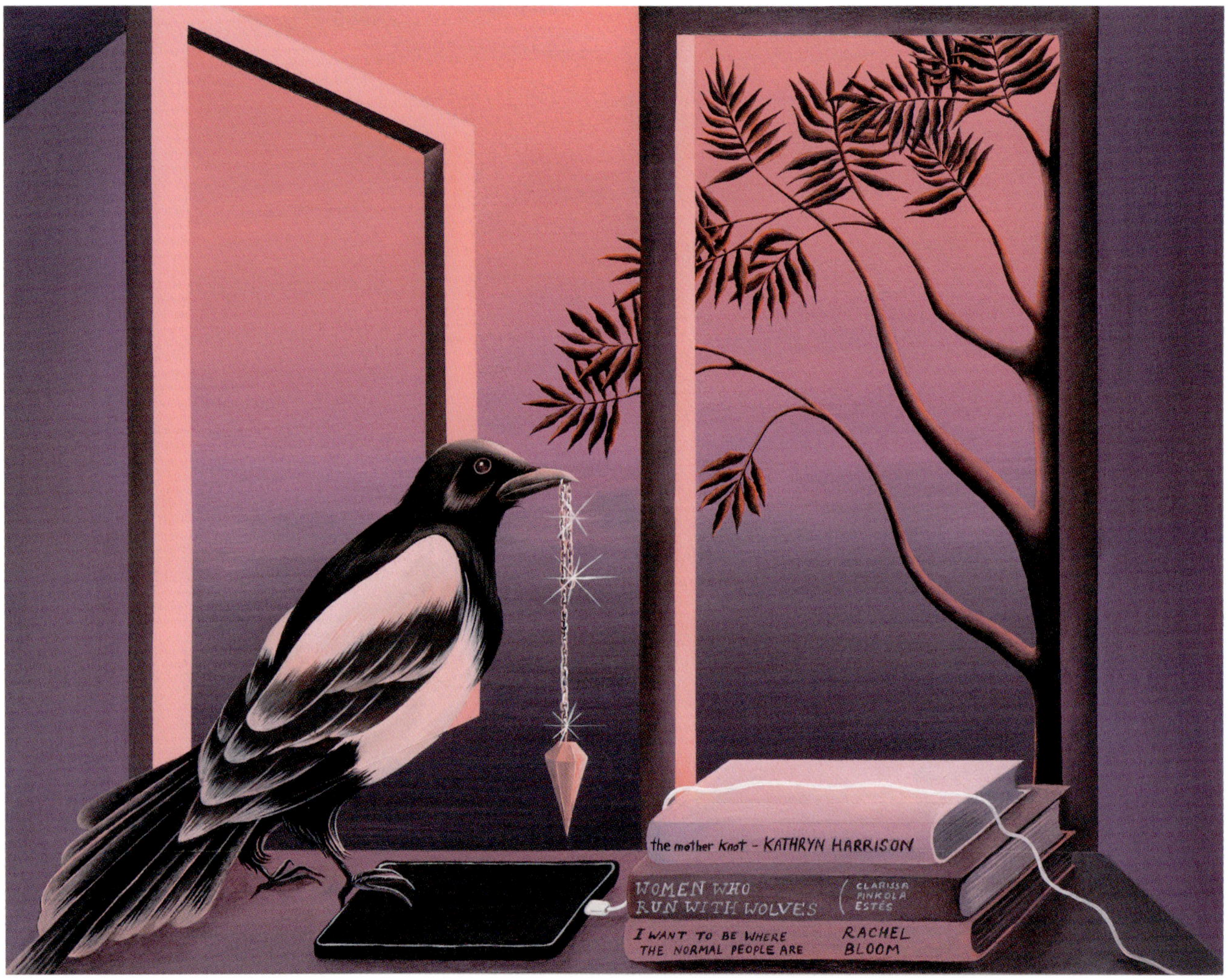

One Is for Sorrow

2024

40 × 50 cm

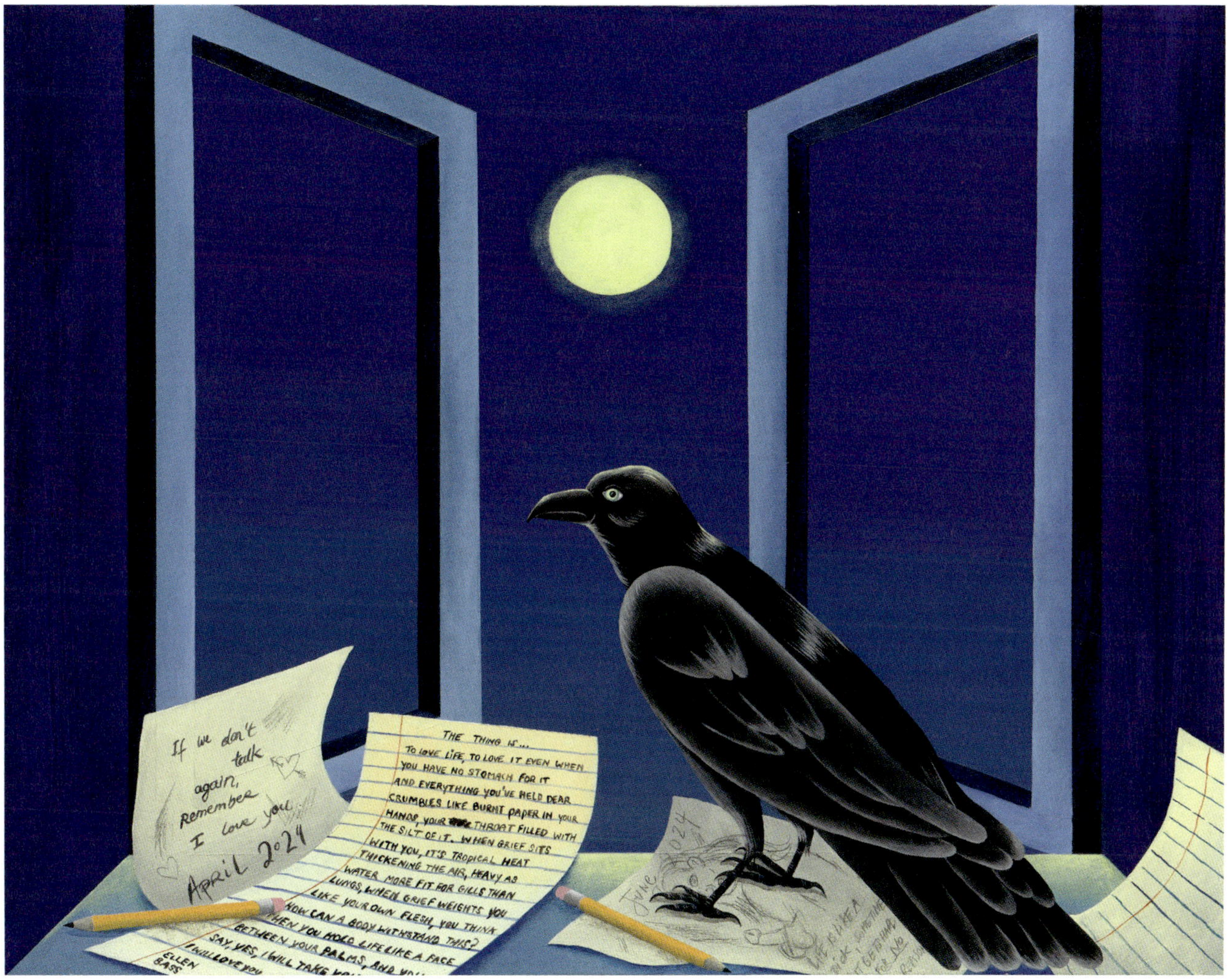

2024

Letters to the Birds

40 × 50 cm

24 × 18 cm

Teardrop

2024

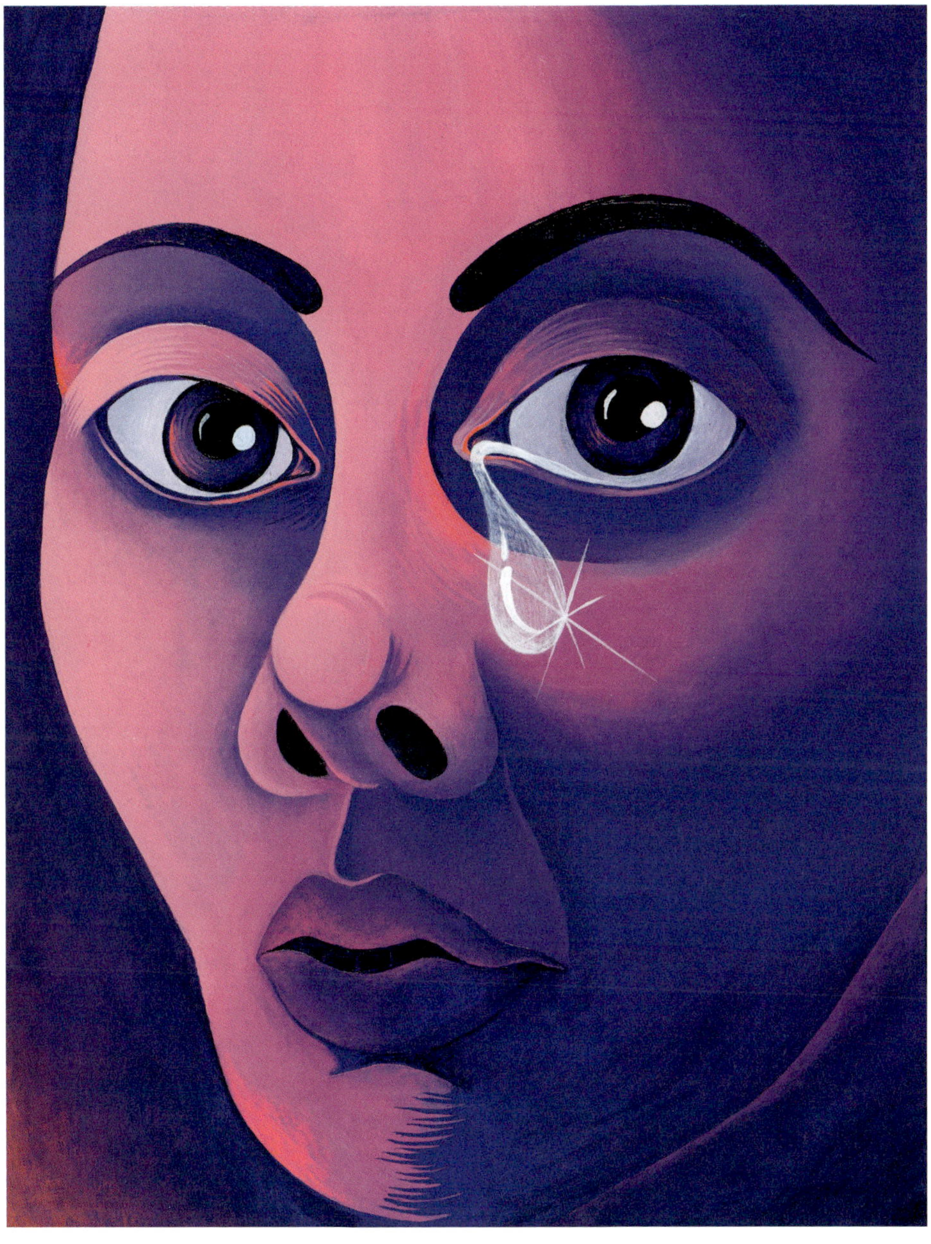

RE

KIND

LING

29.7 × 21 cm

Mourning in Forgetfulness (series)

2024

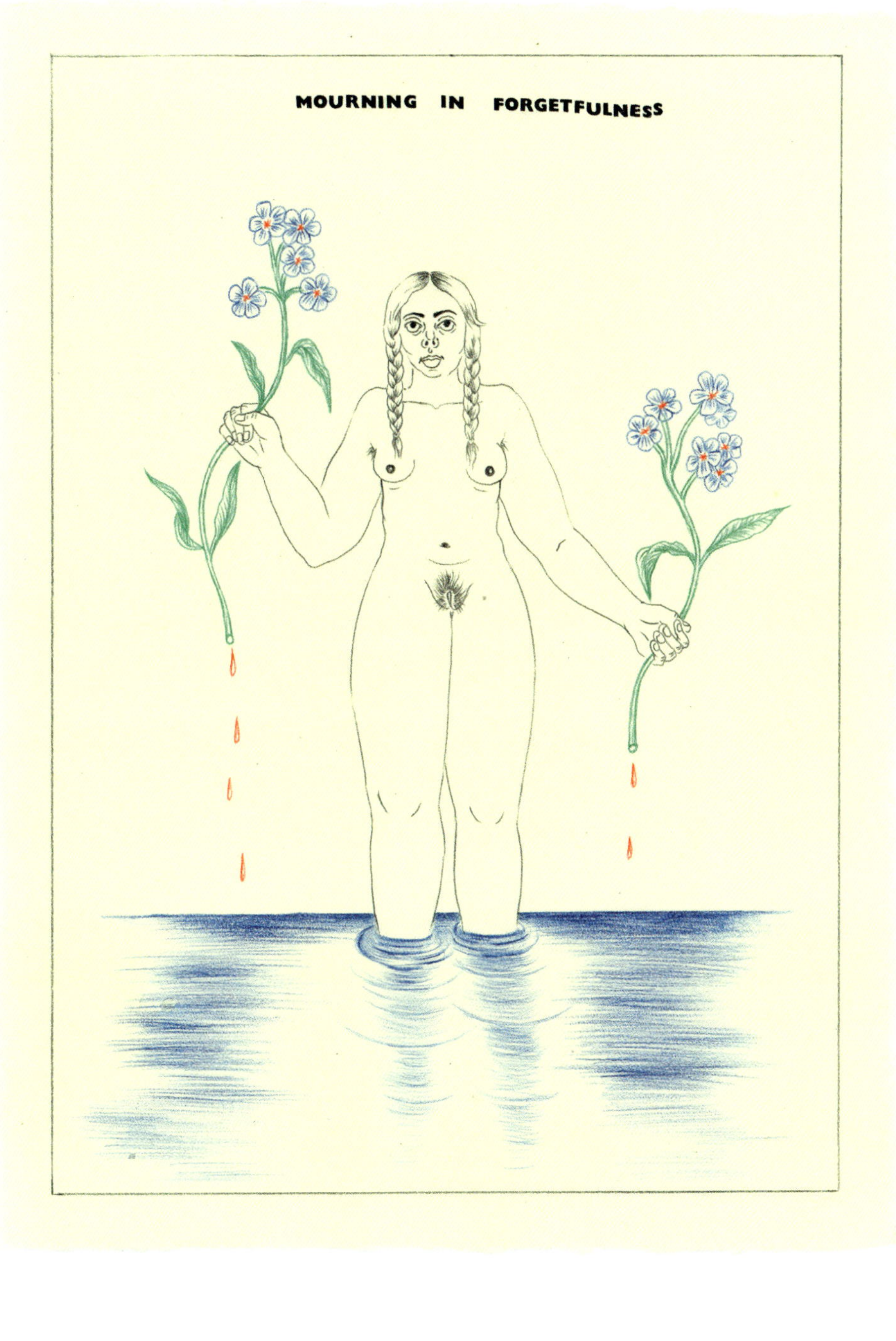
MOURNING IN FORGETFULNESS

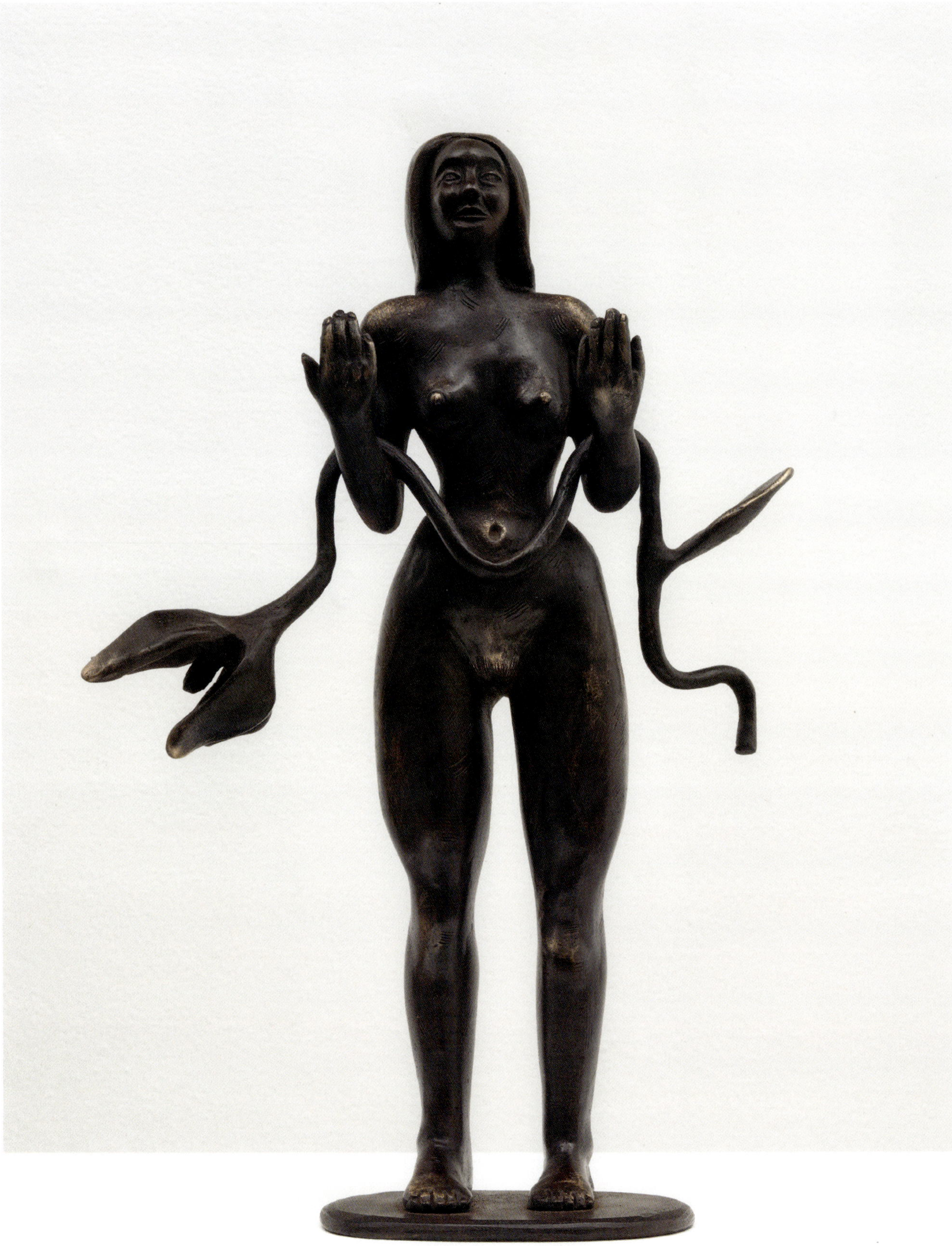

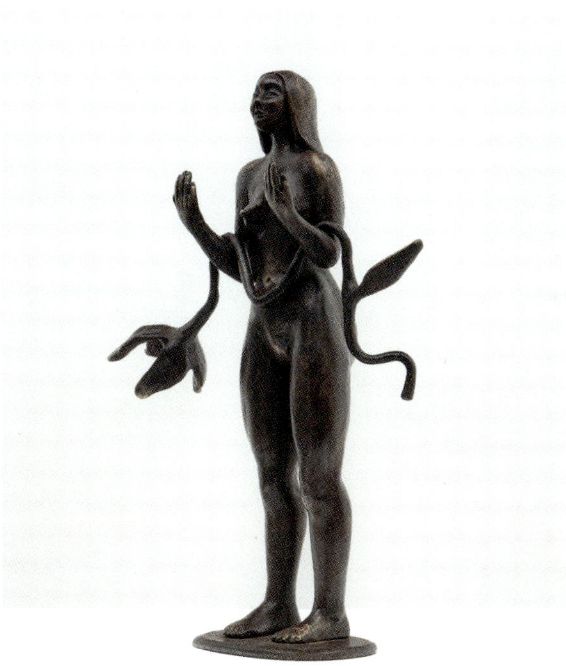
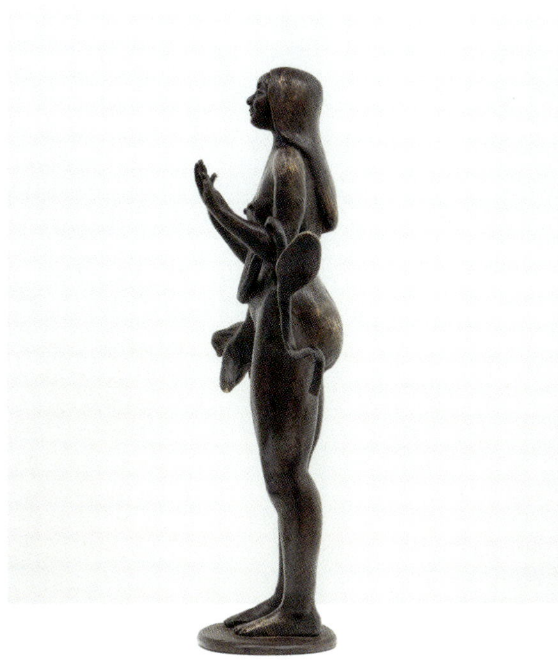
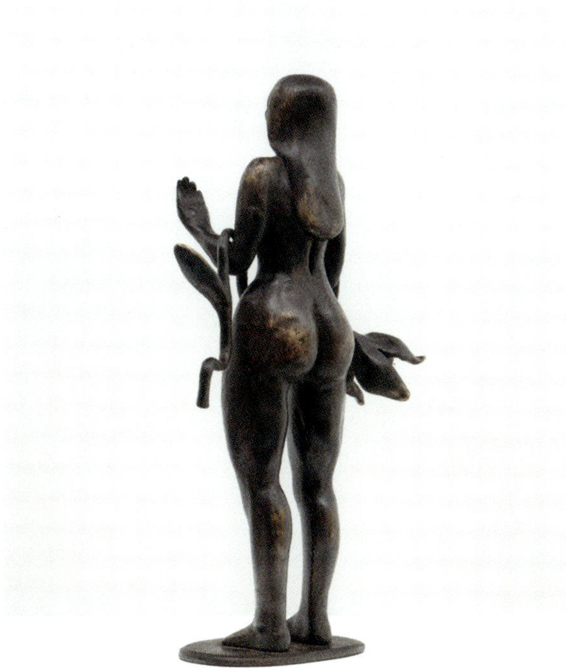
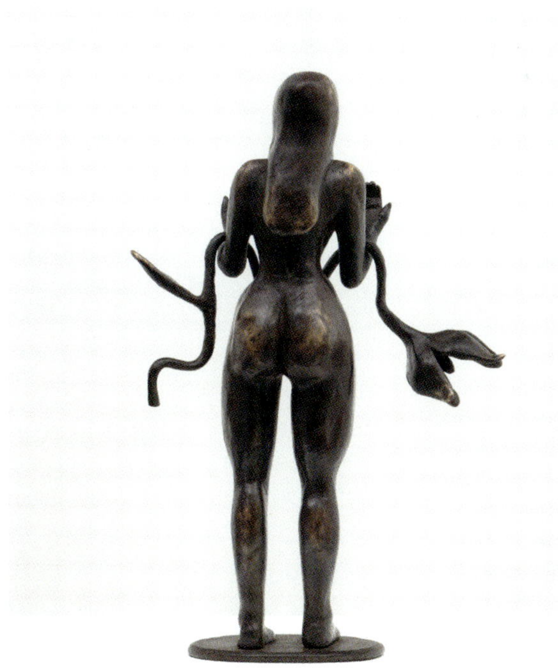

2025

Catharsis 1 (Edition of 8 + 4 AP)

c. 33 × 21,5 × 10 cm

Self-Portrait in Abundance

100 × 80 cm

2025

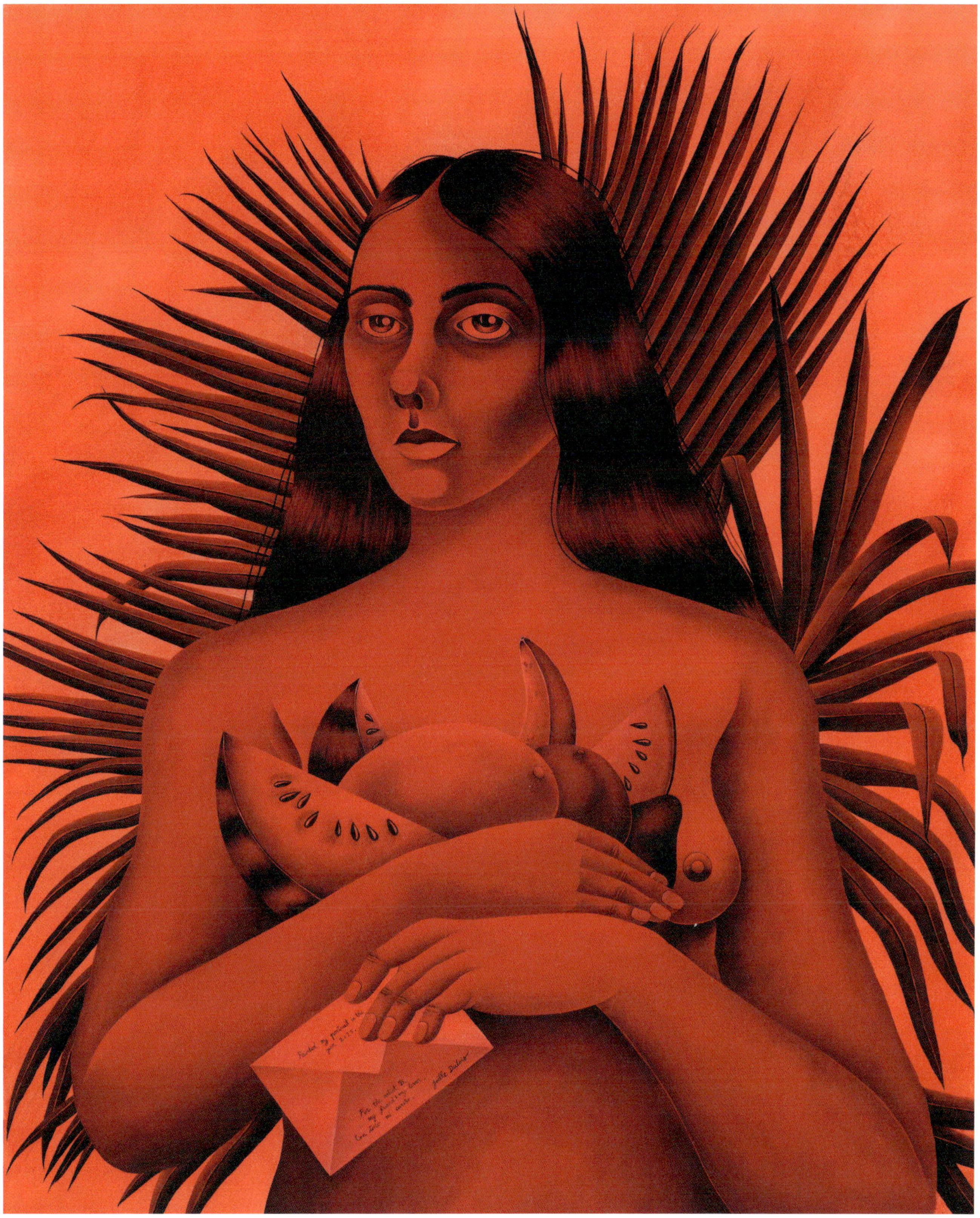

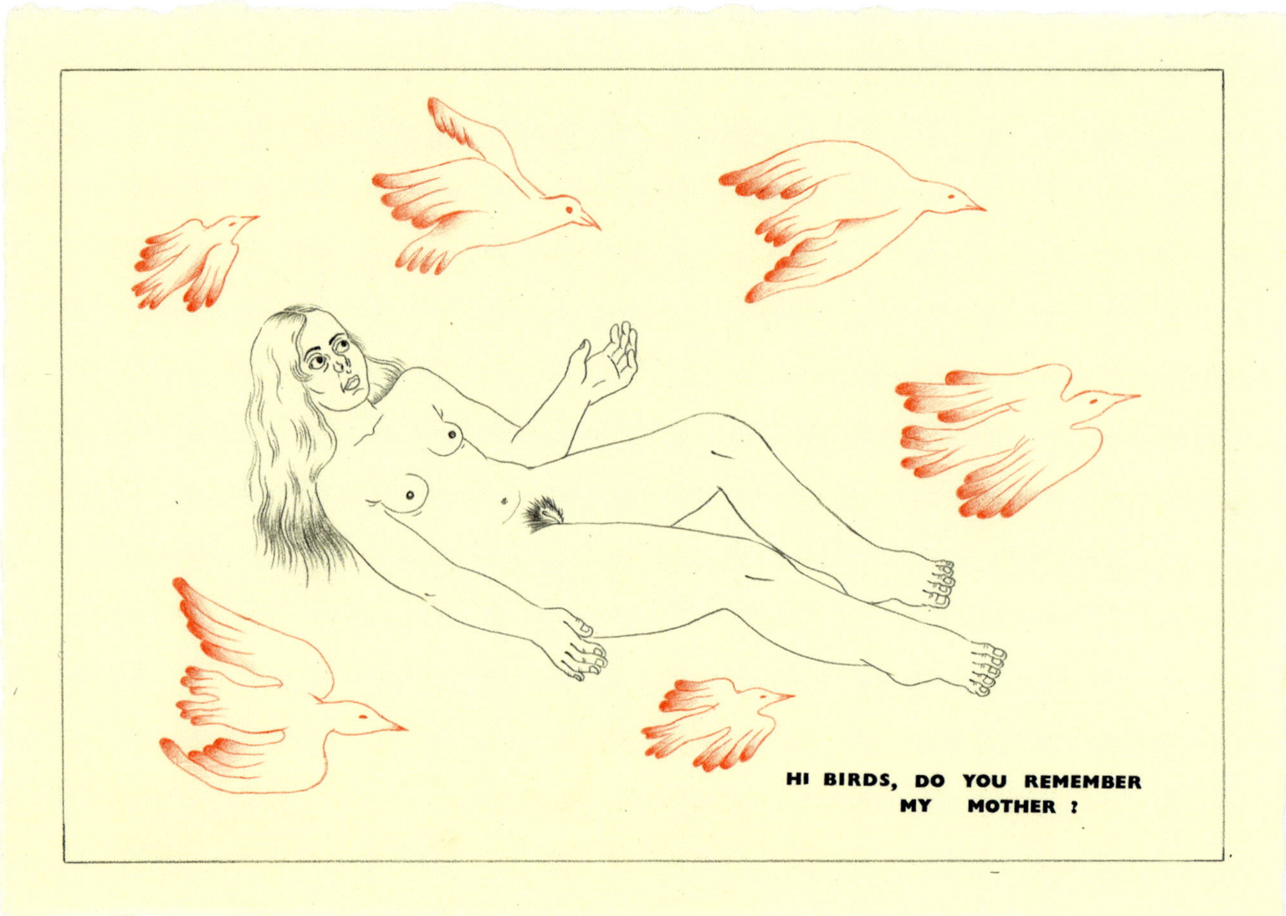

2025

Mourning in Forgetfulness (series) [pp. 144–7]

21 × 29.7 cm (each)

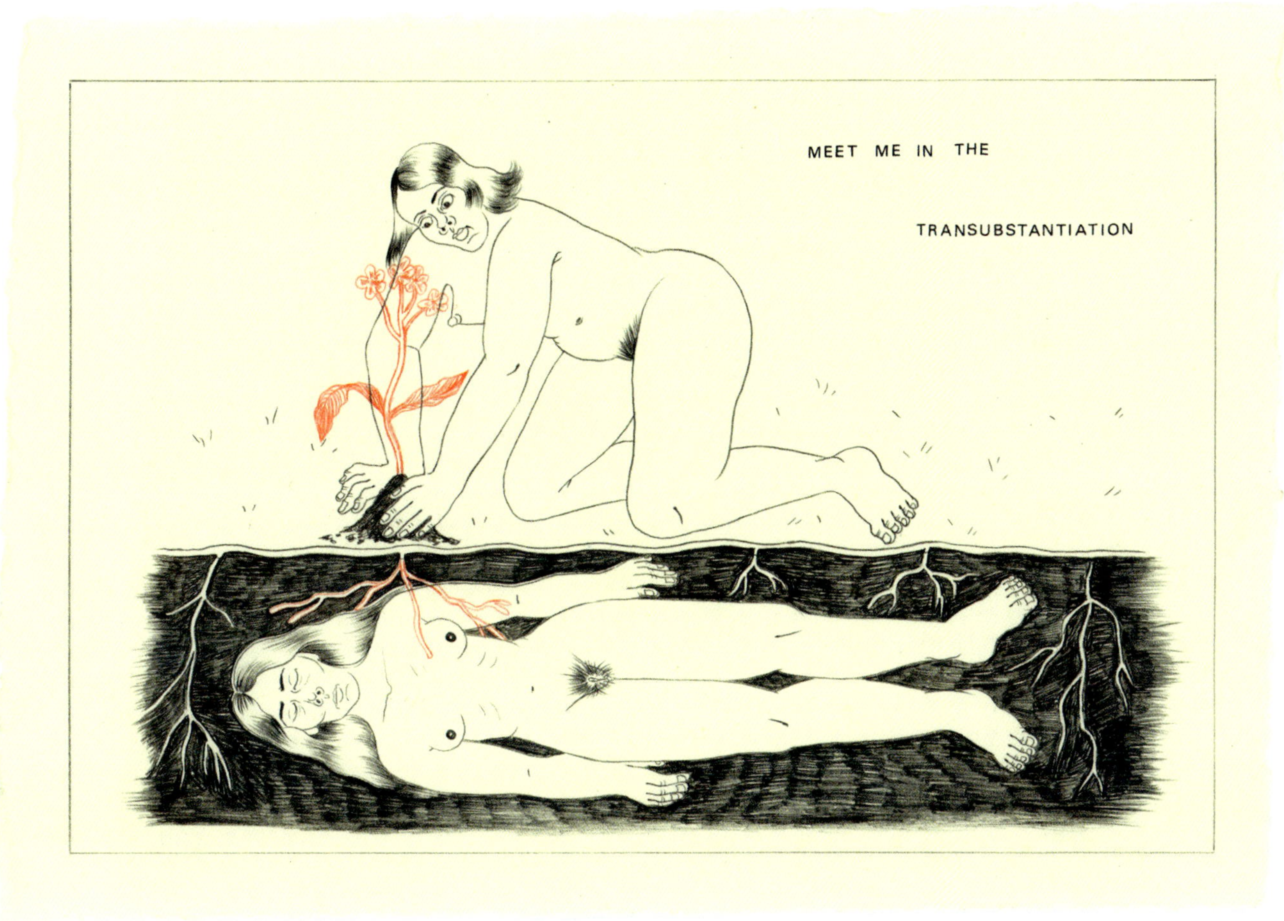
MEET ME IN THE
TRANSUBSTANTIATION

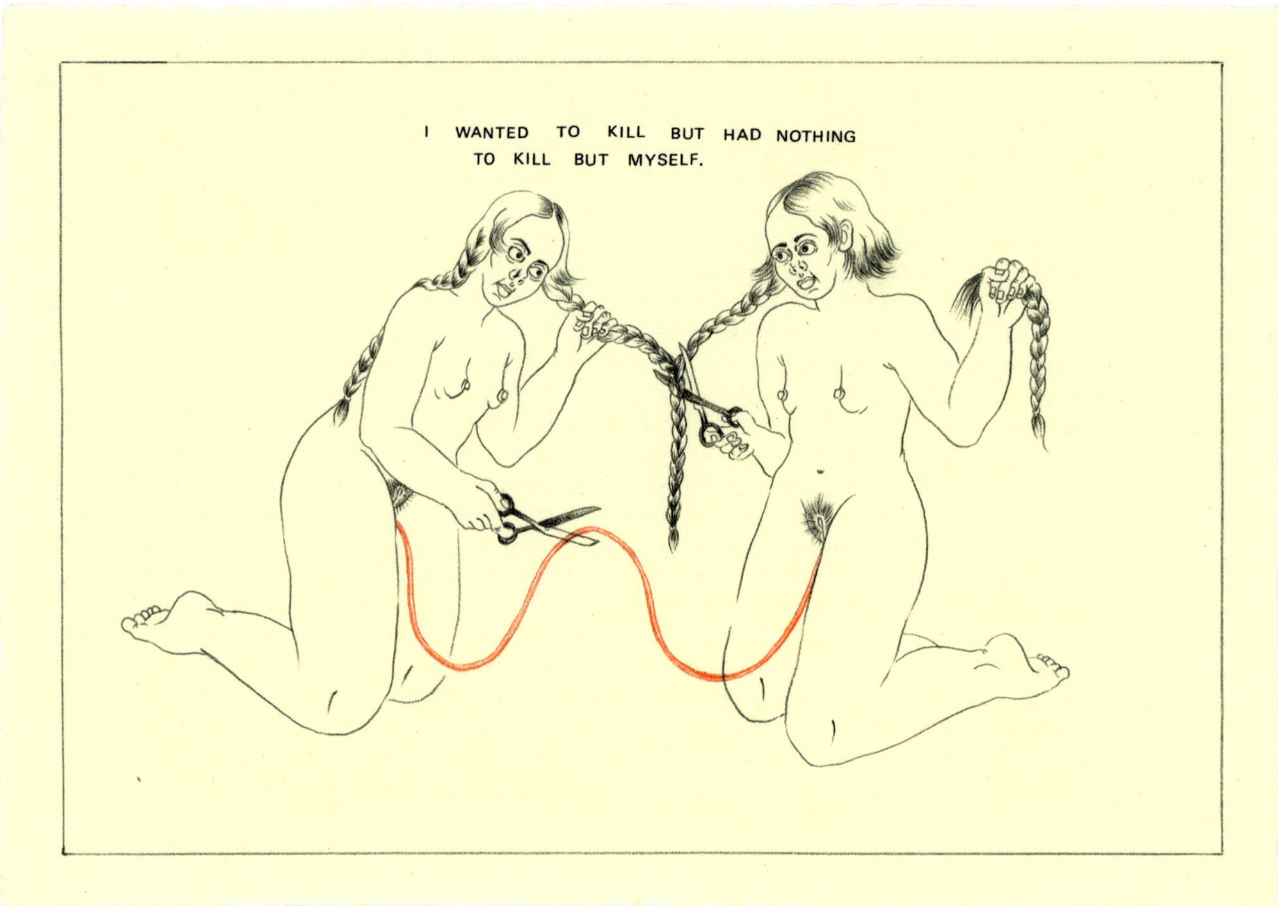
I WANTED TO KILL BUT HAD NOTHING
TO KILL BUT MYSELF.

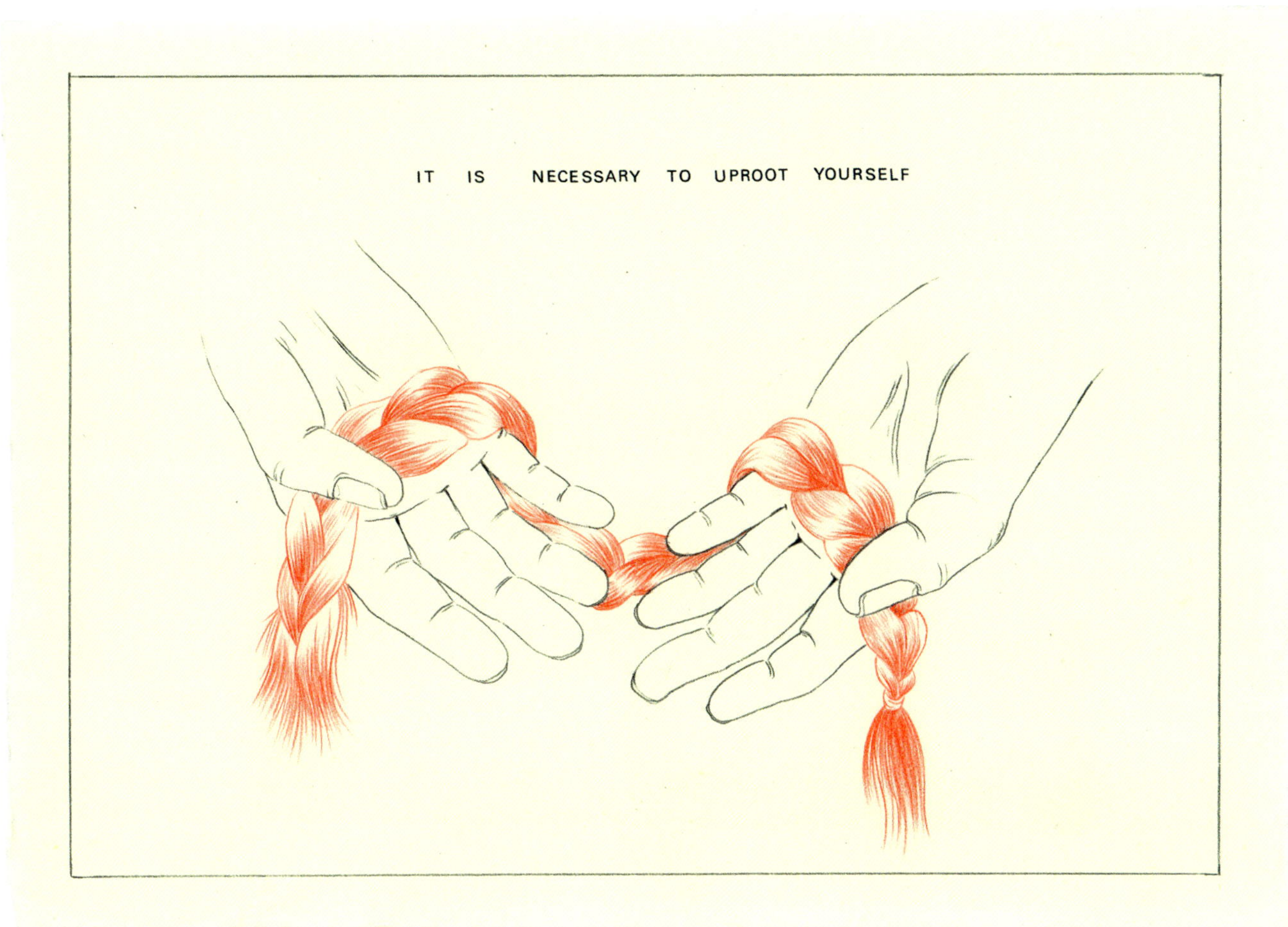
IT IS NECESSARY TO UPROOT YOURSELF

60.5 × 50.5 cm *Galvanised Spirit, My Mother* 2025

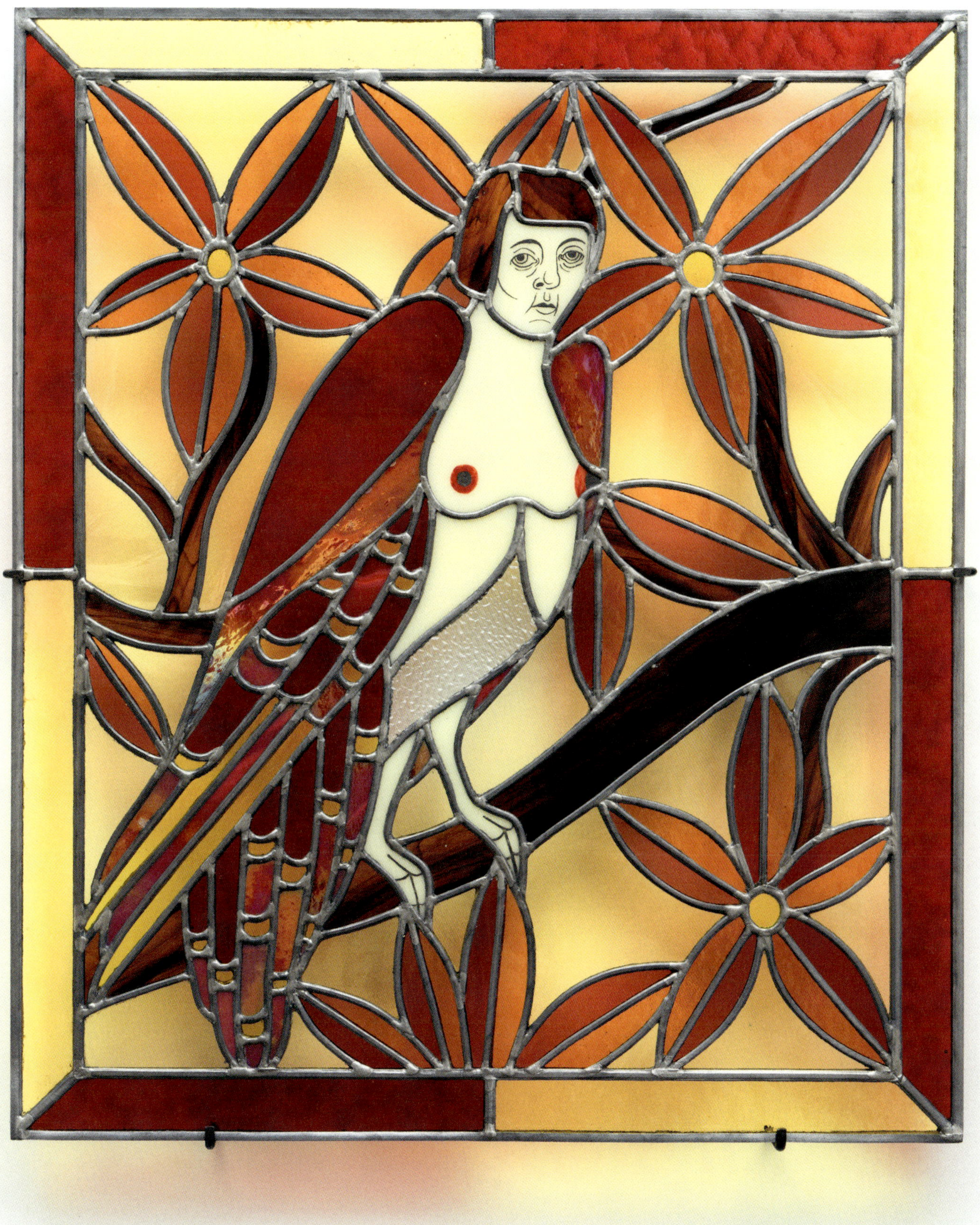

21 × 29,7 cm (each)

Mourning in Forgetfulness (series)

2025

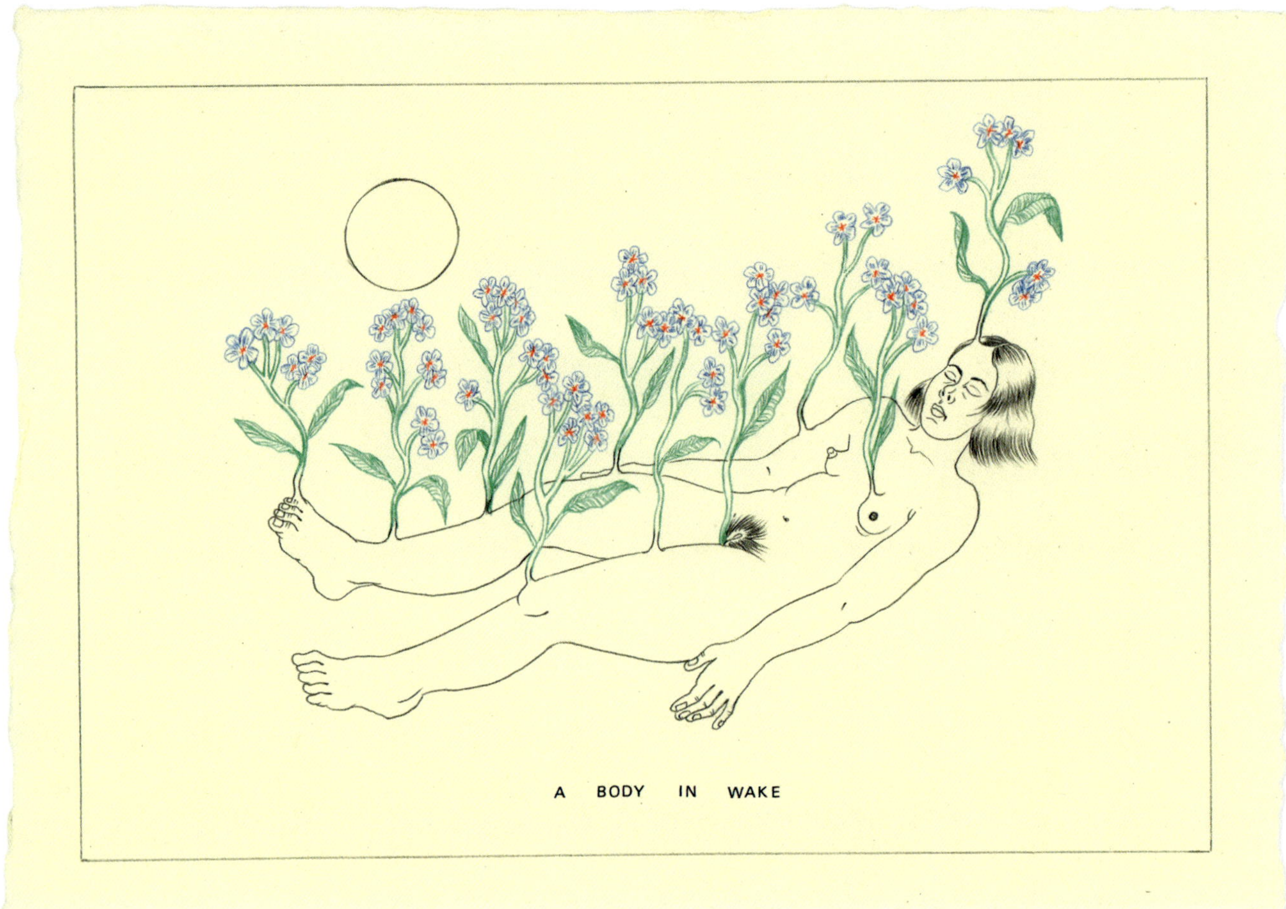

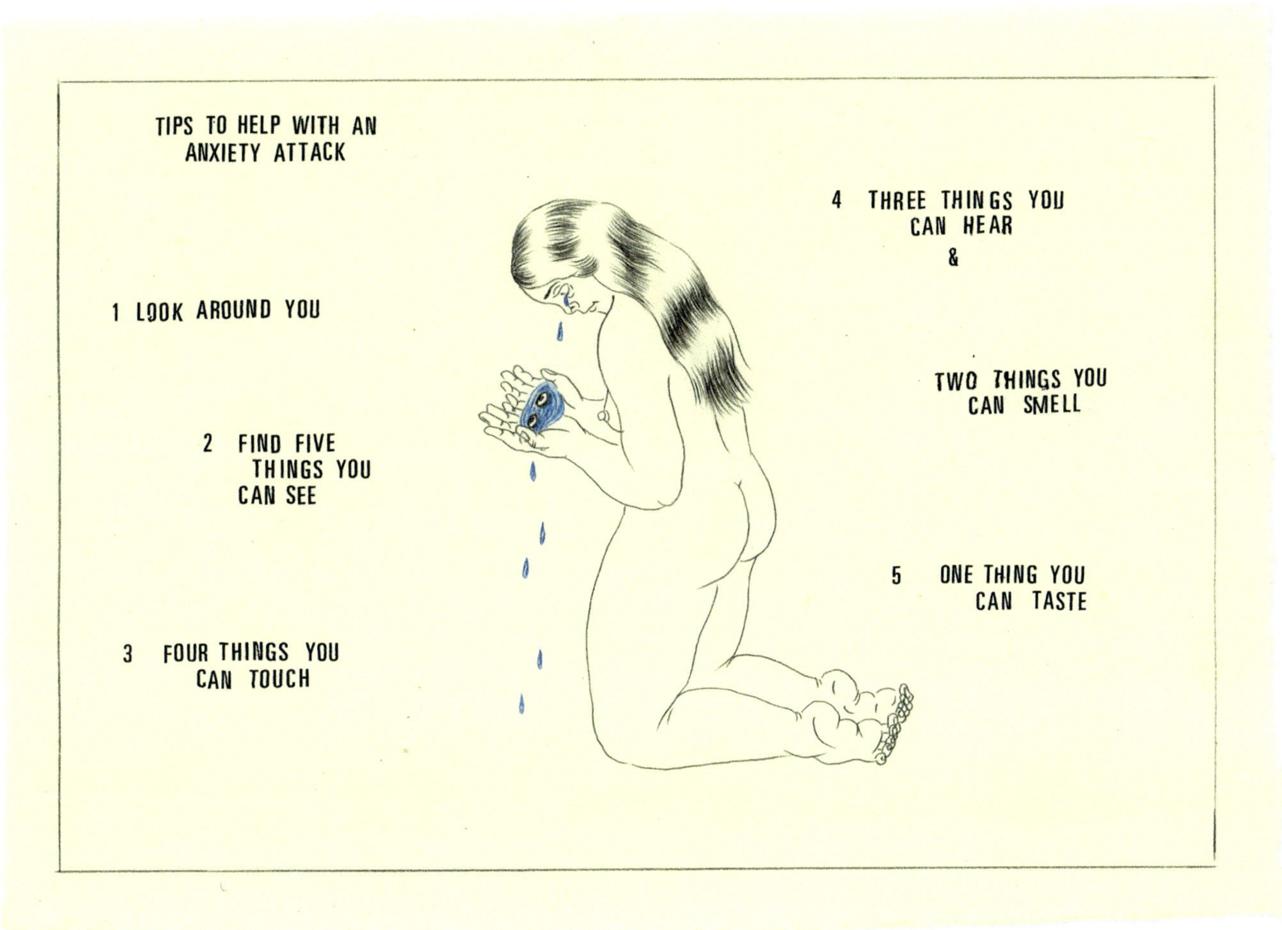
TIPS TO HELP WITH AN
ANXIETY ATTACK
1 LOOK AROUND YOU
2 FIND FIVE
THINGS YOU
CAN SEE
3 FOUR THINGS YOU
CAN TOUCH
4 THREE THINGS YOU
CAN HEAR
&
TWO THINGS YOU
CAN SMELL
5 ONE THING YOU
CAN TASTE

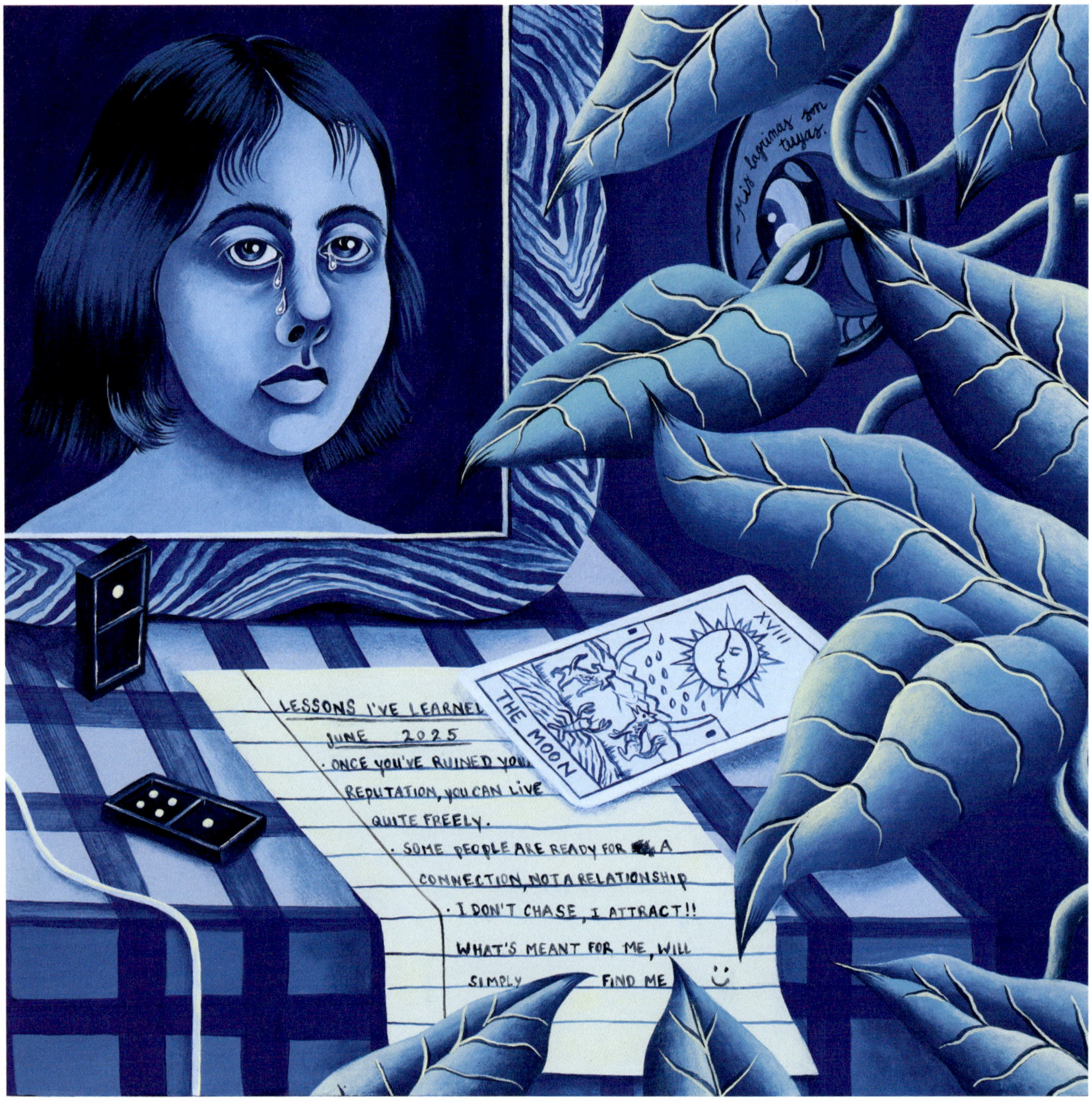

2025

Lessons I've Learnt

30 × 30 cm

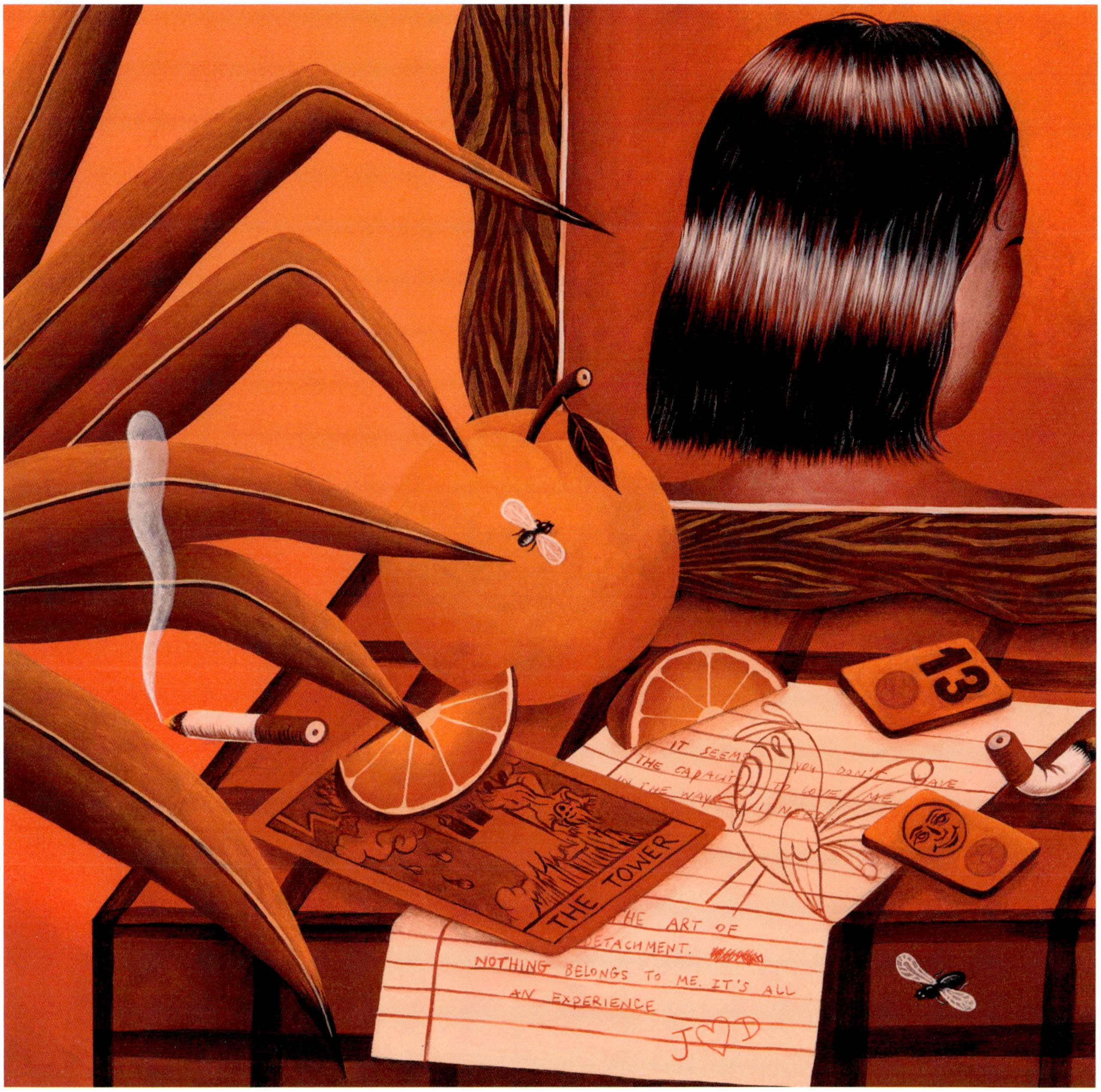

2025

The Art of Detachment

30 × 30 cm

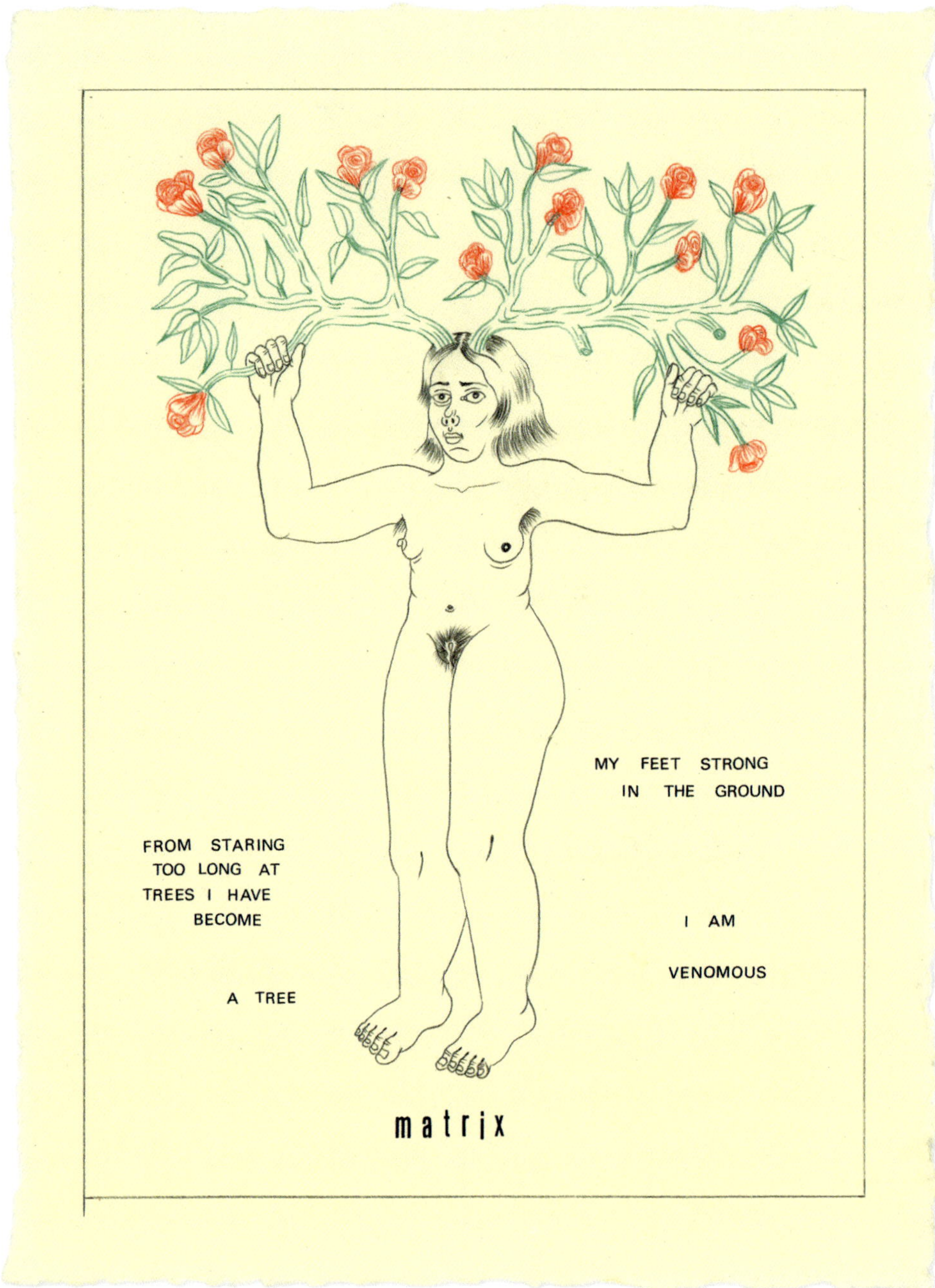

2025

Mourning in Forgetfulness (series)

29.7 × 21 cm (each)

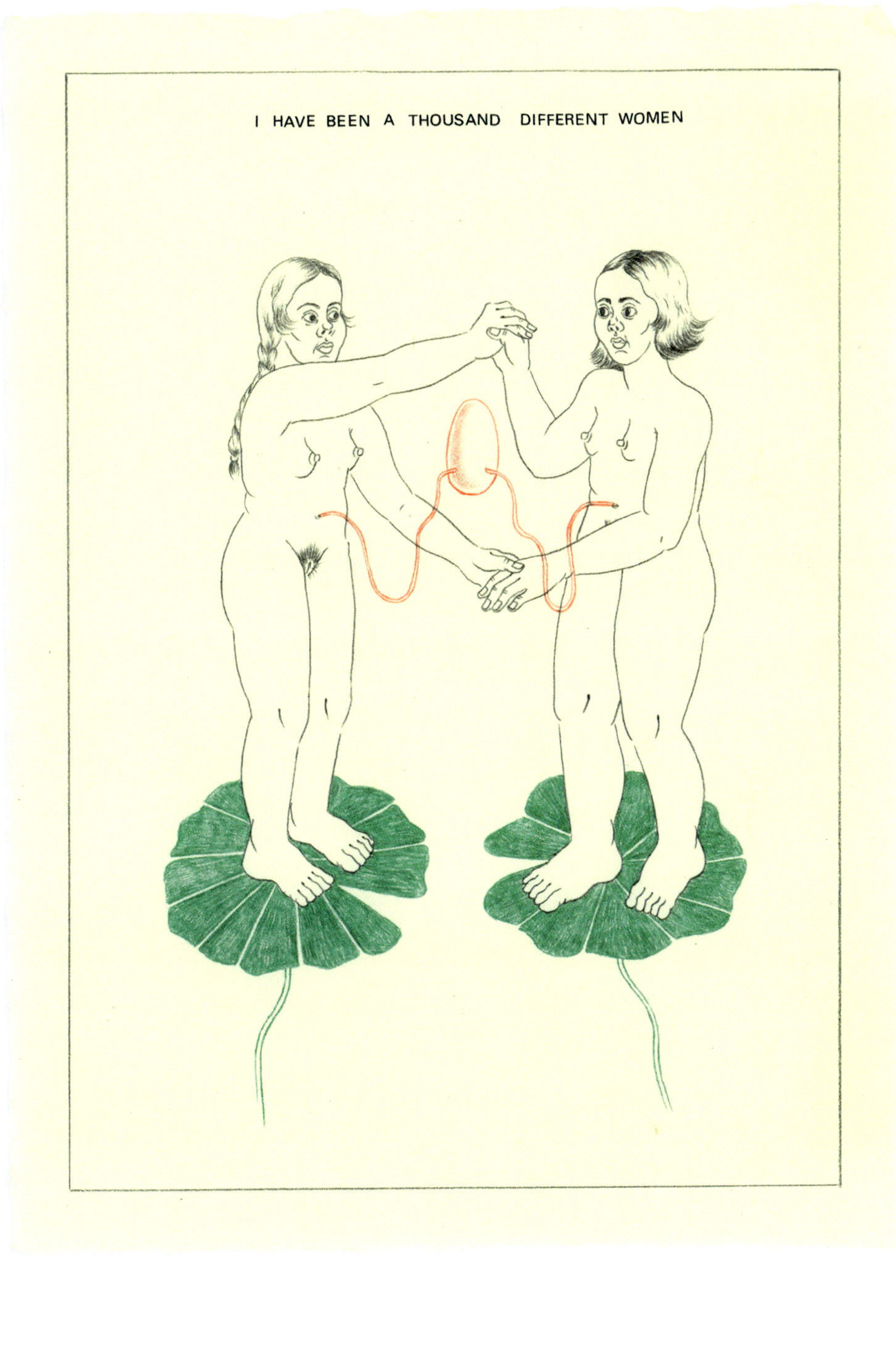
I HAVE BEEN A THOUSAND DIFFERENT WOMEN

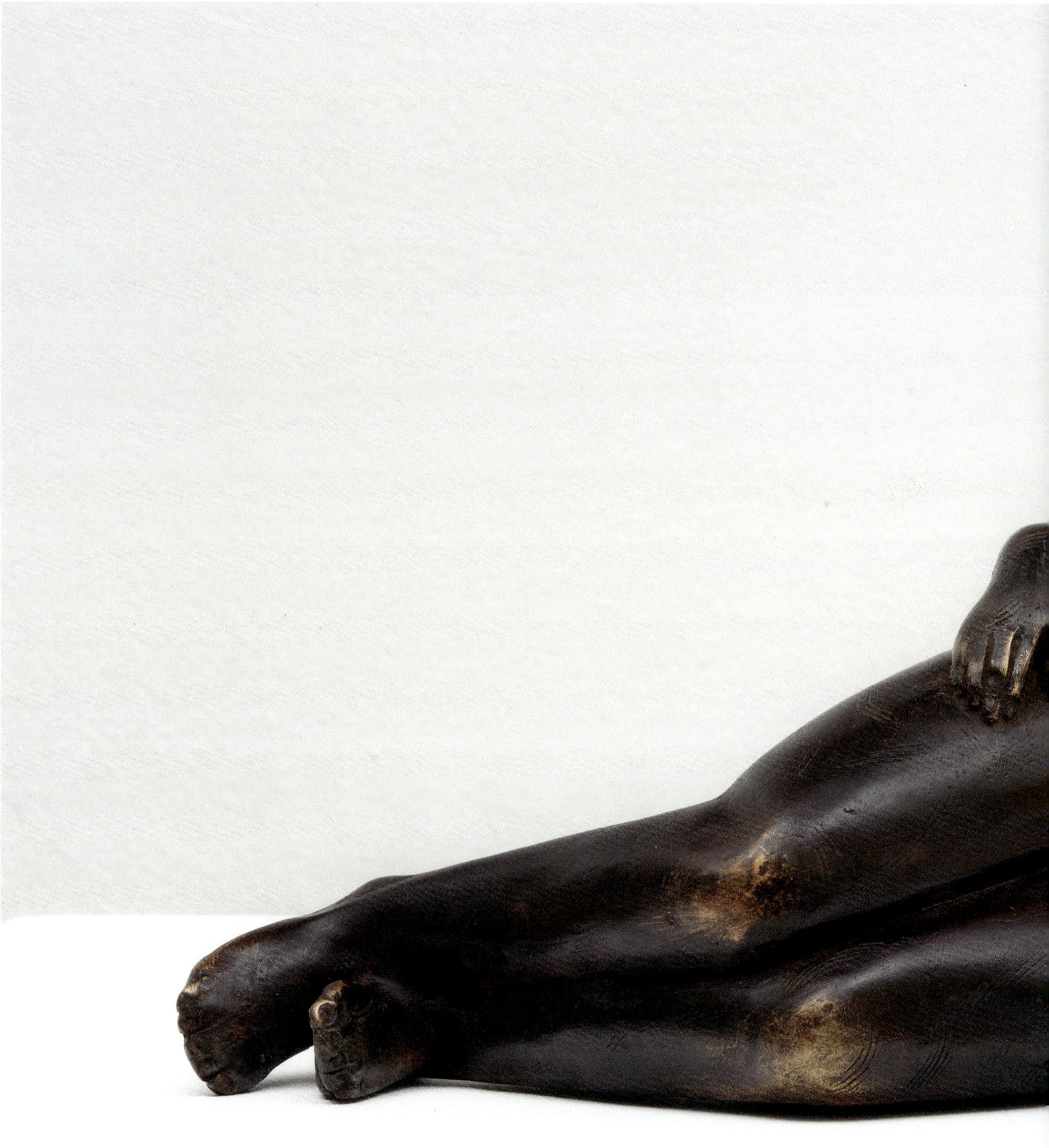

c. 14 × 25 × 17 cm *Catharsis 3* (Edition of 8 + 4 AP) 2025

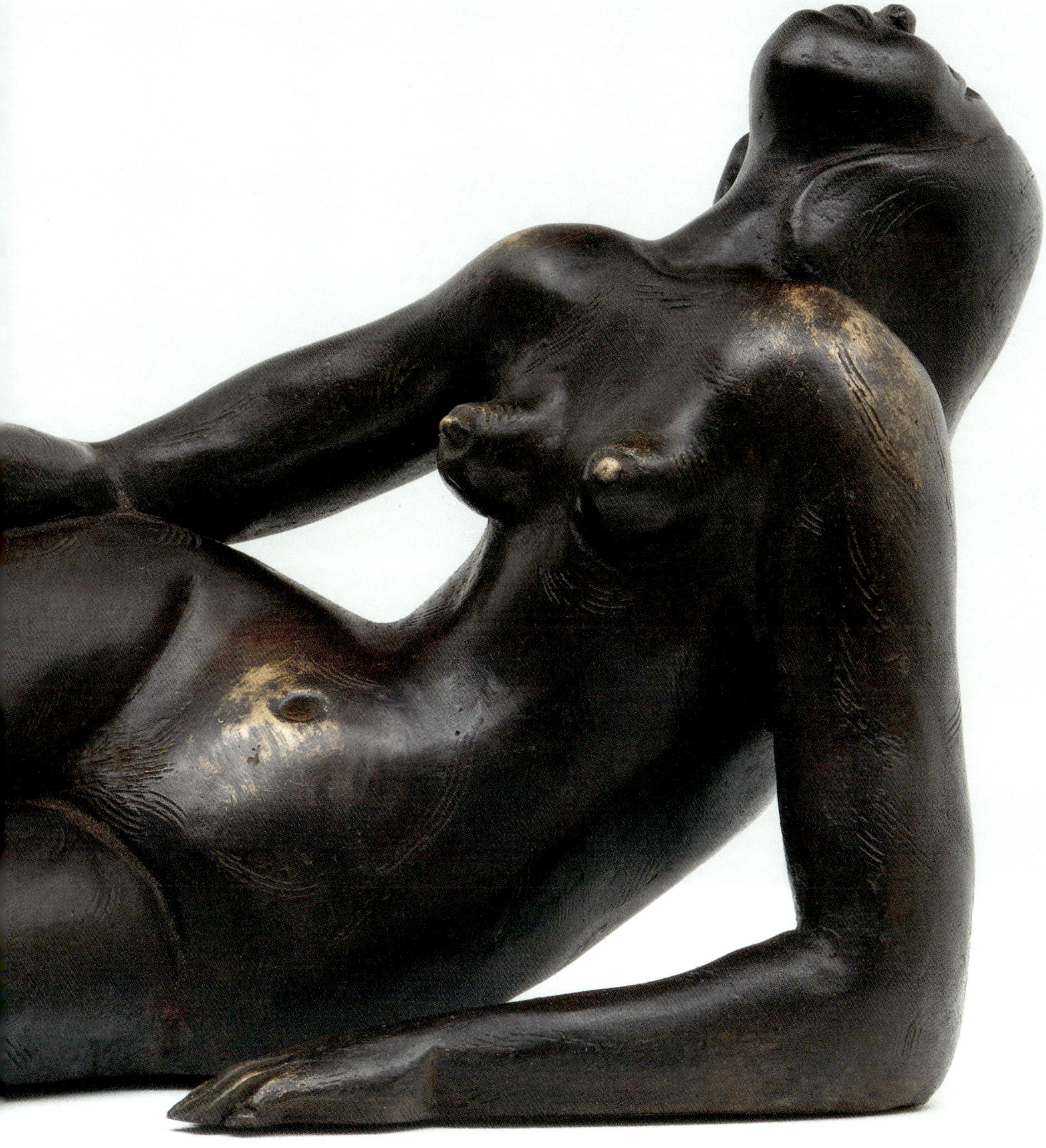

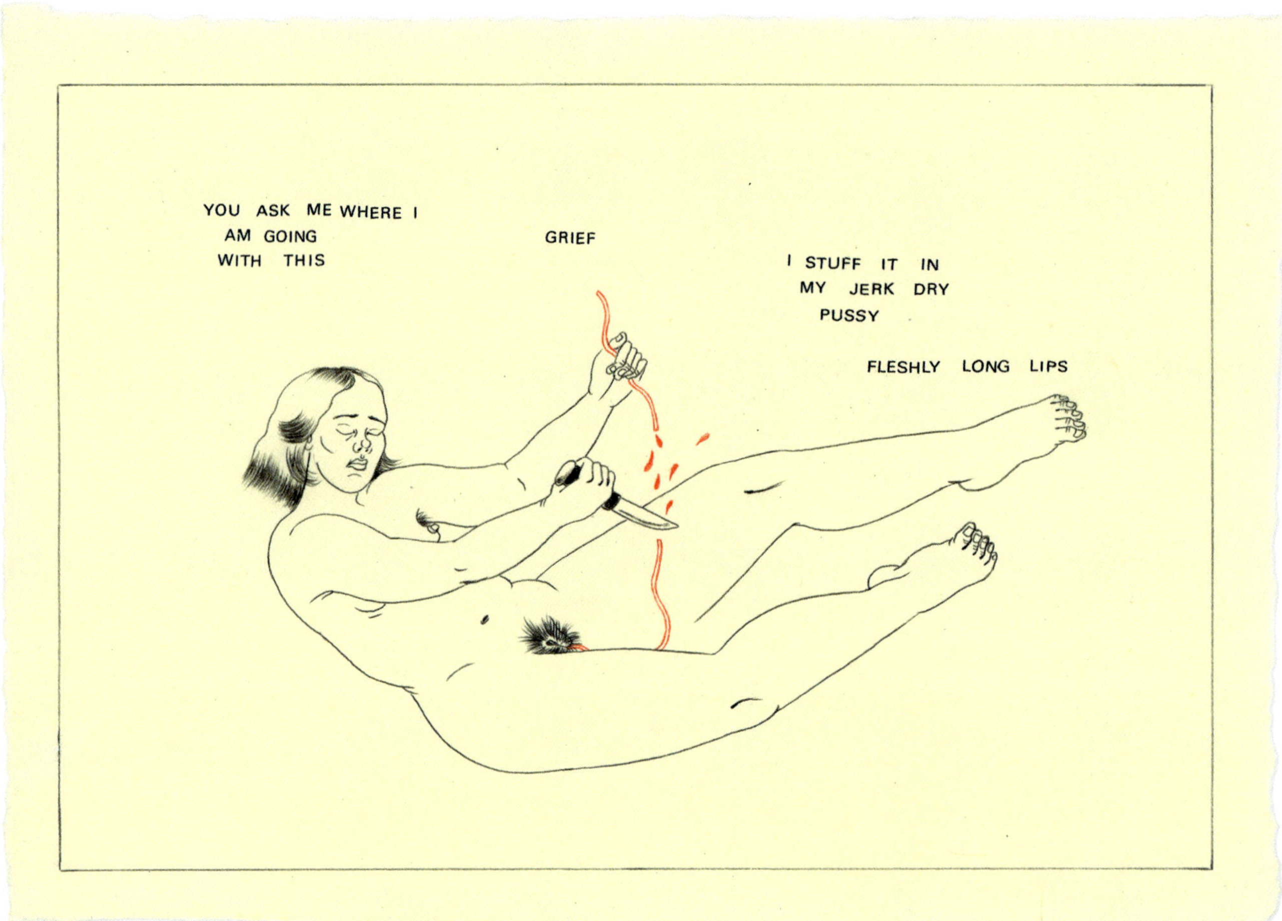

2025

Mourning in Forgetfulness (series)

21 × 29,7 cm (each)

I am my mother's daughter

In this deeply poetic and intimate monograph, Joëlle Dubois (b. 1990, Ghent) explores themes such as loss, grief, memory and love. Using symbols, metaphors and allegories, she processes her mother's Alzheimer's diagnosis and transforms pain into a cathartic journey. Through a wide variety of media such as paintings, drawings, sculptures and a video installation, Dubois reflects on connection, identity and healing. Raw yet tender, empowering yet vulnerable, this body of work reveals the fleeting nature of life and the resilience of the mother–daughter bond.

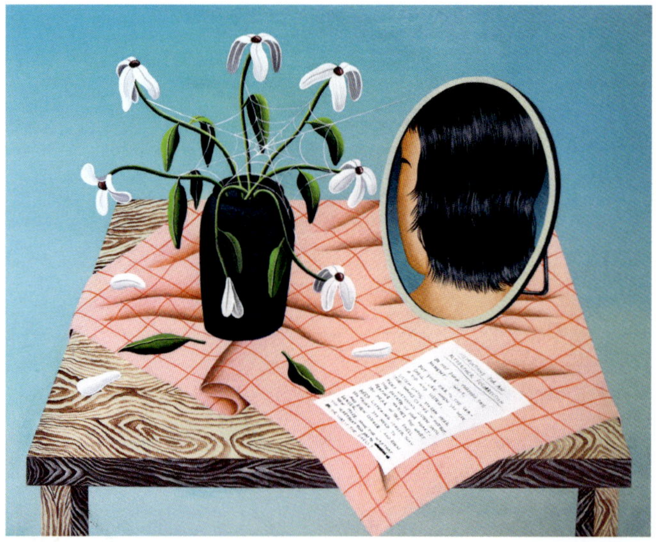

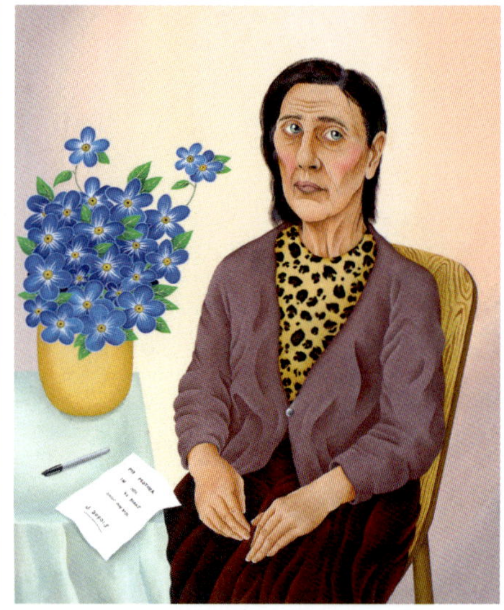

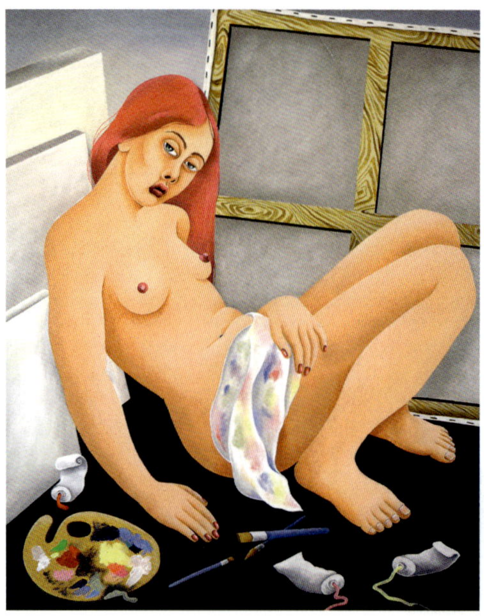

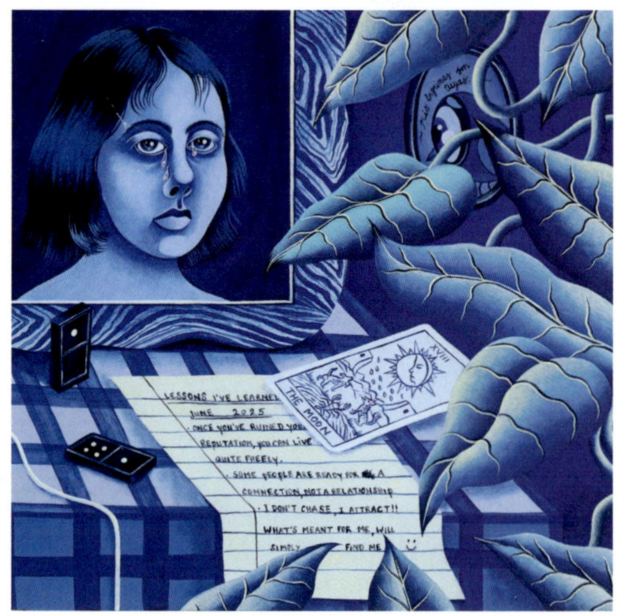

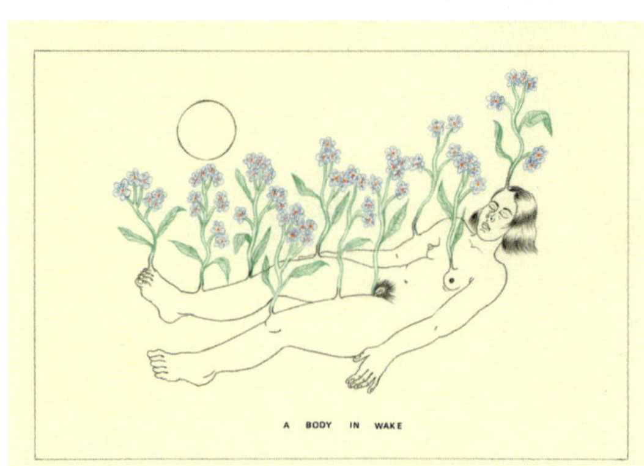

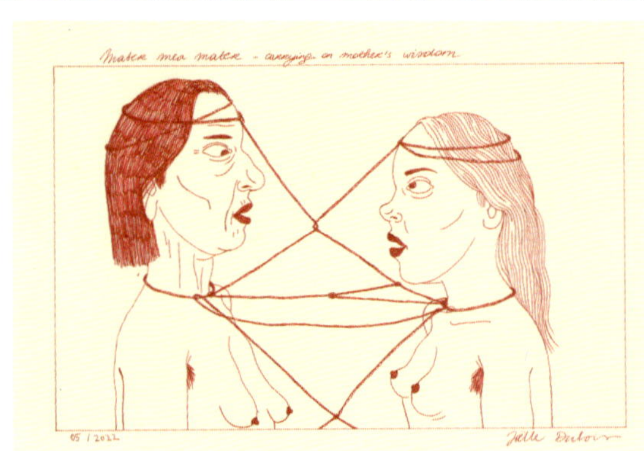

9 789493 416116

HANNIBAL BOOKS

www.hannibalbooks.be

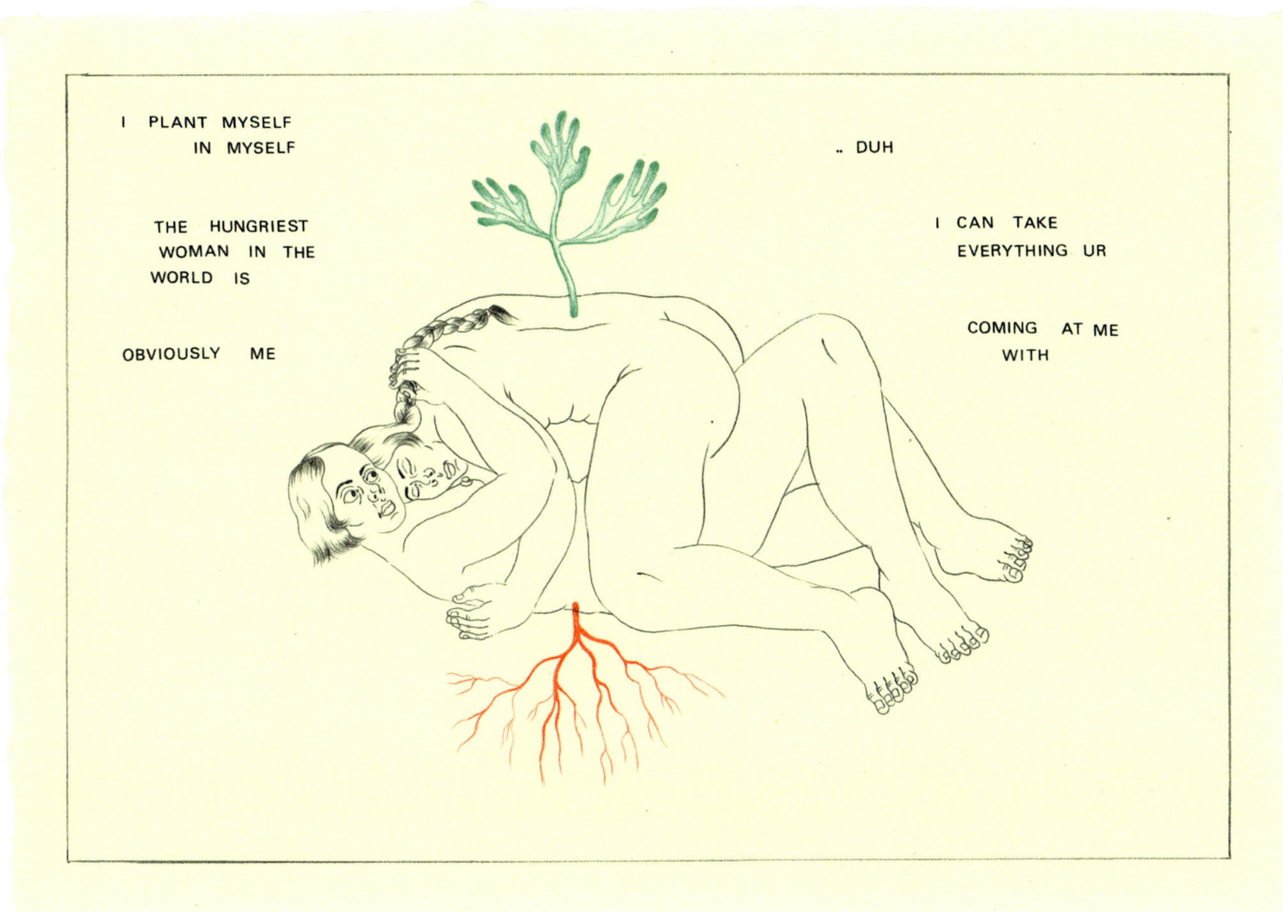
I PLANT MYSELF
IN MYSELF
.. DUH
THE HUNGRIEST
WOMAN IN THE
WORLD IS
OBVIOUSLY ME
I CAN TAKE
EVERYTHING UR
COMING AT ME
WITH

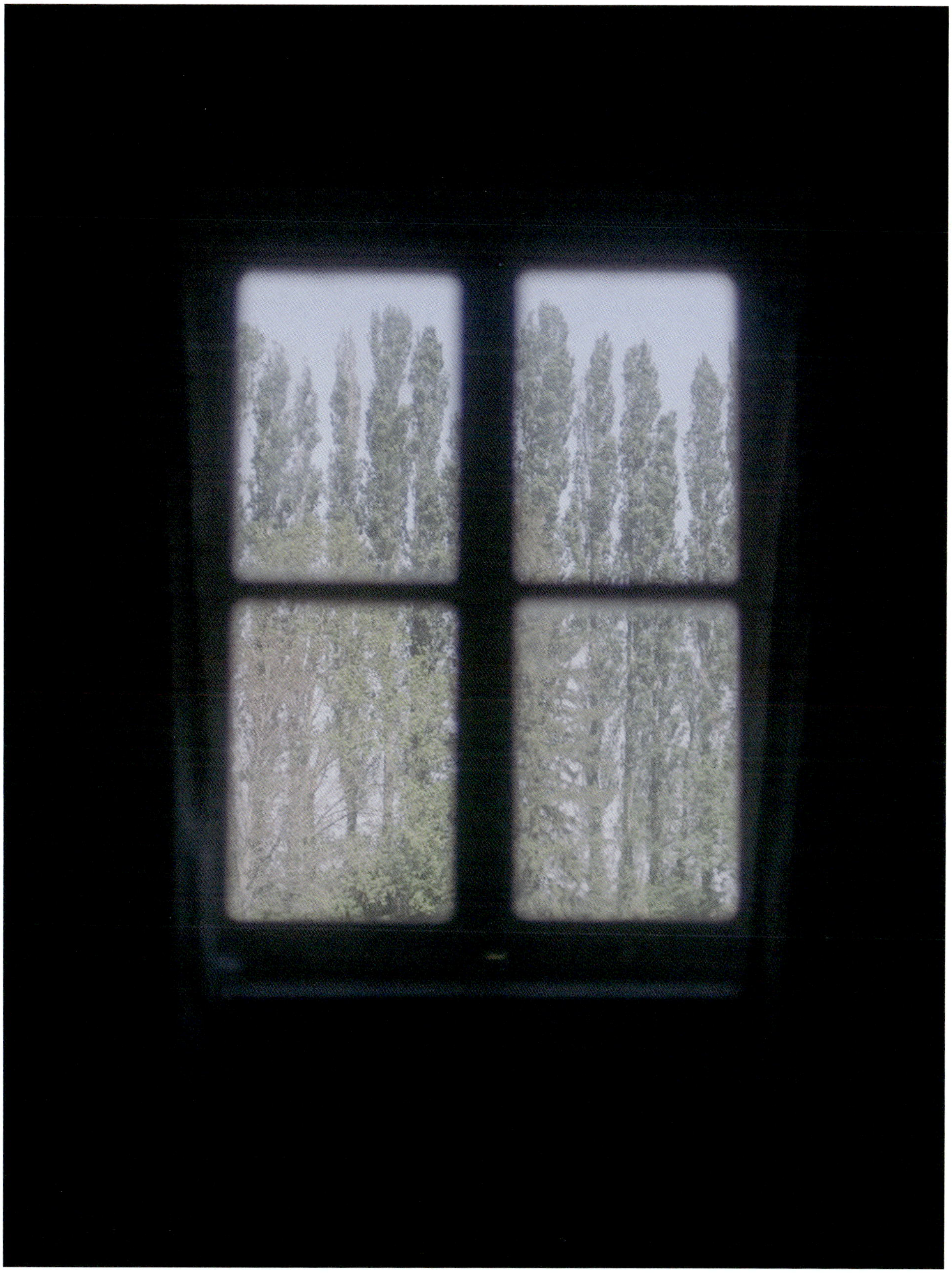

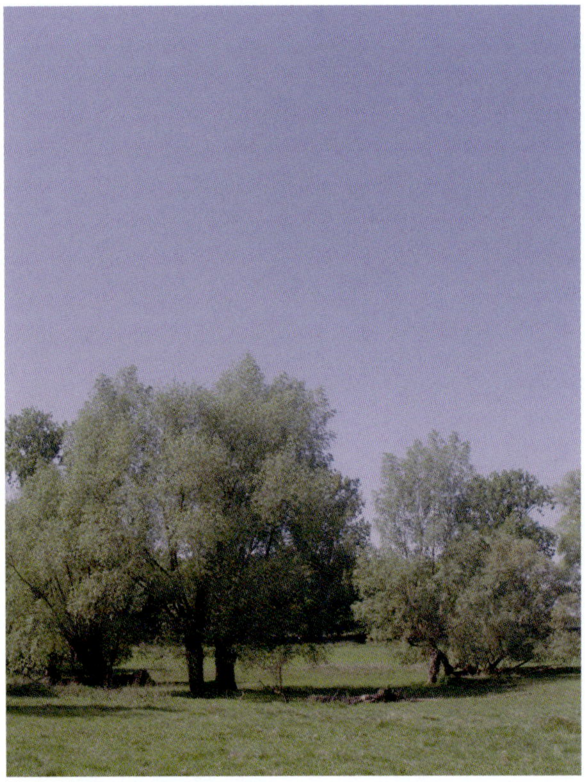

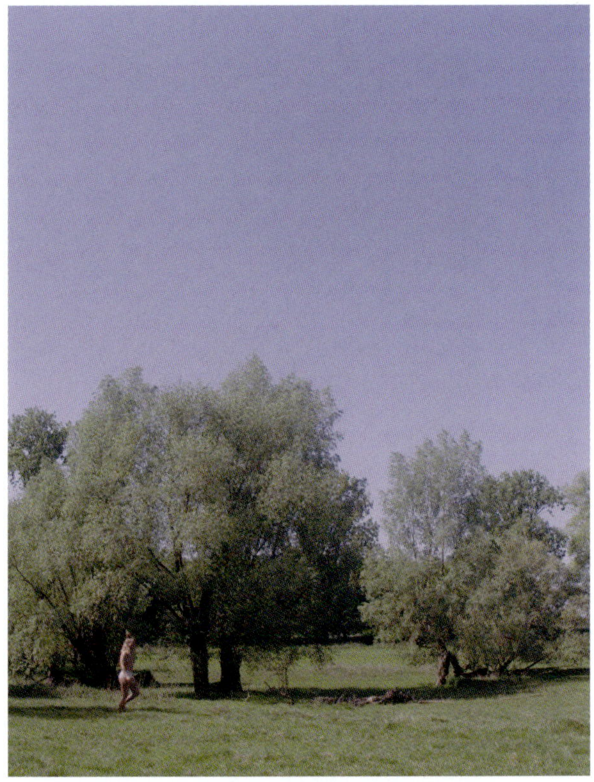

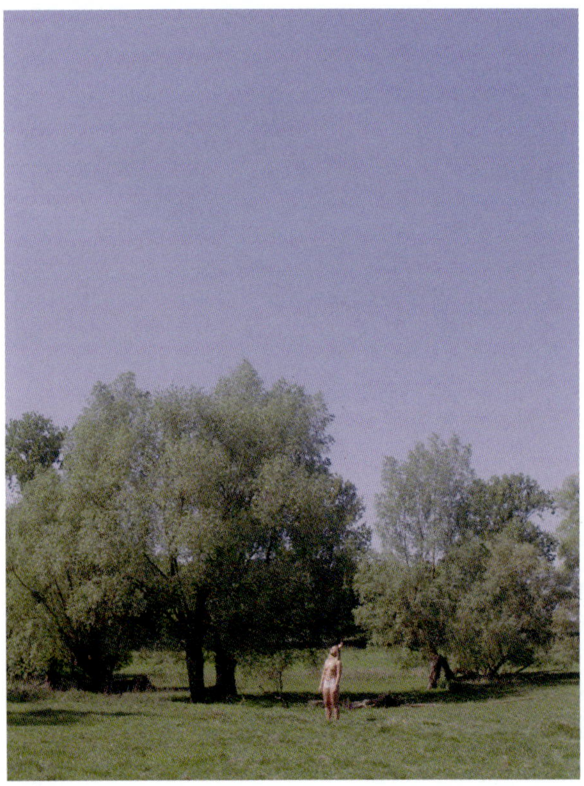

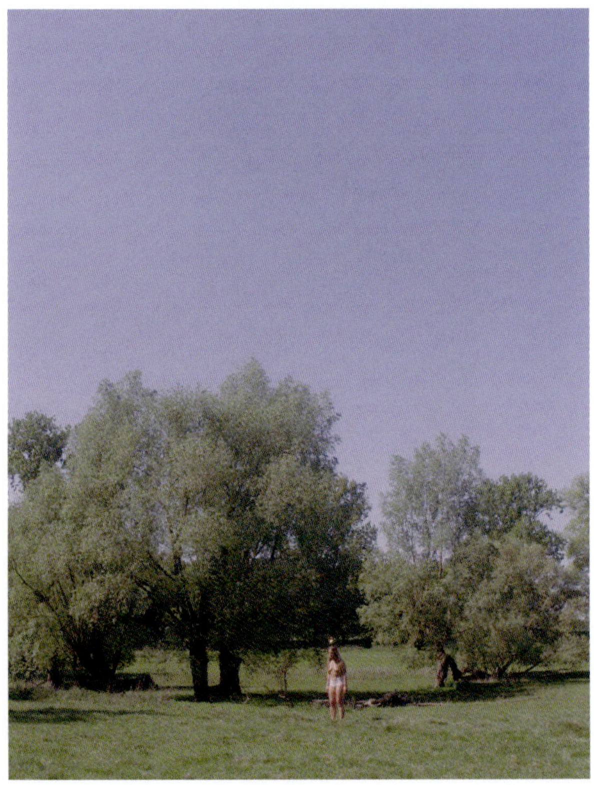

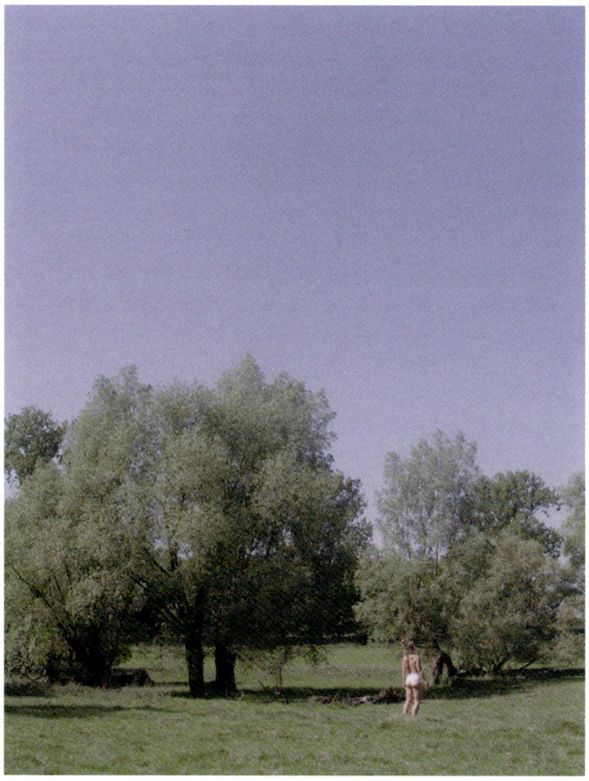
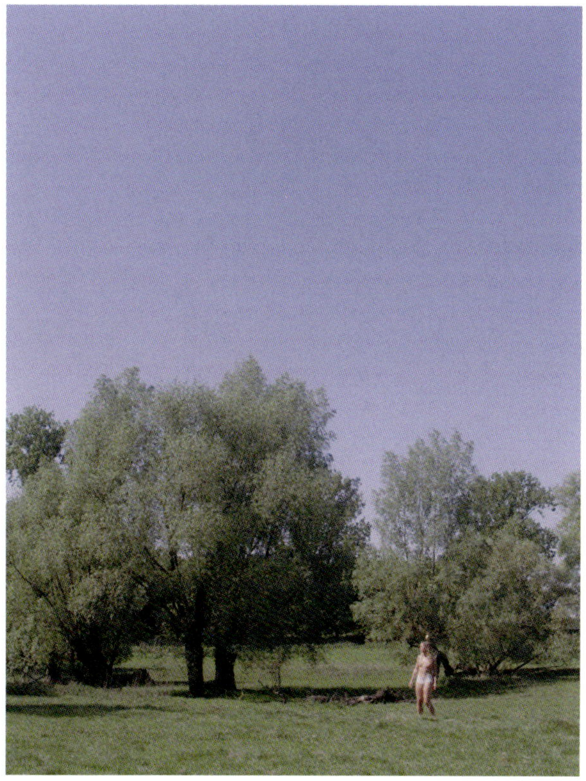
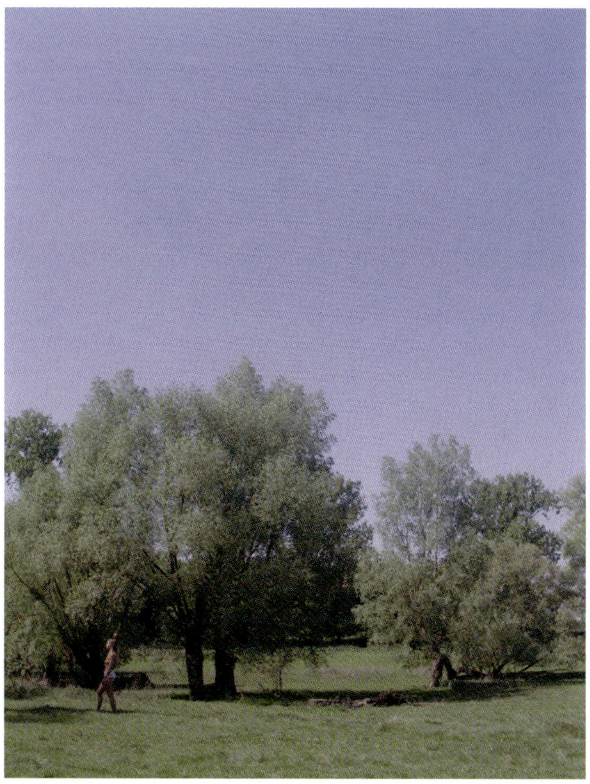
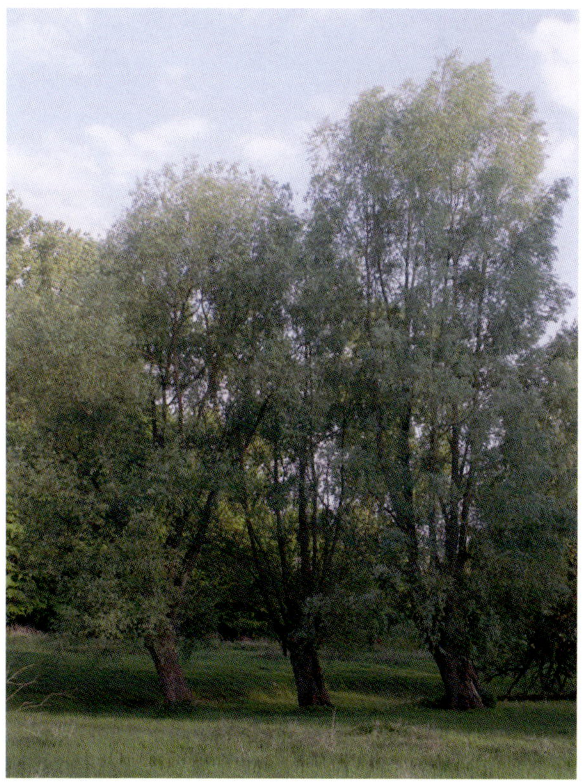

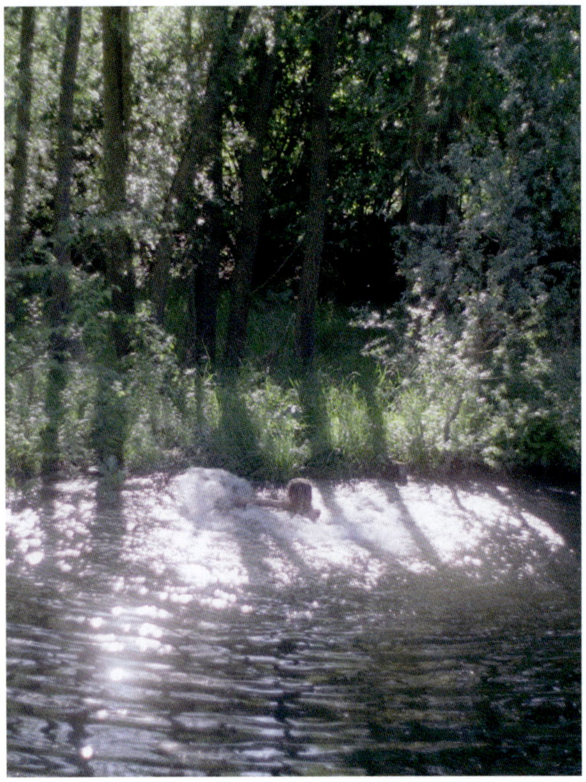

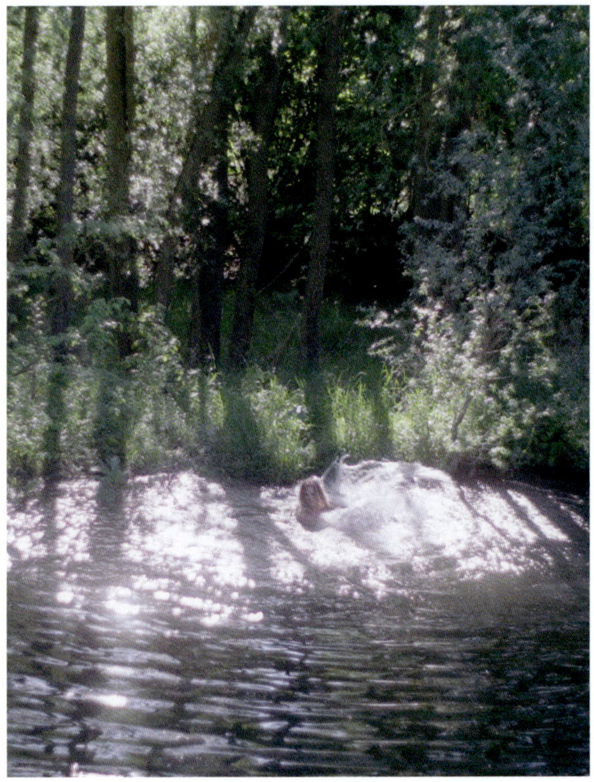

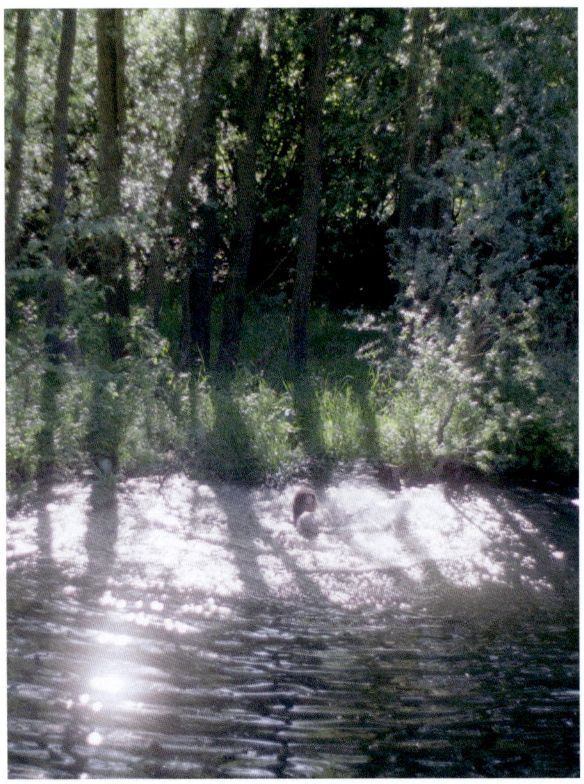

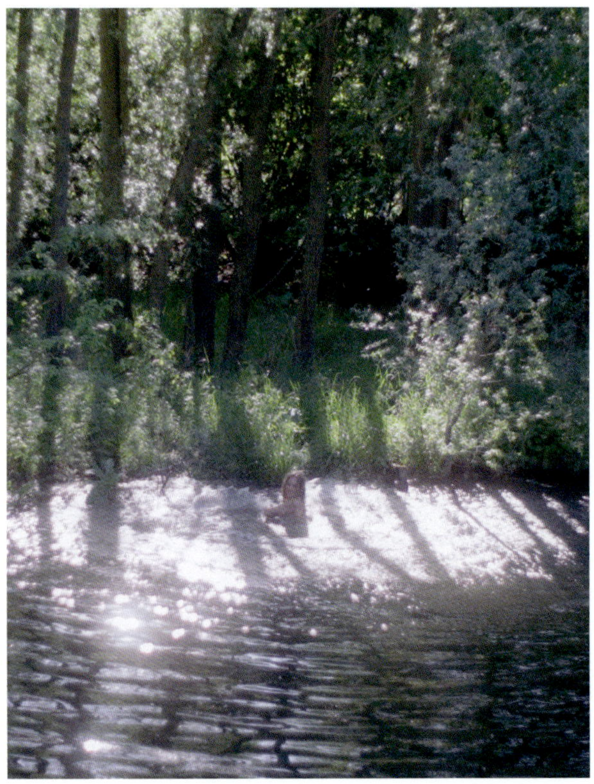

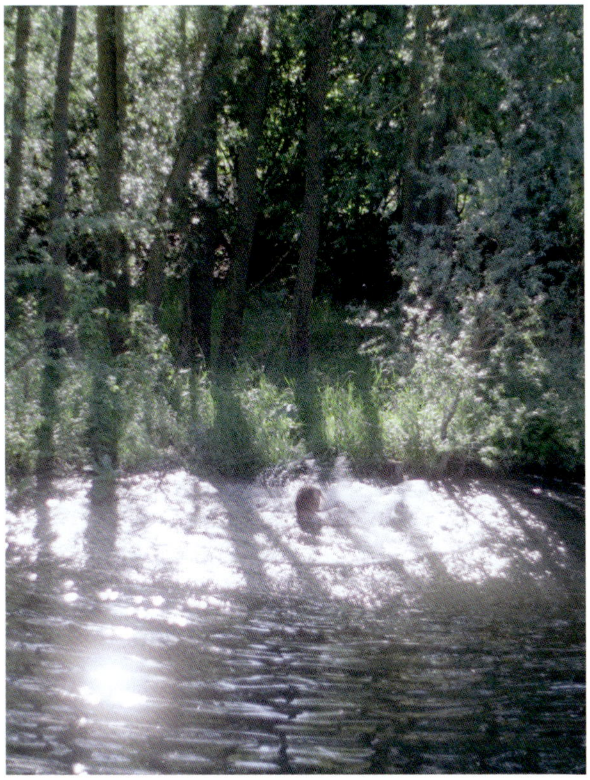
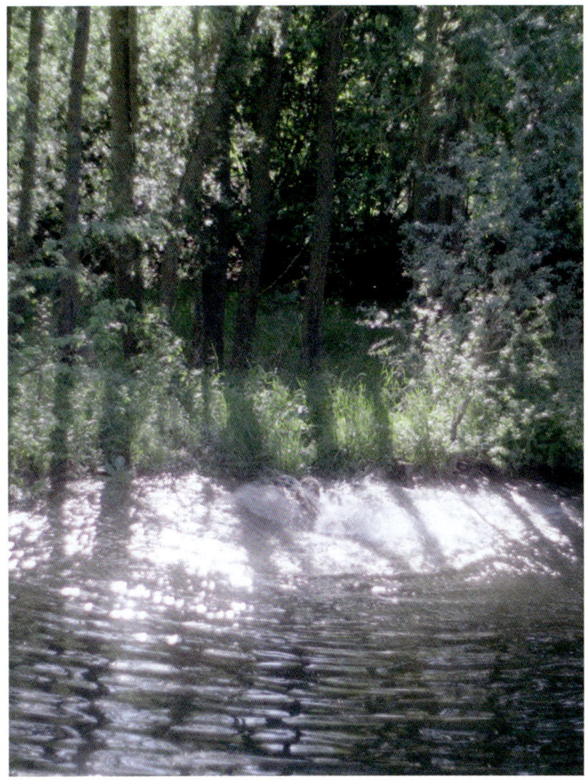
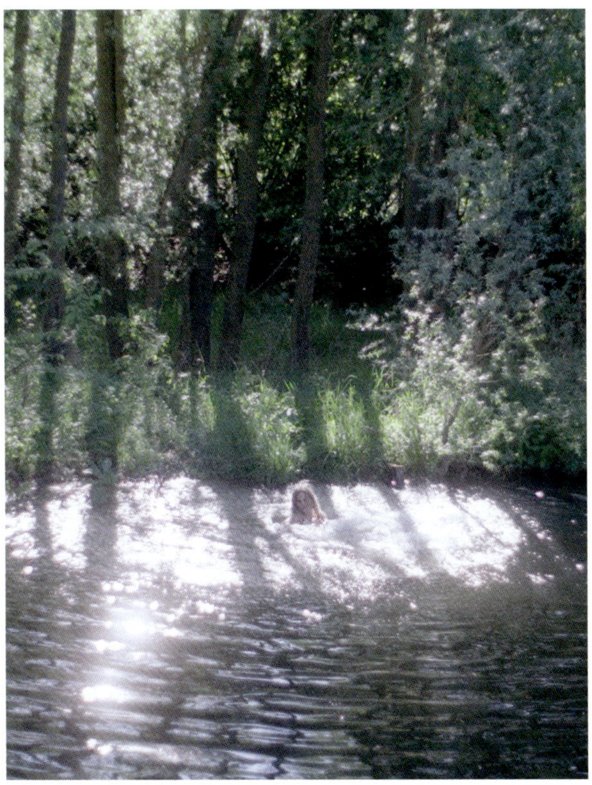
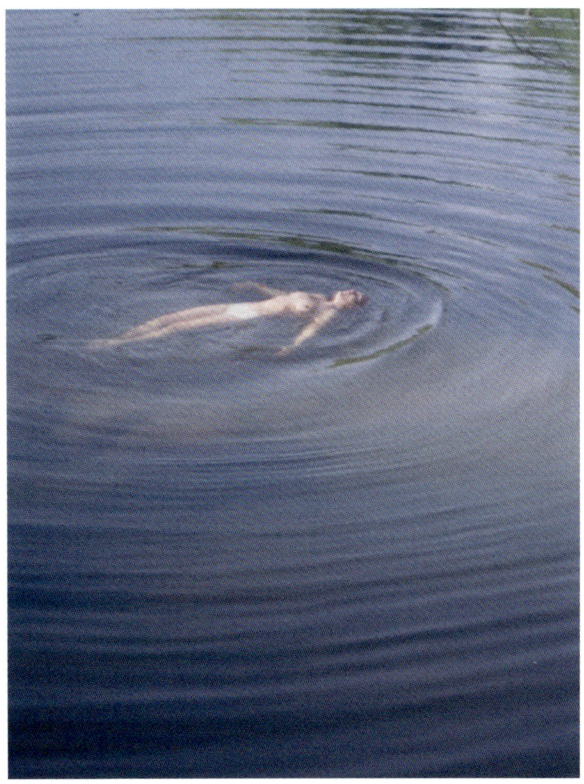

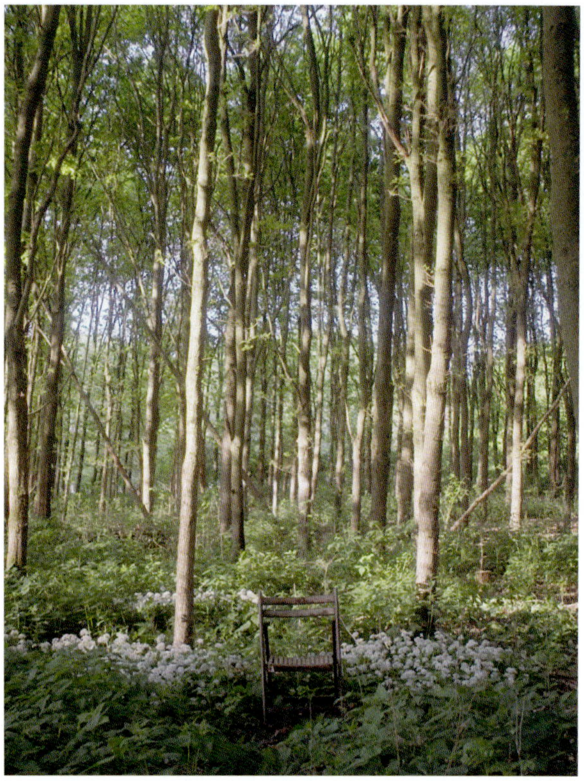

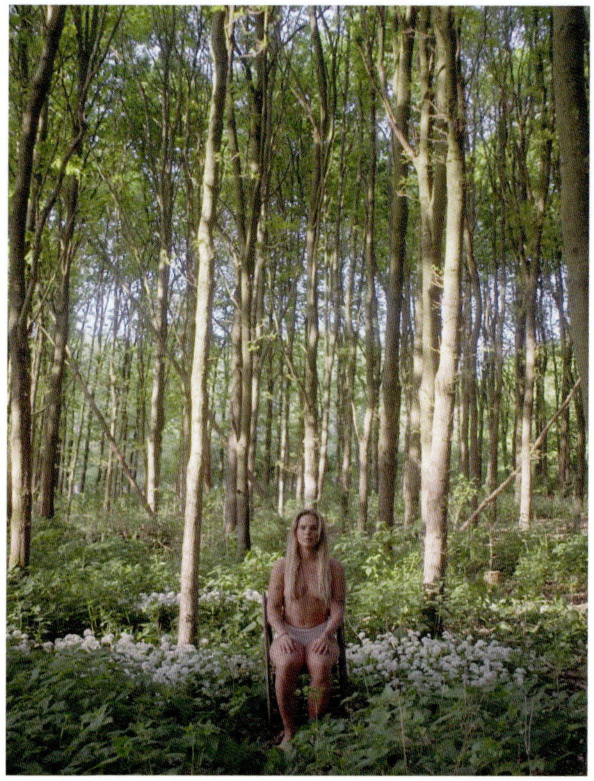

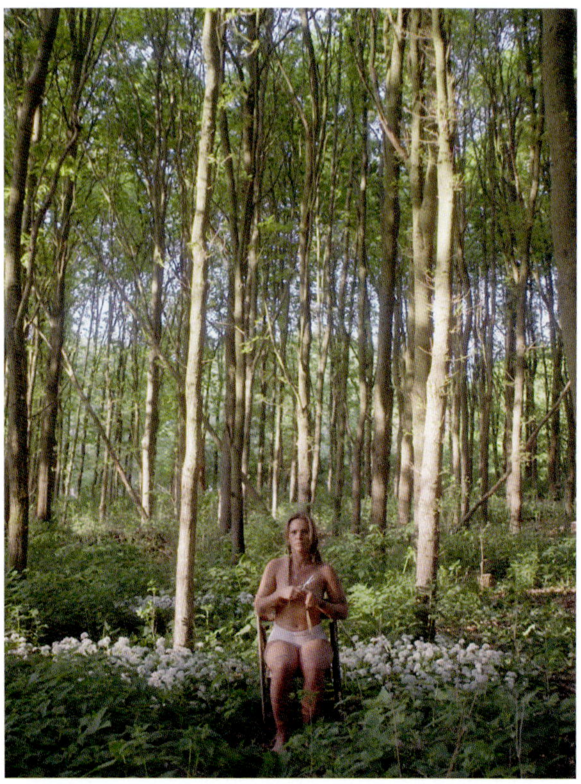

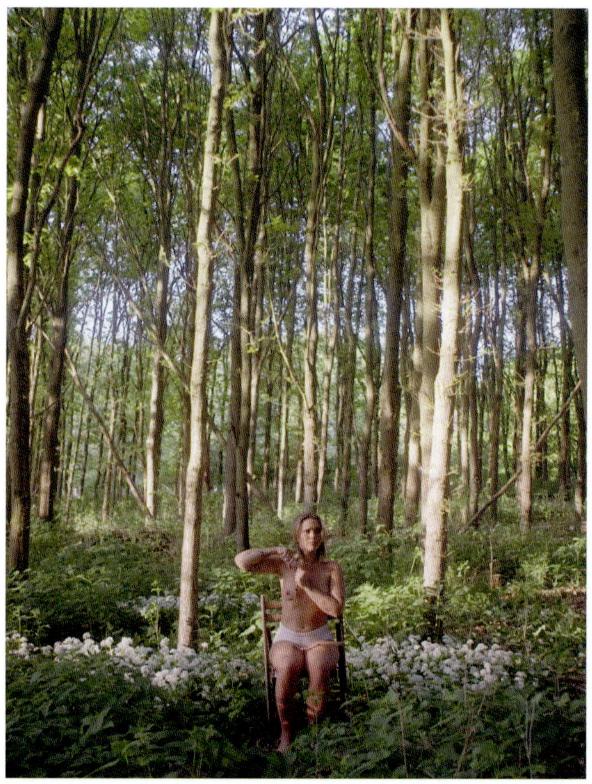

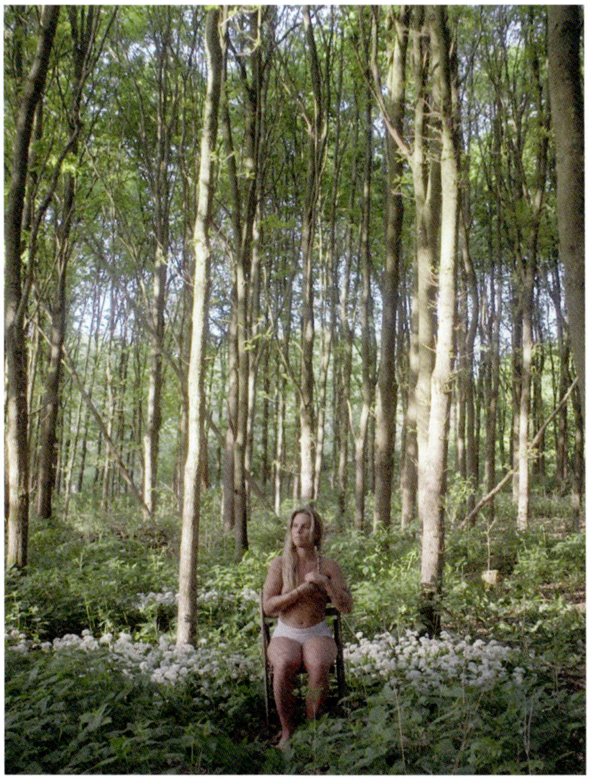

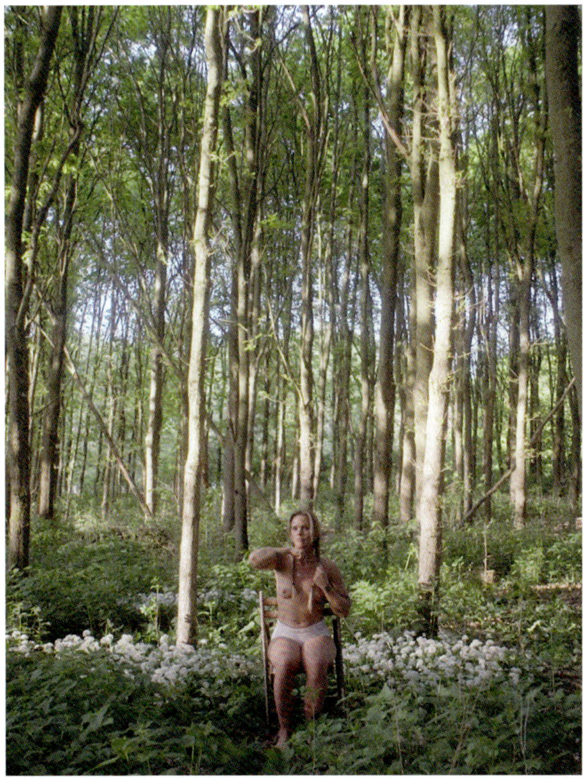

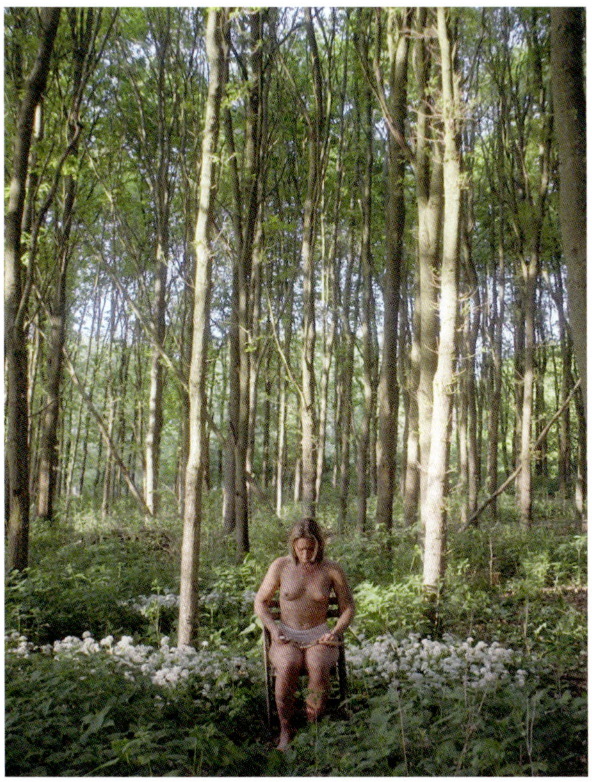

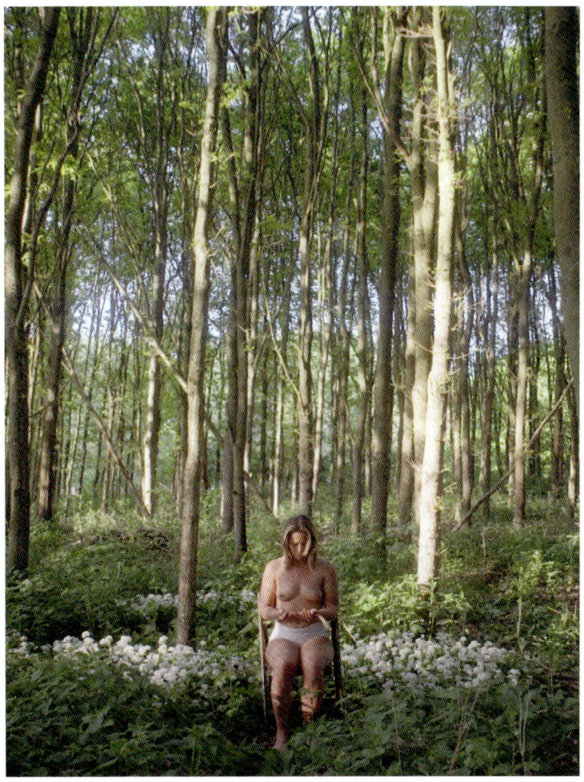

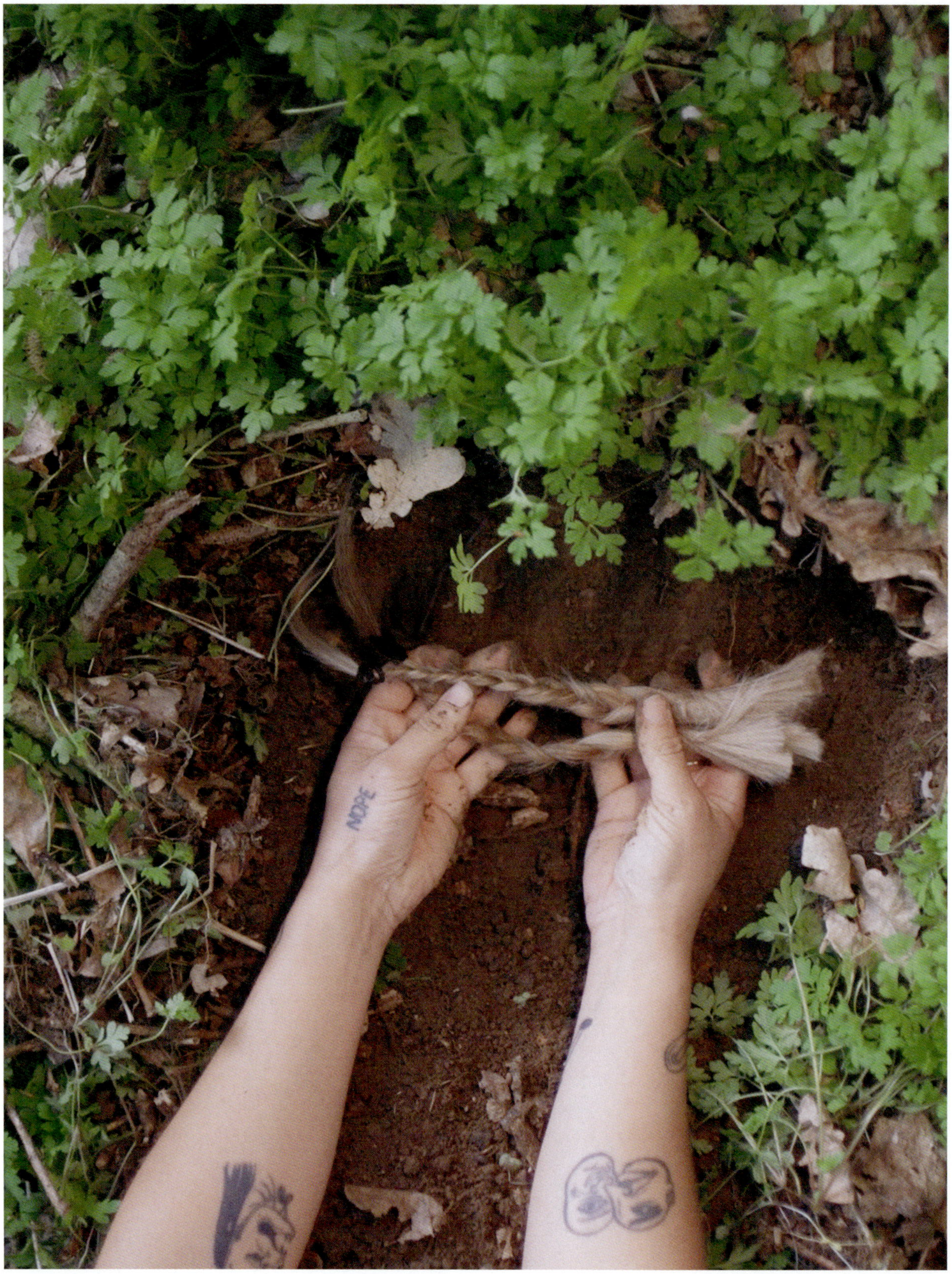
NOPE

24/12/2020 I picked you up to celebrate Christmas Eve

19/01/2021 Bought new shoes

18/02/2021 Walked to your new home, together with Milo

12/05/2021 I washed your hair and we watched TV

03/10/2021

Went for a walk with Anemone, Fee and Nina

11/02/2022 Moved to Eau de Gand

16/08/2022 You were very sad, you were scared

28/11/2022 You ate a cake at De Roos

30/04/2023 We went for a walk, it started to rain, you were too cold

08/05/2023 Nadia visited, sadly Nicole wasn't there

23/12/2023 You didn't say much

20/01/2024 We visited the cafeteria, you were very sad

18/05/2024 Hospital admission, you were very dazed

24/12/2020 I picked you up to celebrate Christmas Eve

19/01/2021 Bought new shoes

18/02/2021 Walked to your new home, together with Milo

12/05/2021 I washed your hair and we watched TV

03/10/2021

Went for a walk with Anemone, Fee and Nina

11/02/2022 Moved to Eau de Gand

16/08/2022 You were very sad, you were scared

28/11/2022 You ate a cake at De Roos

30/04/2023 We went for a walk, it started to rain, you were too cold

08/05/2023 Nadia visited, sadly Nicole wasn't there

23/12/2023 You didn't say much

20/01/2024 We visited the cafeteria, you were very sad

18/05/2024 Hospital admission, you were very dazed

19/12/2020 We looked at old photos together

15/02/2021 Dad and I helped you move, we decorated the room together while you got a tour of the new home

05/04/2021 Went for a long walk

23/04/2021 Talked with Claus about the first restless night

15/09/2021 Visit from Dr Creus, sleep medication adjusted

25/10/2021 We danced and sang together

13/03/2022 We went for a walk and had coffee at De Roos

27/03/2022 The doctor came

07/08/2022 Visited your sister, Martine was there too

19/02/2023 Cathy from London came over, we looked at photos together

26/03/2023 Made a drawing together

02/06/2023 We played a game of pétanque, you cheered us on

11/11/2023 You listened to music, you fell asleep

09/01/2024 You were confused, we didn't go for a walk, we were quiet

03/03/2024 I brought you fresh orange juice

19/12/2020 We looked at old photos together

15/02/2021 Dad and I helped you move, we decorated the room together while you got a tour of the new home

05/04/2021 Went for a long walk

23/04/2021 Talked with Claus about the first restless night

15/09/2021 Visit from Dr Creus, sleep medication adjusted

25/10/2021 We danced and sang together

13/03/2022 We went for a walk and had coffee at De Roos

27/03/2022 The doctor came

07/08/2022 Visited your sister, Martine was there too

19/02/2023 Cathy from London came over, we looked at photos together

26/03/2023 Made a drawing together

02/06/2023 We played a game of pétanque, you cheered us on

11/11/2023 You listened to music, you fell asleep

09/01/2024 You were confused, we didn't go for a walk, we were quiet

03/03/2024 I brought you fresh orange juice

26/12/2020 I read my book to you

11/01/2021 You took a shower and I washed your hair, we picked an outfit together

16/02/2021 We ate sandwiches with tuna and a cookie for dessert

09/03/2021 Watched television together

08/05/2021 Helped cut the vegetables for dinner

10/06/2021 Went for a long walk

12/07/2021 Visit with sweets, brought the laundry basket

11/09/2021 Bought slippers together

10/10/2021 Ate shrimp croquettes with a small salad, you enjoyed it

26/11/2021 Went to the city to buy a new phone, you found it difficult

12/01/2022 I brushed your hair while you cuddled with Milo

01/06/2022 Had a coffee at De Roos

30/07/2022 Visited with Nina, you were happy to see baby Lewis

31/07/2022 I joined you in bed, I showed you my latest work

09/11/2022 I read the newspaper to you

31/12/2022 We celebrated Christmas and New Year together

05/03/2023 You listened to music. We laughed a lot

28/03/2023 Watched the cycling race

26/05/2023 Cake again, things weren't going too well

27/08/2023 You cried a lot, we listened to music

20/10/2023 We lay in bed together

12/01/2024 You were sleeping on the couch

05/02/2024 You were angry

07/03/2024 I had to comfort you, I gave you a hug

26/12/2020 I read my book to you

11/01/2021 You took a shower and I washed your hair, we picked an outfit together

16/02/2021 We ate sandwiches with tuna and a cookie for dessert

09/03/2021 Watched television together

08/05/2021 Helped cut the vegetables for dinner

10/06/2021 Went for a long walk

12/07/2021 Visit with sweets, brought the laundry basket

11/09/2021 Bought slippers together

10/10/2021 Ate shrimp croquettes with a small salad, you enjoyed it

26/11/2021 Went to the city to buy a new phone, you found it difficult

12/01/2022 I brushed your hair while you cuddled with Milo

01/06/2022 Had a coffee at De Roos

30/07/2022 Visited with Nina, you were happy to see baby Lewis

31/07/2022 I joined you in bed, I showed you my latest work

09/11/2022 I read the newspaper to you

31/12/2022 We celebrated Christmas and New Year together

05/03/2023 You listened to music. We laughed a lot

28/03/2023 Watched the cycling race

26/05/2023 Cake again, things weren't going too well

27/08/2023 You cried a lot, we listened to music

20/10/2023 We lay in bed together

12/01/2024 You were sleeping on the couch

05/02/2024 You were angry

07/03/2024 I had to comfort you, I gave you a hug

28/12/2020 I came over for coffee and we ate chocolate

11/03/2021 Went for a short walk **07/04/2021** Moved from Tijgerstraat to Blaisanthuis

06/06/2021 Visited your sister, sat in the sun together

07/07/2021 Cut fruit for fresh pancakes **03/08/2021** You told me you felt lonely

14/10/2021 Went for a walk **02/11/2021** You were quiet

04/12/2021 Talk with the doctor about your mood swings

15/01/2022 I painted your nails in blue

29/06/2022 We ate a Cornetto together in the garden **29/07/2022** You were very anxious, I comforted you

06/09/2022 I washed your hair, you looked beautiful **05/10/2022** Sat on the terrace at De Roos with baby Lewis

13/01/2023 Visited with a Belgian waffle **28/02/2023** You fell on your head, you were tired

07/04/2023 Bought new glasses, you found it confusing

25/06/2023 We celebrated my birthday on the terrace at De Roos **19/07/2023** I brought fresh flowers, you didn't say much **08/09/2023** Had drinks at De Roos with baby Lewis

07/02/2024 Visited with Lewis, you didn't say much

28/12/2020 I came over for coffee and we ate chocolate

11/03/2021 Went for a short walk 07/04/2021 Moved
from Tijgerstraat to Blaisanthuis

06/06/2021 Visited your sister, sat in the sun together

07/07/2021 Cut fruit for fresh pancakes 03/08/2021 You
told me you felt lonely

14/10/2021 Went for
a walk 02/11/2021 You were quiet

04/12/2021 Talk with the doctor about your mood swings

15/01/2022 I painted your nails in blue

29/06/2022 We ate a Cornetto together in the garden 29/07/2022
You were very anxious, I comforted you

06/09/2022 I washed your hair, you looked beautiful 05/10/2022 Sat on the terrace at De Roos with baby Lewis

13/01/2023
Visited with a Belgian waffle 28/02/2023 You fell on your head,
you were tired

07/04/2023 Bought new glasses, you found it confusing

25/06/2023 We celebrated my birthday on the terrace at De Roos 19/07/2023 I brought fresh flowers, you didn't
say much 08/09/2023 Had drinks at De Roos with baby Lewis

07/02/2024 Visited with Lewis, you didn't say much

19/05/2024 You closed your eyes

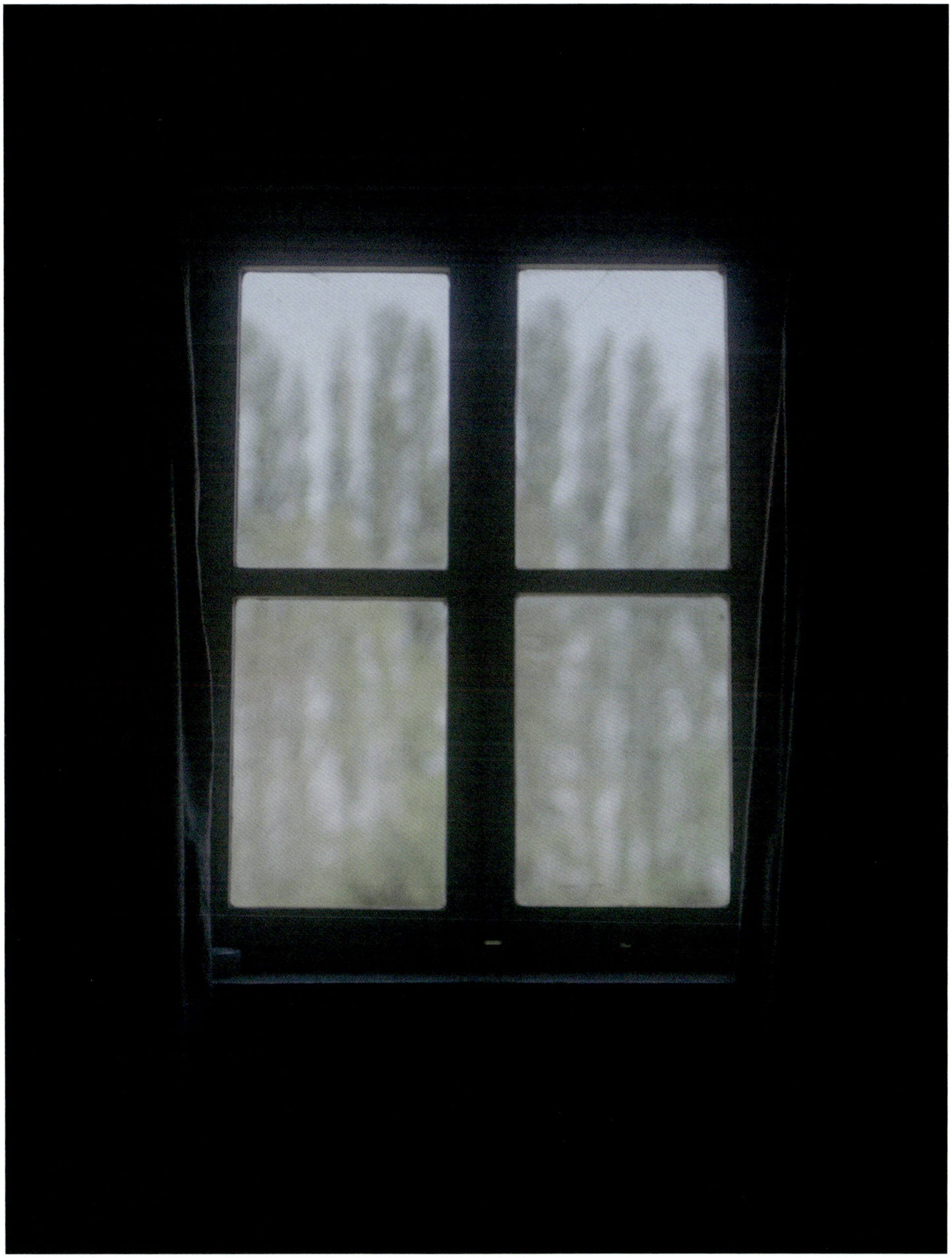

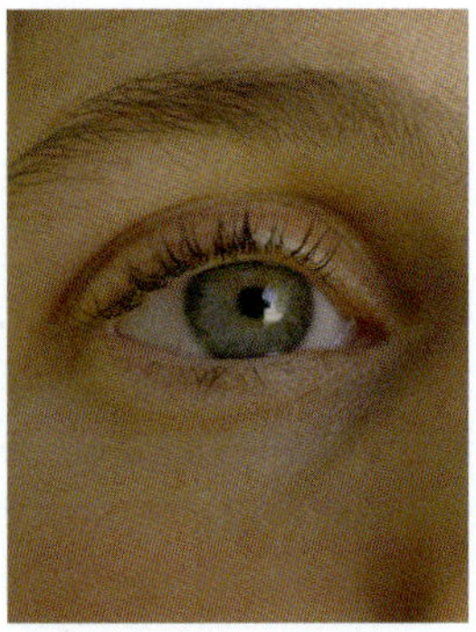
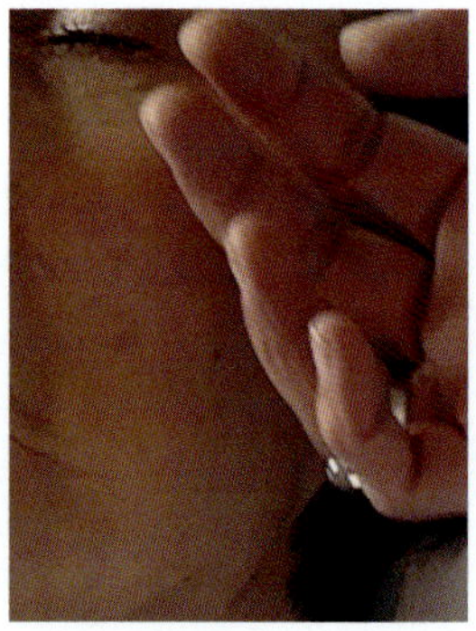

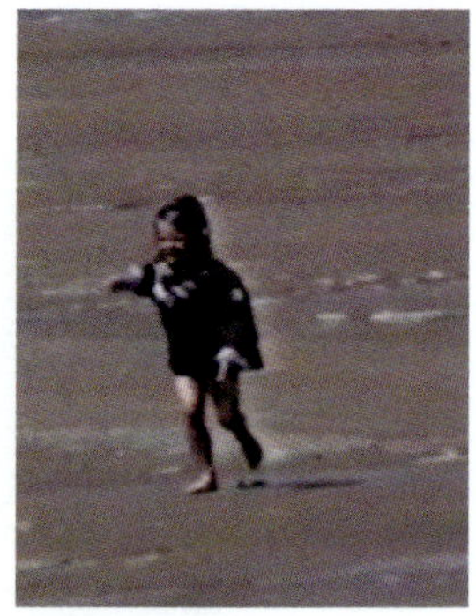
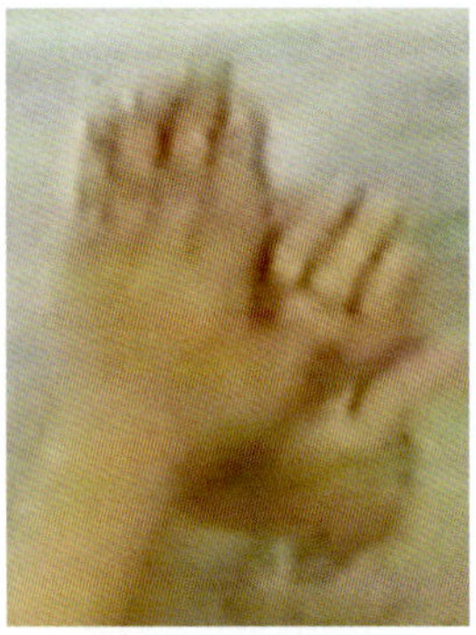
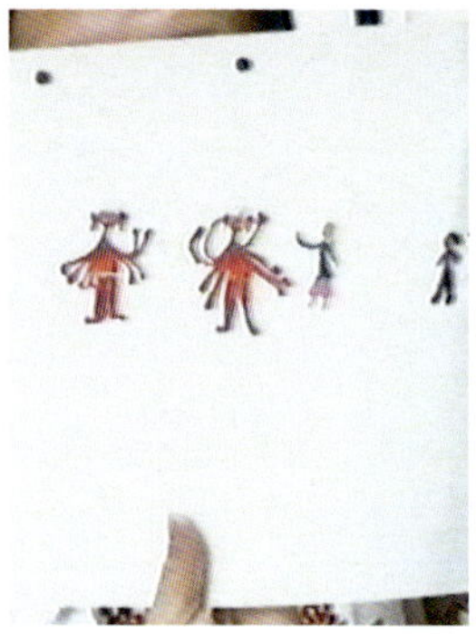
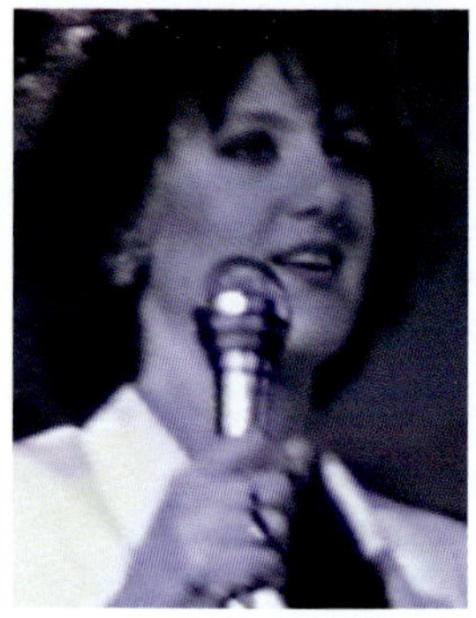
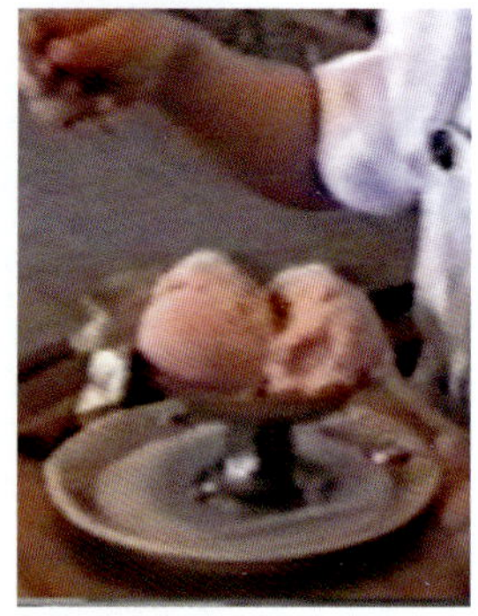
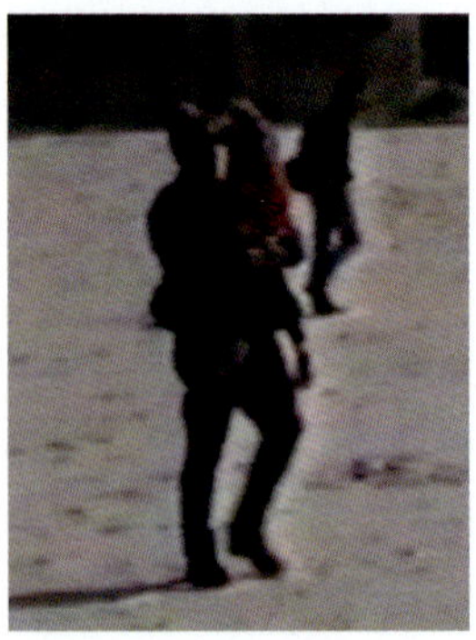
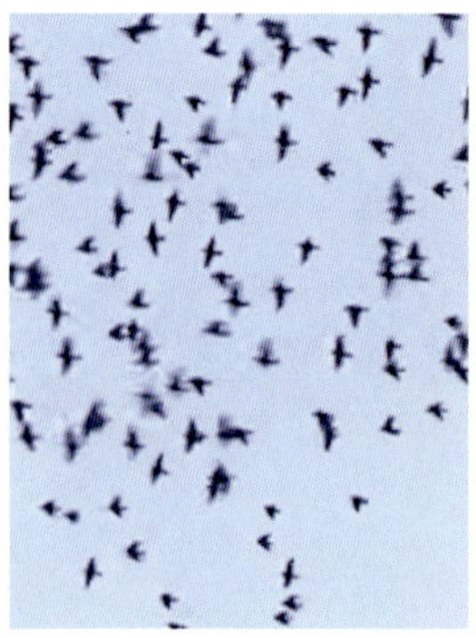

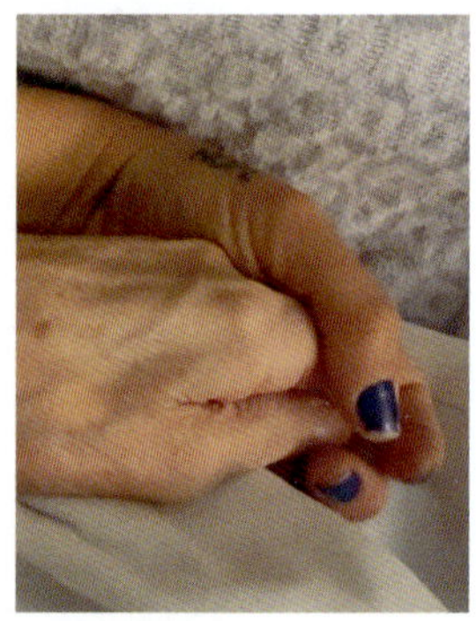
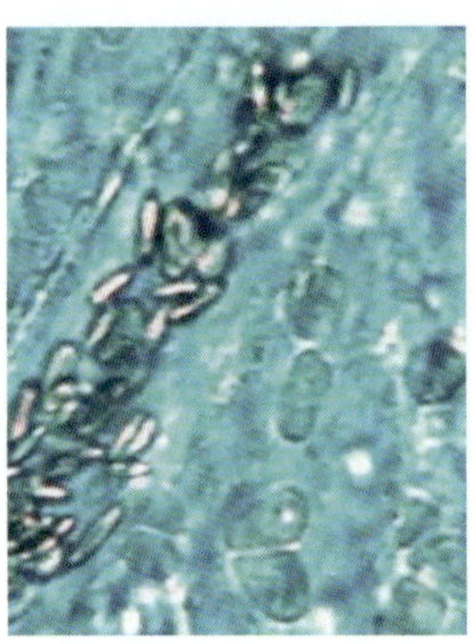
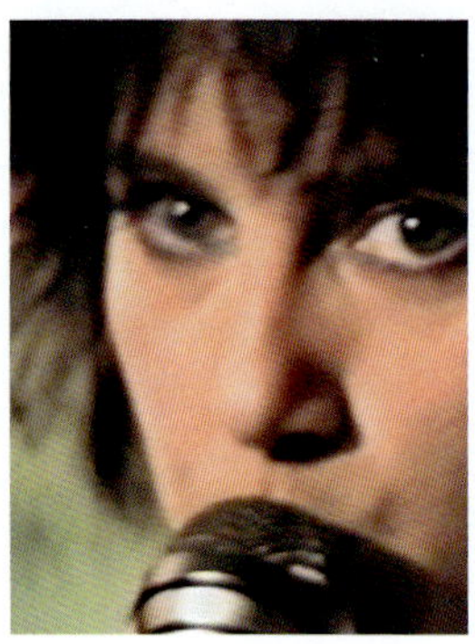
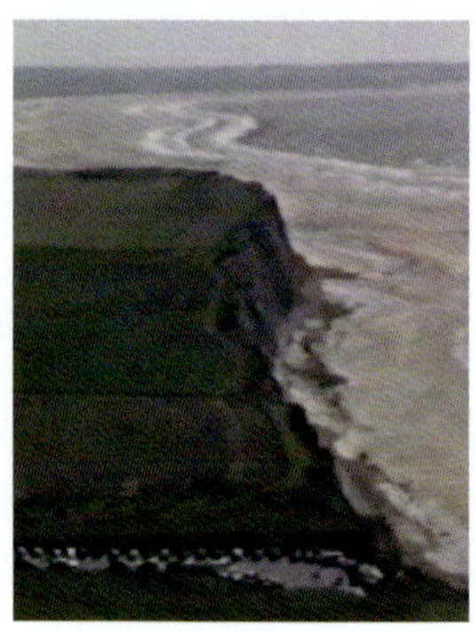
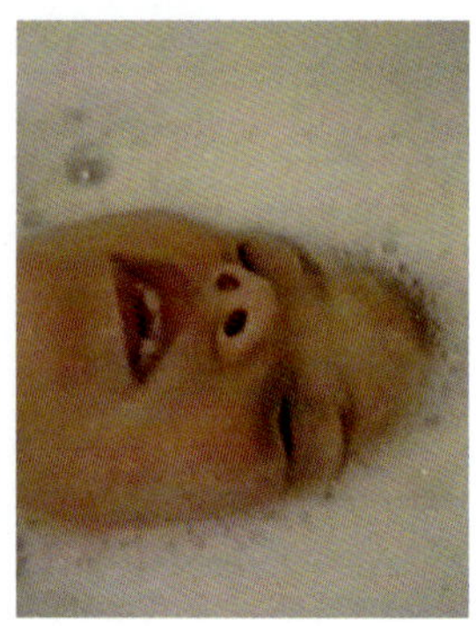

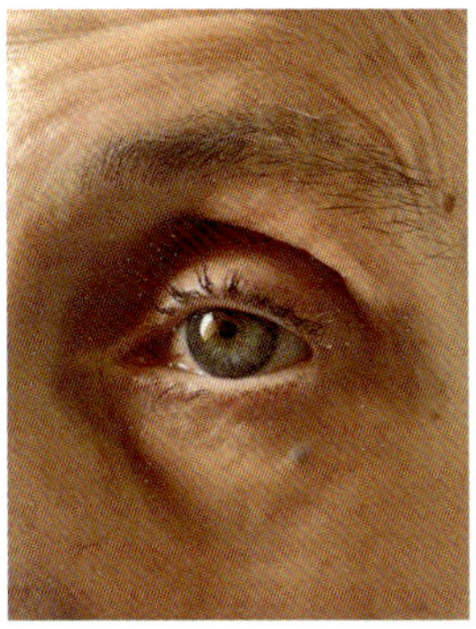
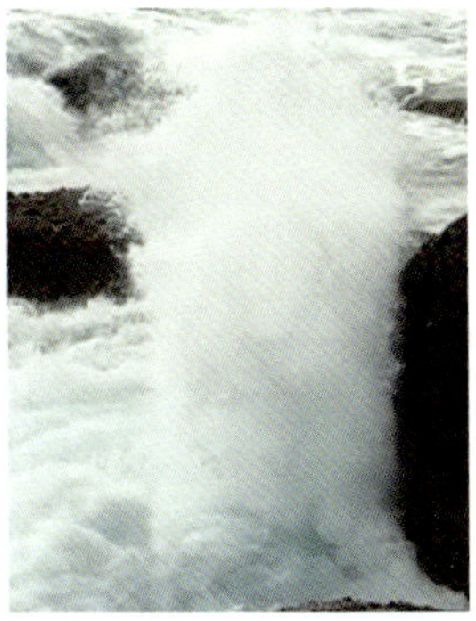
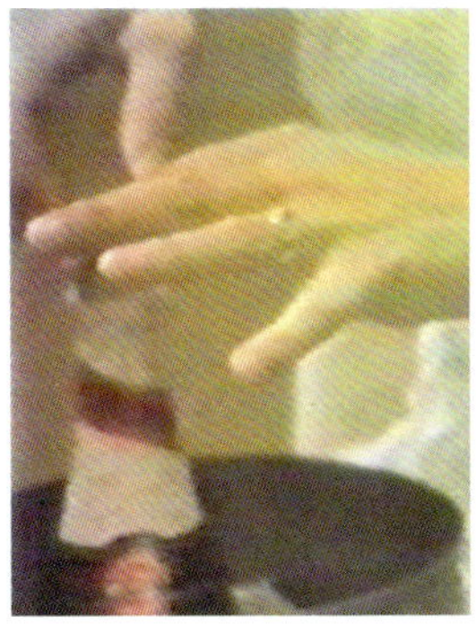
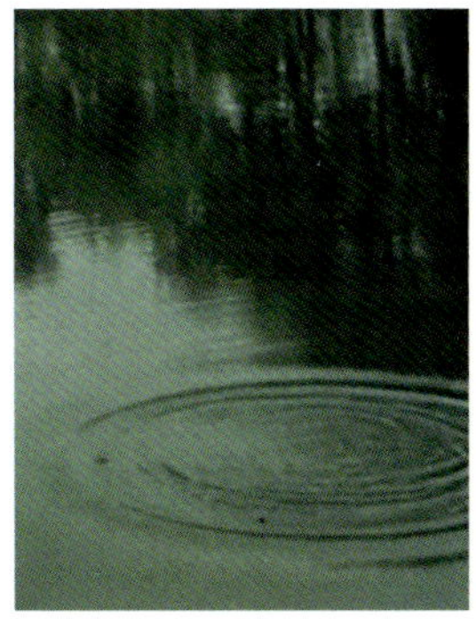
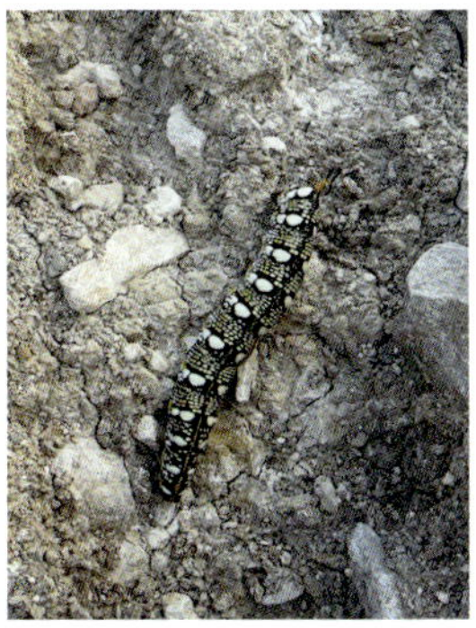
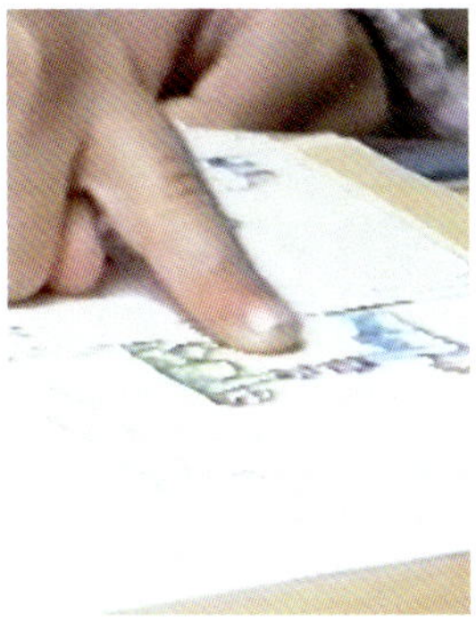
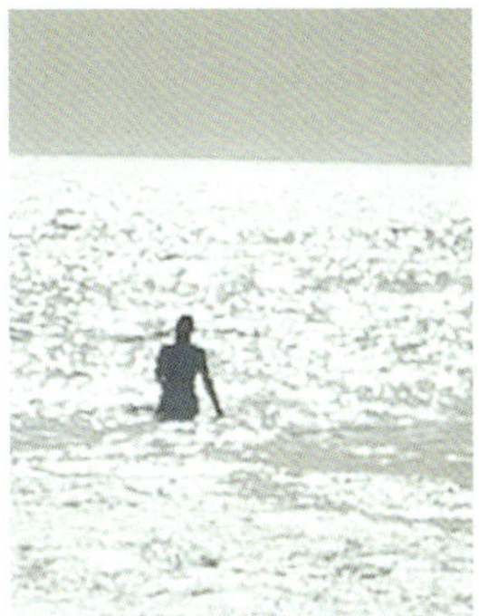
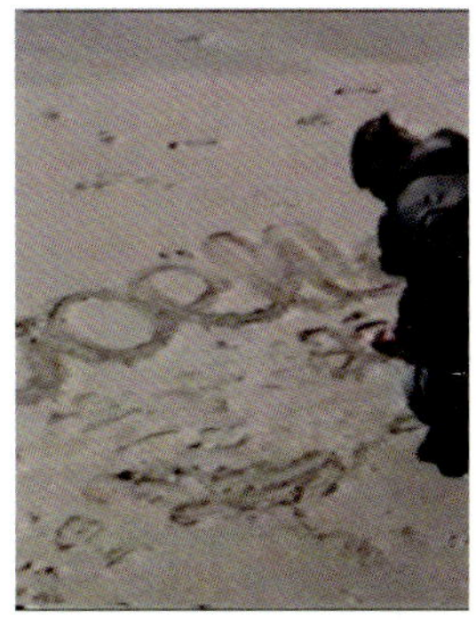
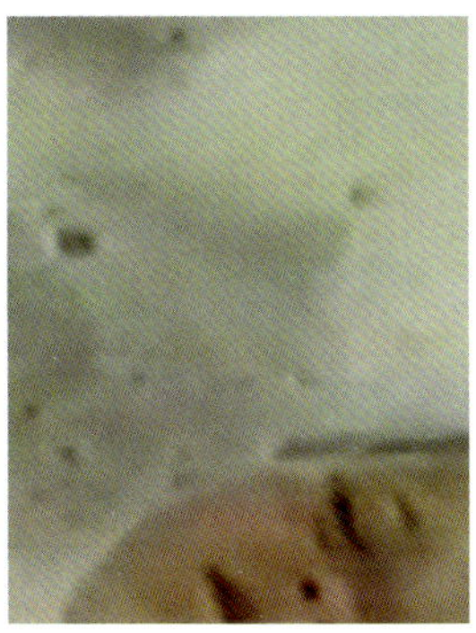
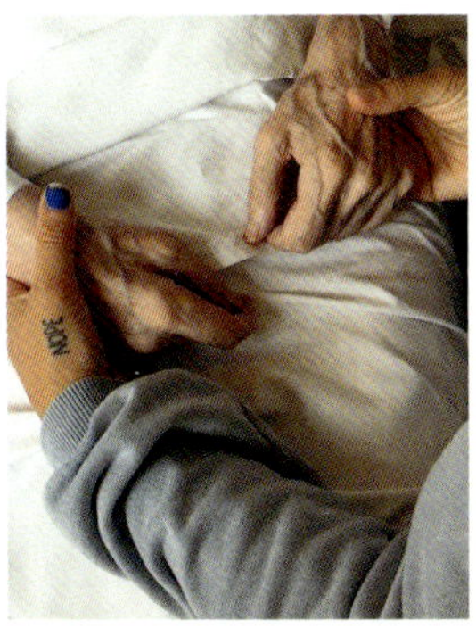
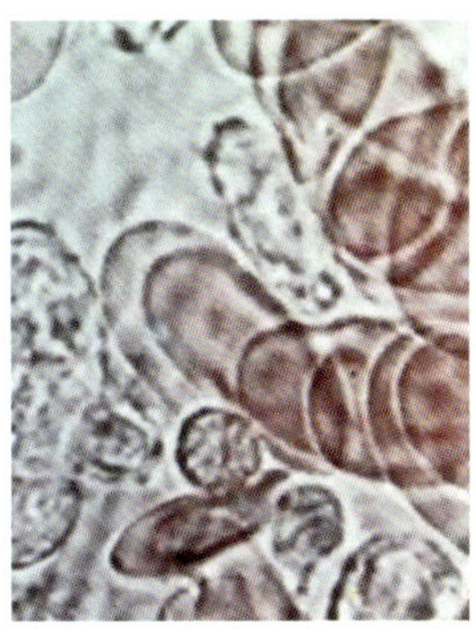
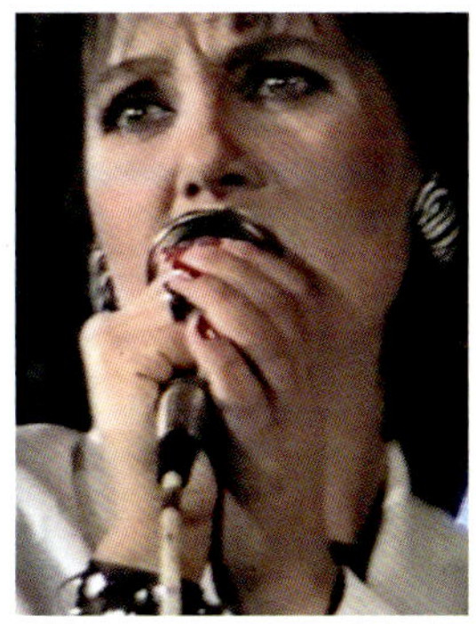
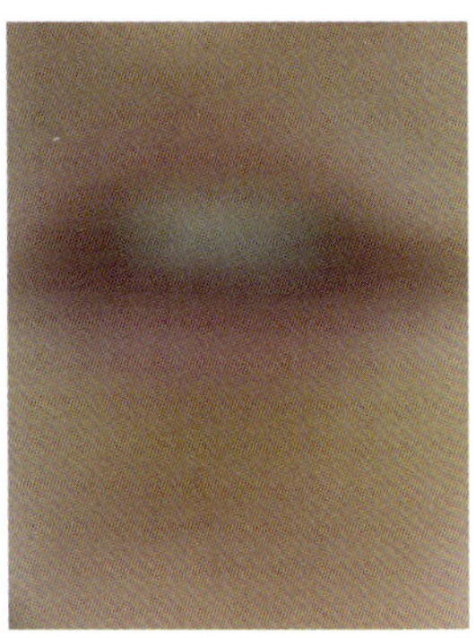
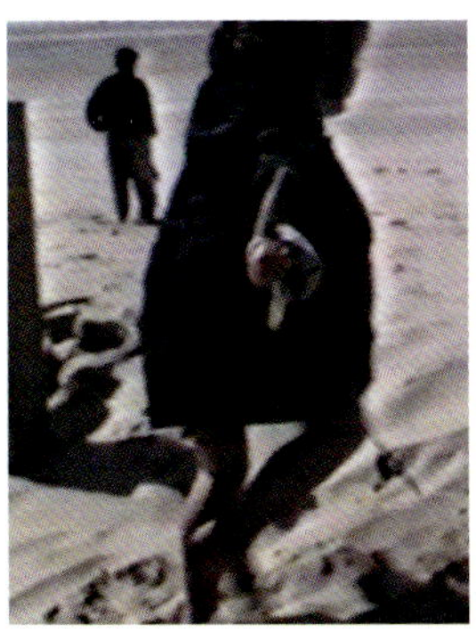
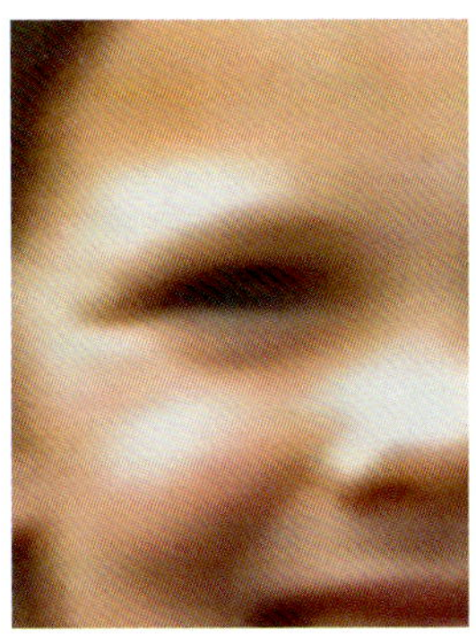
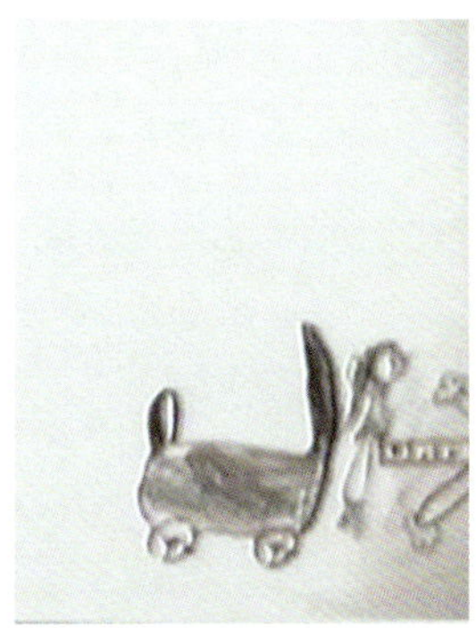

27·05·2024 – GENT

LIEVE MAMA,

IK VIND HET MOEILYK DE JUISTE WOORDEN TE VINDEN. WANT SPREKEN DOEN WE DE AFGELOPEN TWEE JAAR DAN OOK NAUWELYKS. DE LAATSTE JAREN WAS HET MOEILYK EN PYNLYK OM NIET MET JE TE KUNNEN PRATEN. DIE VERPLETTERENDE STILTE. NU IK ERAAN TERUGDENK WAS HET EEN WOORDELOOS GESPREK. WE SPRAKEN, MAAR MET ONZE OGEN. WE HEBBEN GELEERD ELKAAR TE VERSTAAN OP EEN ANDER NIVEAU. IK MIS HET OM JE STEM TE HOREN, TE LUISTEREN NAAR JE TALRYKE VERHALEN OVER JE KINDERTYD. JE GEKKE VERHALEN, JE AVONTUREN. JE LAS ME OOK NIET VAAK BOEKJES VOOR TYDENS HET SLAPENGAAN. JIJ VERTELDE. OVER JE TYD IN LONDEN, OVER HANDLEZEN EN TAROT, HOROSCOPEN. FLOWER-POWER EN VROUWENRECHTEN. "NOG EEN KEERTJE" ZEI IK DAN IN BED. MYN KINDERLYF DAT VAN GENOEGEN SPINT EN VERSLAPT VAN PLEZIER EN NIET WILT GAAN SLAPEN. DE 60'S ROCK & ROLL. LUCY IN THE SKY WITH DIAMONDS. DE VERZAMELING LP'S ONDERAAN IN HET REK, IN ONS HUIS WAAR IK UREN VOOR ZAT. JE LEERDE ME AL SNEL DE NAALD VAN DE PLATENSPELER CORRECT GEBRUIKEN. IK KOOS 'AN YOUR SISTER' EN ZONG LUIDKEELS MEE. GE HEBT MY OOK GELEERD HOE BELANGRYK HUMOR IS IN HET LEVEN. NIEMAND ANDERS HAD ZOVEEL ZELFSPOT ALS JIJ. JE HAD OOK HET VREEMDE IDEE DAT JE IMUUN WAS VOOR DEMENTIE. HET HEEFT JE NIET GEDEFINIEERD. JE GELOOFDE DE DIAGNOSE NIET. JE GAF NIET OP. VALLEN EN OPSTAAN, MET KNEUZINGEN EN BREUKEN TOT GEVOLG. JE EIGEN STIGMATA. JE HEBT ME LEREN VERTROUWEN OM IN HET MOMENT TE LEVEN, OOKAL LUKT ME DAT NOG NIET ZO GOED. ALS IK BIJ

JE WAS, HEERSTE ER ENKEL NU. WE STAARDEN DOOR HET RAAM. WE KEKEN HOE DE WIND DOOR DE BOMEN WAAIDE EN HOE DE VOGELS HUN LIED ZONGEN. JE HEBT ME GELEERD HOE IK DICHTER KON STAAN BIJ JOU, ZONDER WOORDEN. DUS BEN IK JOU BEGINNEN SCHILDEREN EN IK GA BLIJVEN SCHILDEREN MAMA. JIJ HEBT MIJ GEDRAGEN EN VOOR MIJ GEZORGD. IK HEB VOOR U GEZORGD EN HEB U GEDRAGEN. DE CIRKEL IS ROND. ZOALS KUNSTHISTORICUS HANNE HAGENAARS HET ZO MOOI ZEGT:

JE MOEDER IS AANWEZIG IN JE BOTTEN. DAT LIJKT ME HET MEEST DIEPE DIEP VAN MIJN LICHAAM, DAT WAT ME OVEREIND HOUDT EN WAT ONDER DE GROND HET LANGST OVERBLIJFT. DAT JE MOEDERS GEEST IN JE BOTTEN IS GEKROPEN, DAT ZEGT IETS OVER HET ONVERBREEKBARE, DE INTENSE VERBONDENHEID, DAT GAAT NIET MEER OVER HERINNEREN OF HOUDEN VAN, MAAR OVER HET ONVERBREKELIJKE. ALS IK MAAR WIJSHEID WIL ONTVANGEN, MAAK IK CONTACT MET MIJN BOTTEN. MAAR HOE IK CONTACT MOET MAKEN MET MIJN BOTTEN, ZONDER ZE TE BREKEN OF KNEUZEN, OM ZE TE VOELEN, DAAROVER HEB IK GEEN IDEE. IK ZOU KUNNEN GAAN MEDITEREN (OF IN MIJN GEVAL, SCHILDEREN), MAAR IK KAN HET OOK ZO LATEN. WIJ HEBBEN GEEN WOORDEN MEER NODIG MAMA, ENKEL NOG VOGELS EN HUN LIED. IK HOOP DAT ZE JOUW LIED MEENEMEN NAAR HUN VOLGENDE BESTEMMING, ERGENS EXOTISCH, VER WEG.

IK HOU VAN JOU MAMA ♡♡♡♡♡

Dear mum,

I find it difficult to find the right words. Because for the past two years, speaking is something we've hardly done. Those final years, it was difficult and painful not being able to talk with you. That crushing silence. Now when I think back, it was a wordless conversation. We spoke, but with our eyes. We learnt to understand each other on another level. I miss hearing your voice, listening to your many stories about your childhood. Your crazy stories, your adventures. You also hardly ever read me children's books at bedtime. You were doing the storytelling. About your time in London. About reading palms and tarot and horoscopes. Flower-power and women's rights. 'One more time' I'd say in bed. My little body purring with pleasure and going limp with delight, not wanting to go to sleep. The 60s, rock & roll. 'Lucy in the Sky with Diamonds'. The collection of LPs at the bottom of the rack, in our house where I'd sit for hours. You taught me early on how to use the record player needle properly. I'd choose And Your Sister and sing along at the top of my voice. You also taught me how important humour is in life. Nobody else had as much sense for self-deprecating humour as you. You also held the strange idea that you were immune to dementia. It hasn't defined you. You didn't believe the diagnosis. You didn't give up. Falling and getting back up, resulting in bruises and fractures. Your own stigmata. You taught me to trust living in the moment, even though I'm not very good at it yet. When I was with you, only the present moment reigned. We stared through the window. We watched how the wind blew through the trees and how the birds sang their song. You taught me how to get closer to you, without words. So I've started painting you and I'm going to keep painting. Mum you carried me and cared for me I cared for you and carried you the circle is complete. As art historian Hanne Hagenaars puts it so beautifully: 'Your mother is present in your bones. ... That seems to me to be the deepest depths of my body, it's what holds me up and it's what remains intact in the ground for longest. The fact that your mother's spirit has crept into your bones says something about the unbreakable, intense connection; it's no longer about remembering or loving but about what cannot be broken. ... If you want to receive her wisdom from the ancestral field, make contact with your bones. ... But I have no idea how to make contact with my bones so I can feel them, without breaking or bruising them. I could go and meditate [or in my case, paint]. I can also leave things as they are.' We don't need words anymore mum only birds and their song. I hope they take your song with them to their next destination, somewhere exotic, far away.

I love you Mama ♥♥♥♥♥

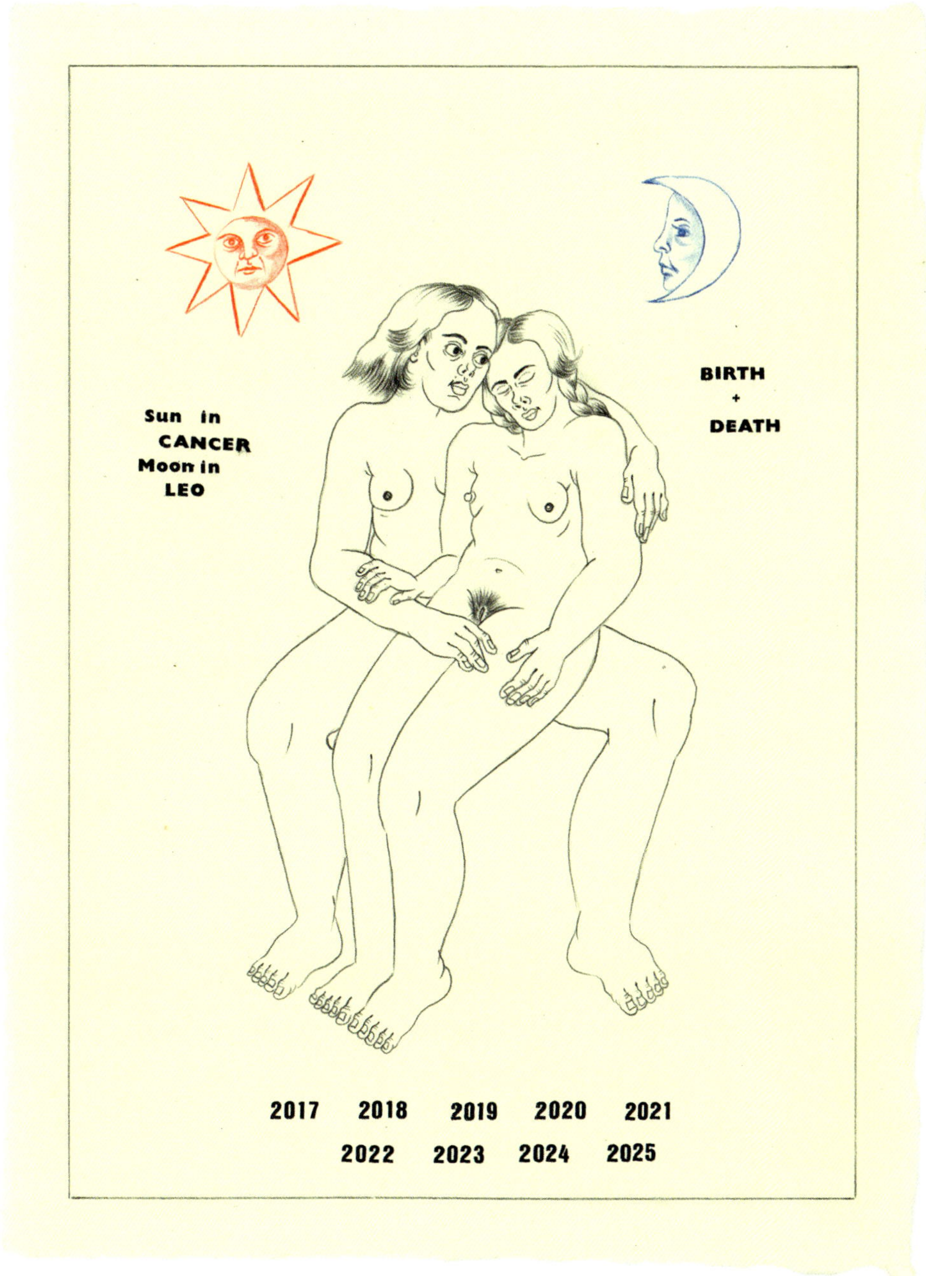

2025

Mourning in Forgetfulness (series)

29,7 × 21 cm

2025

Mourning in Forgetfulness (series)

29.7 × 21 cm (each)

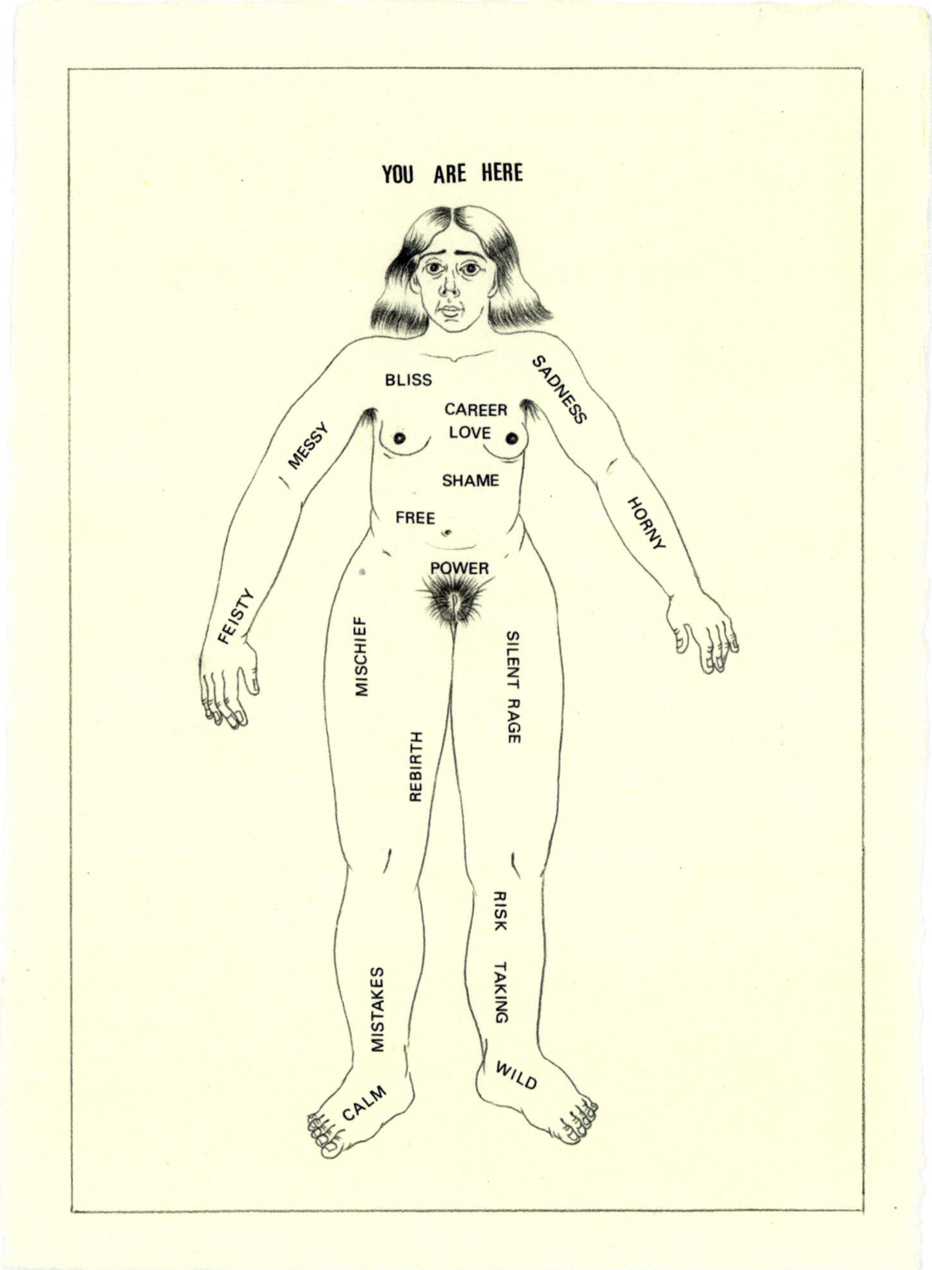

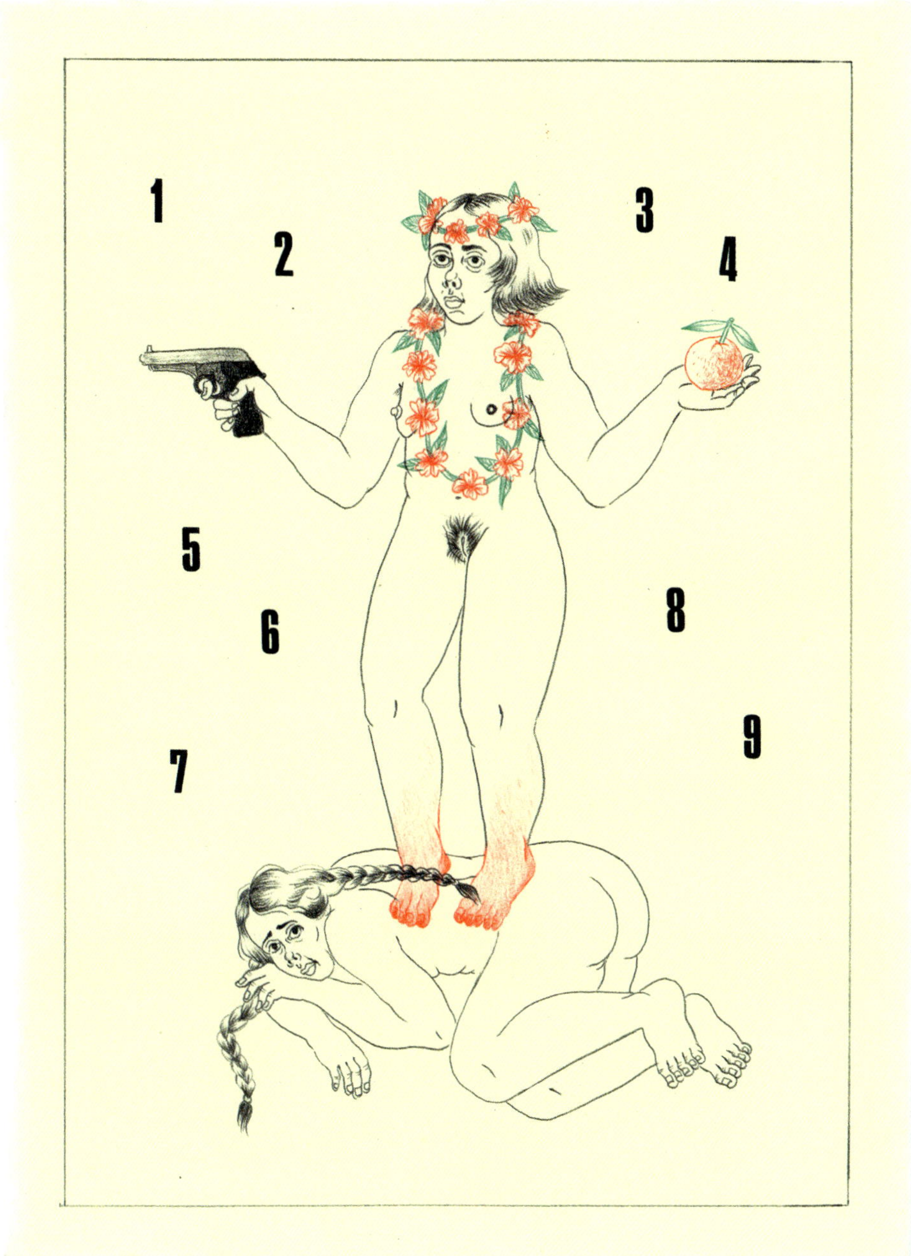
1
2
3
4
5
6
7
8
9

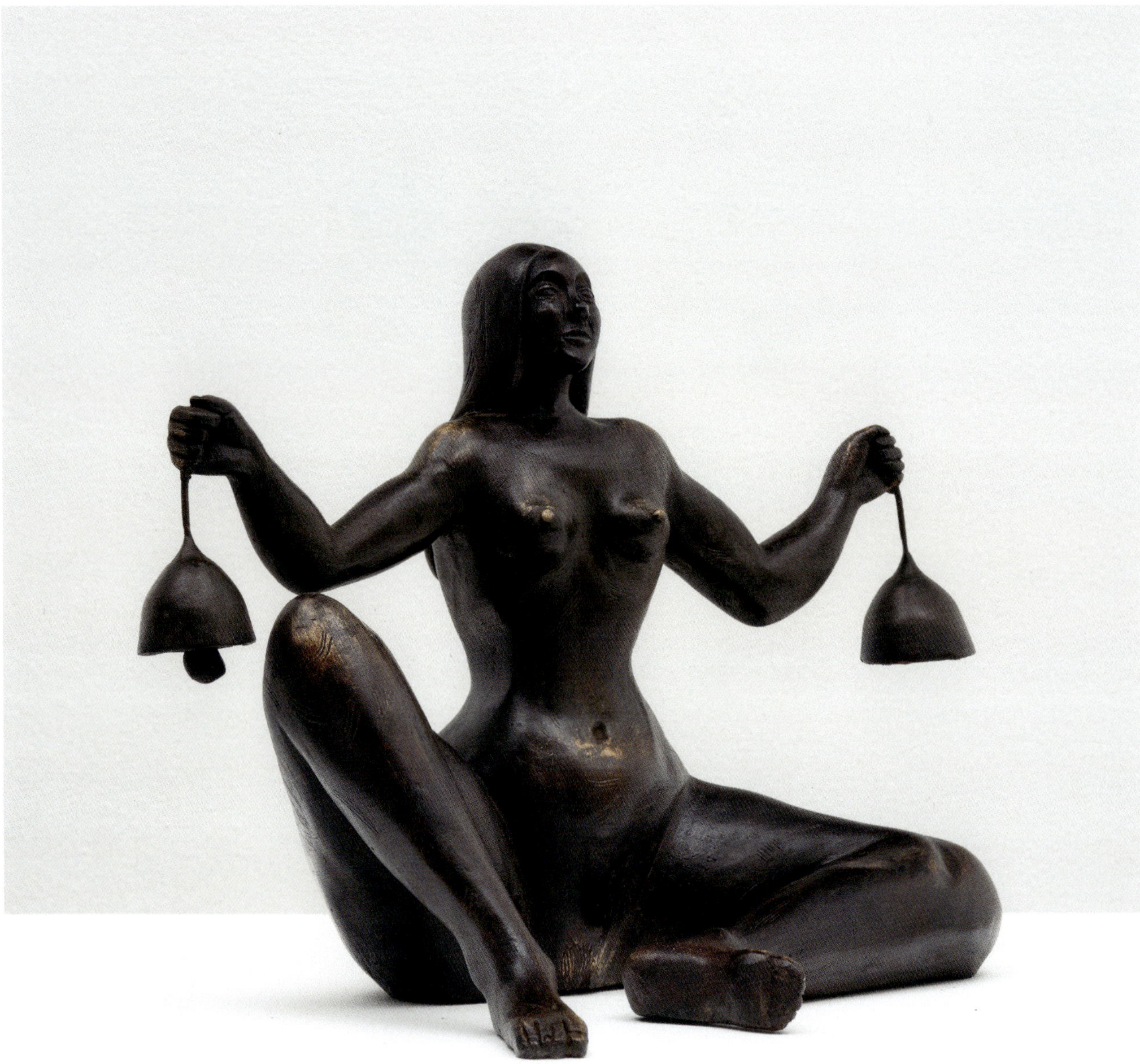

Catharsis 2 (Edition of 8 + 4 AP)

2025

c. 21.5 × 27.5 × 17 cm

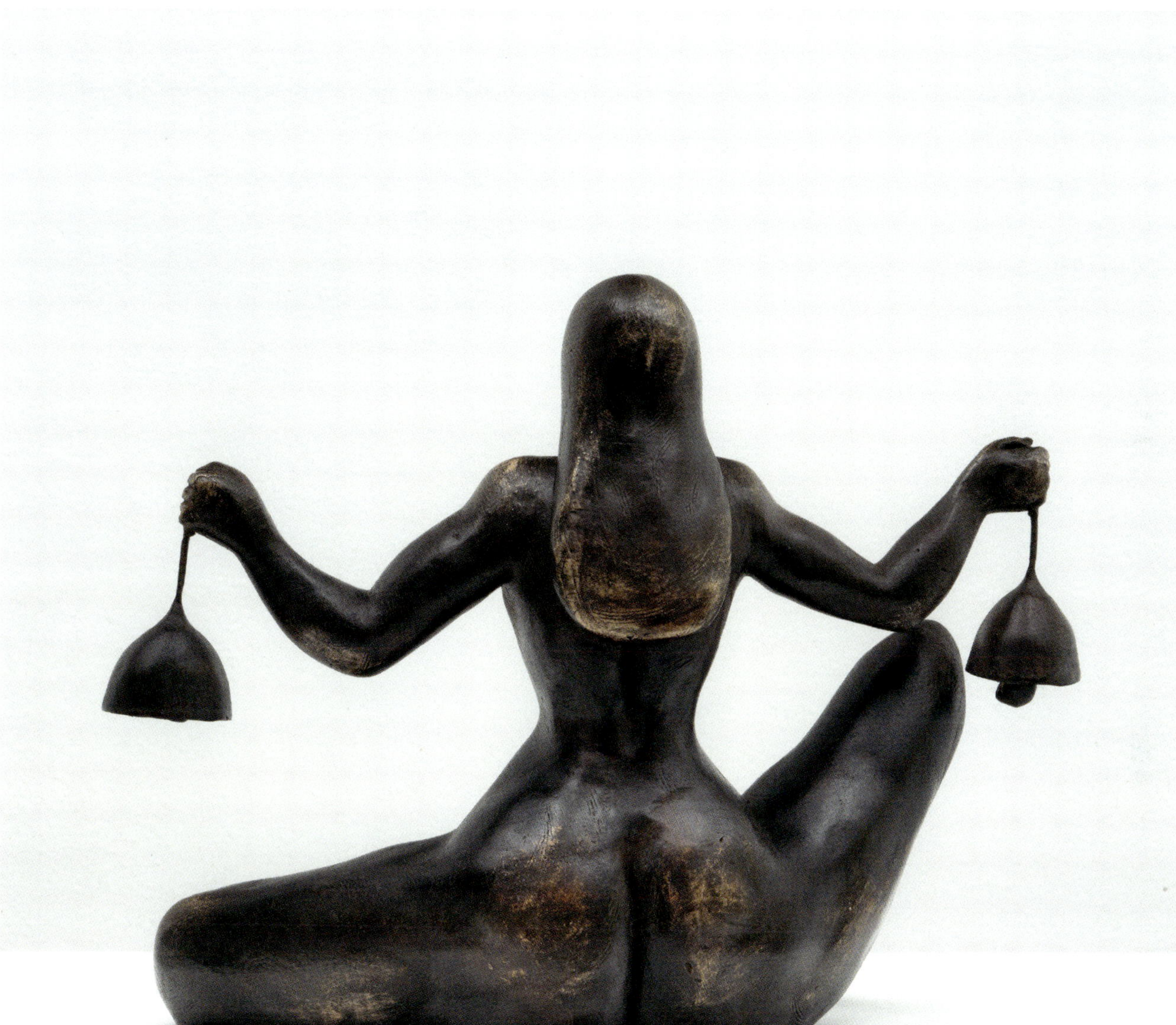

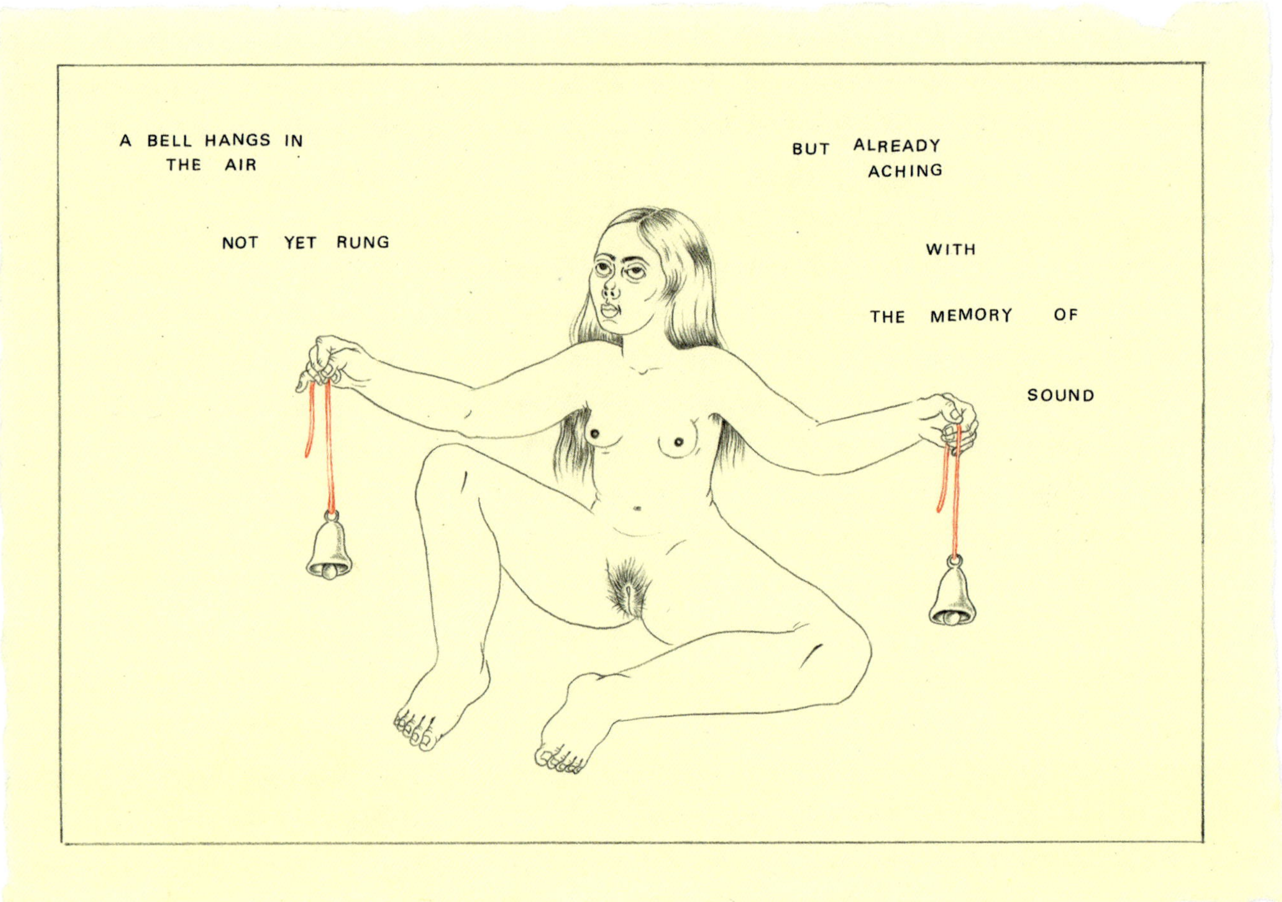

Mourning in Forgetfulness (series)

2025

21 × 29,7 cm (each)

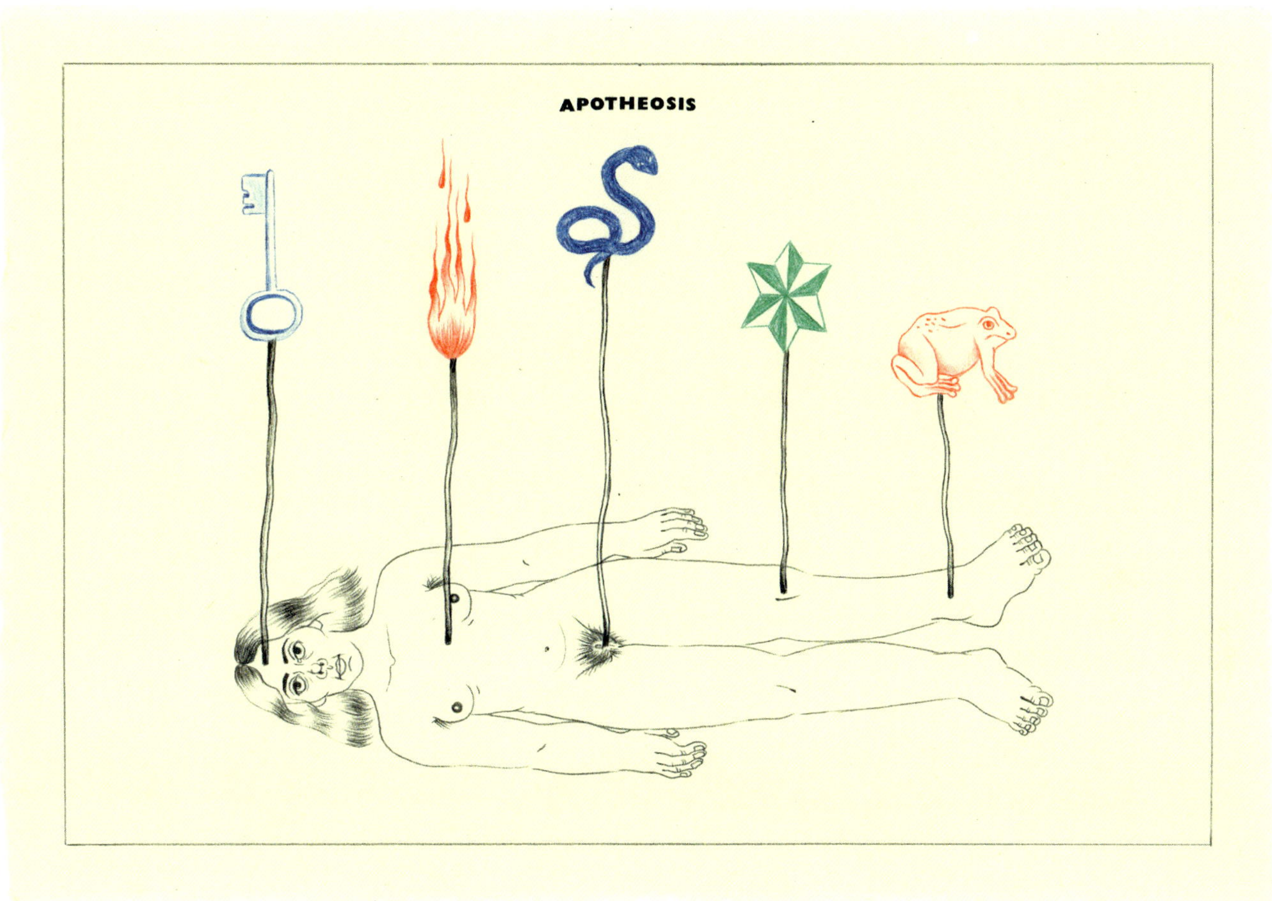
APOTHEOSIS

60 × 50 cm

Galvanised Spirit

2025

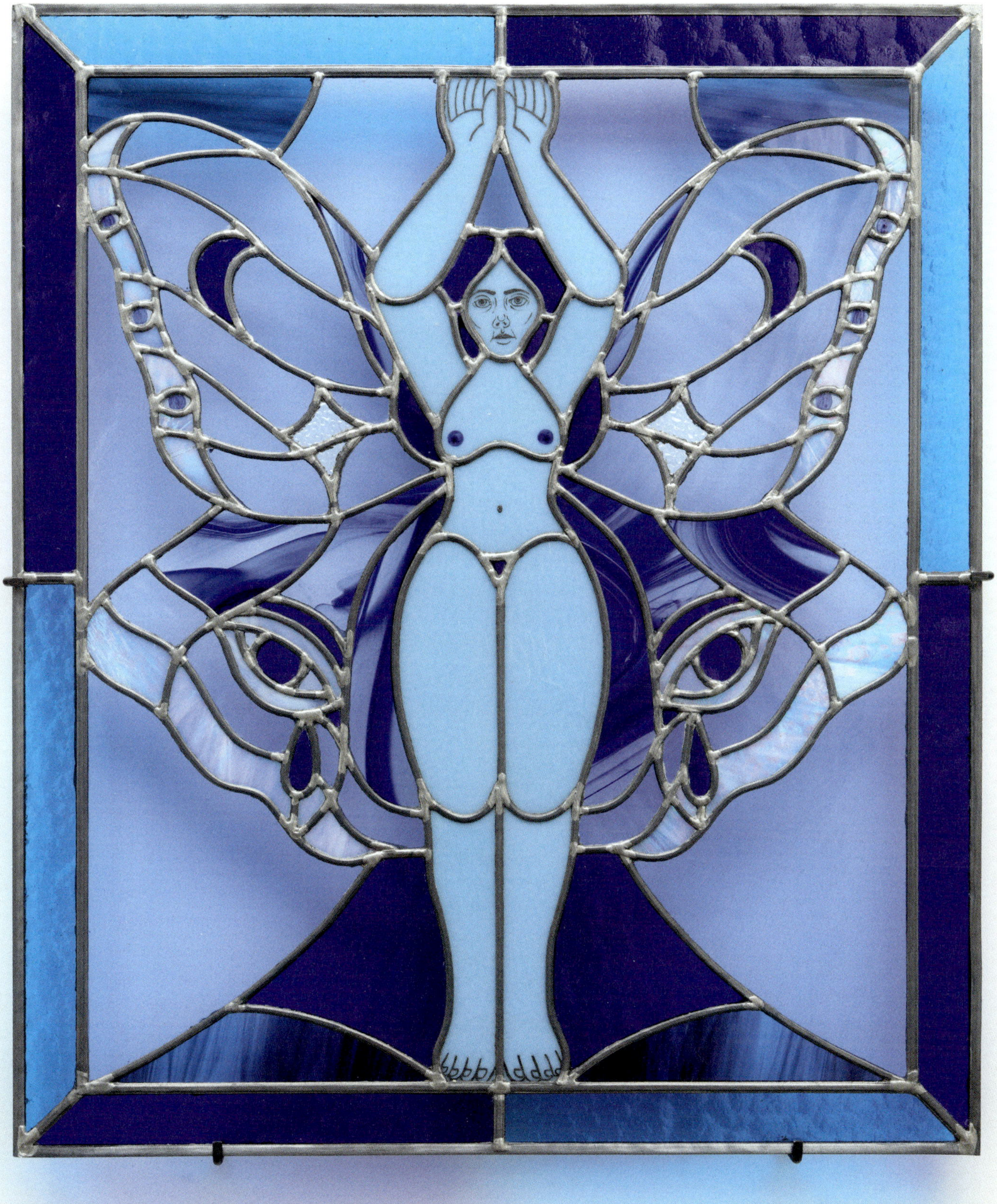

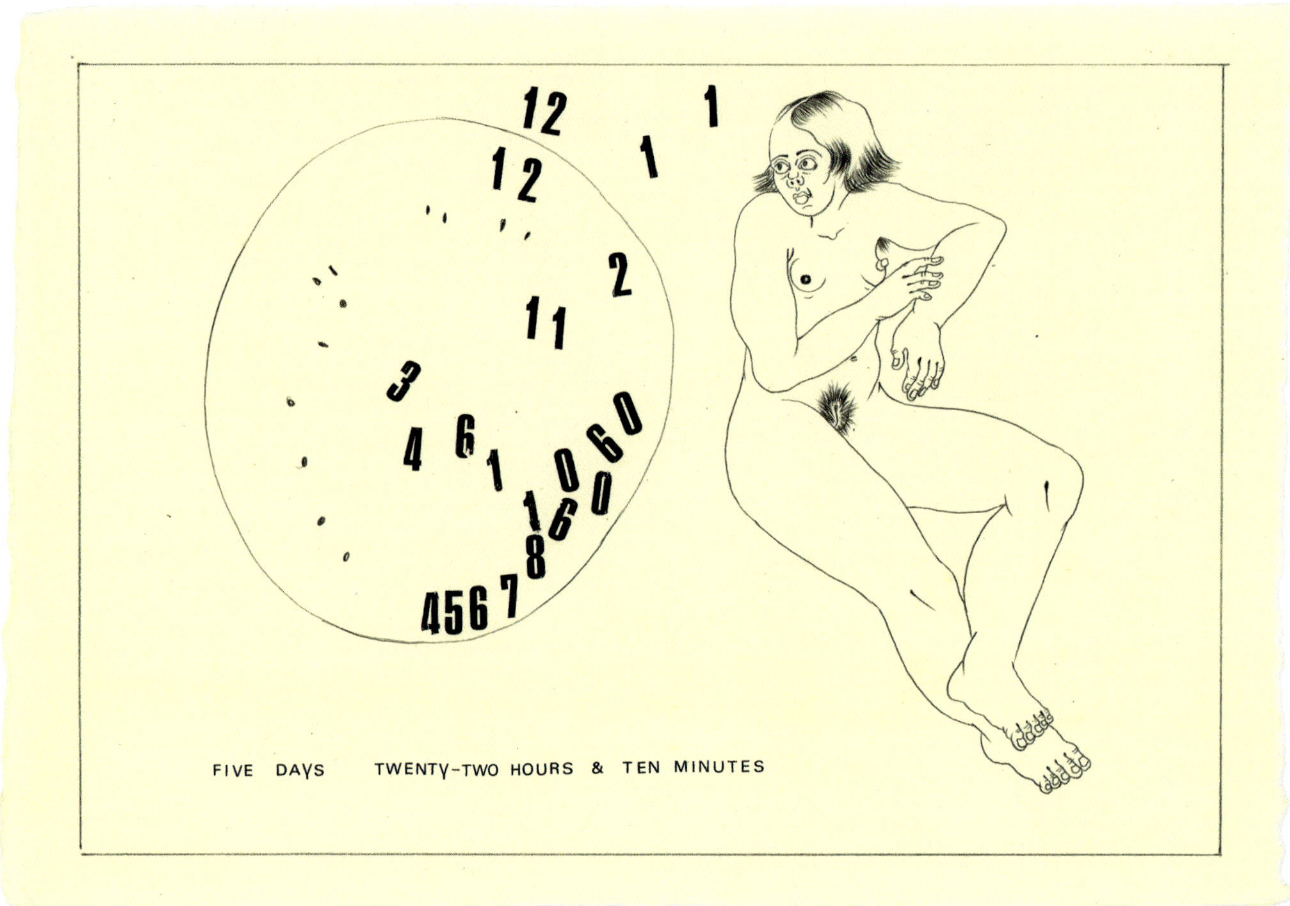

2025

Mourning in Forgetfulness (series)

21 × 29,7 cm (each)

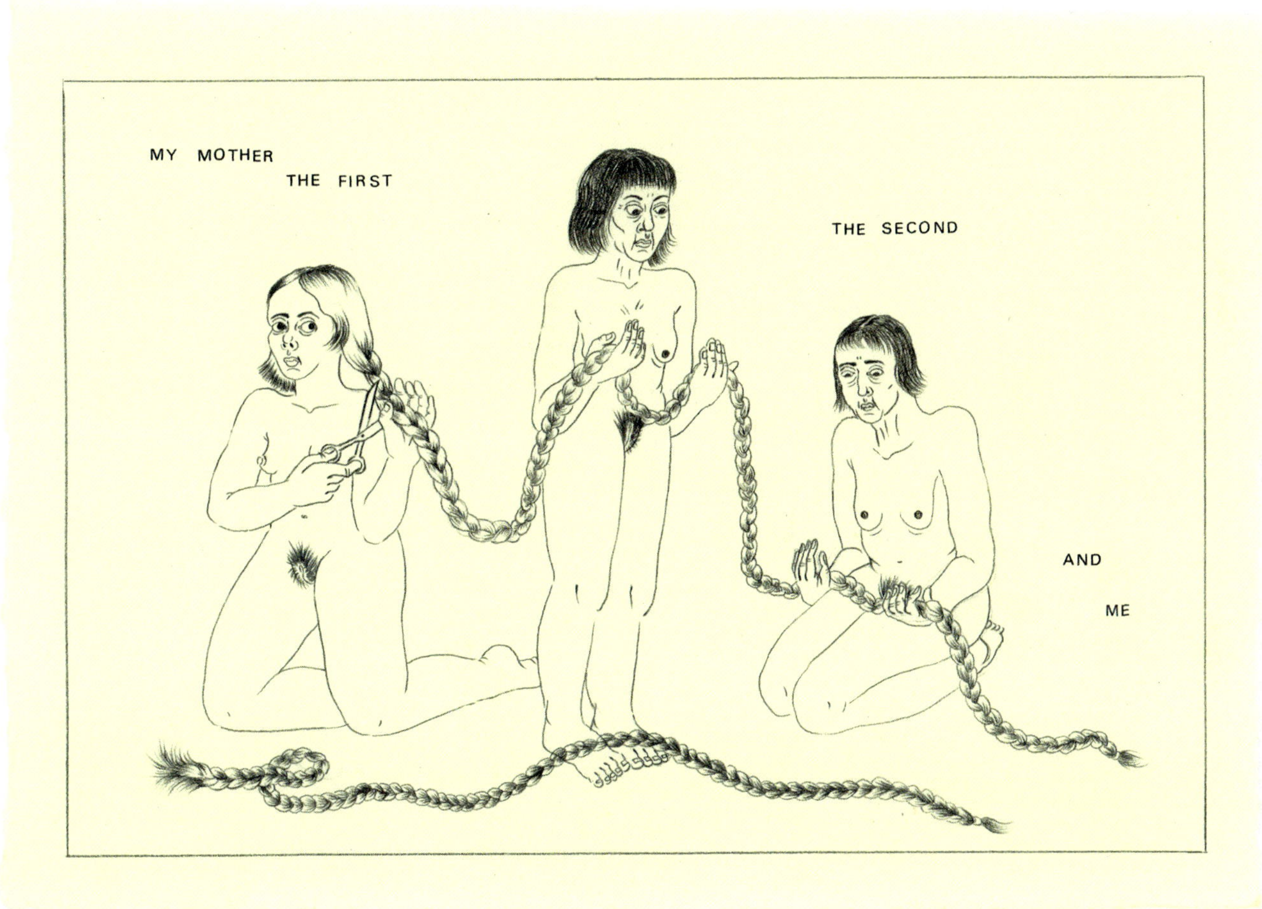
MY MOTHER
THE FIRST
THE SECOND
AND
ME

EPILOGUE

'I am my mother['s] daughter, but your death has left me feeling alone
I will never see your pretty face again or hear your sweet voice on my phone'
Gloria Gatica, 2013

I'm reading Karl Ove Knausgård's *A Death in the Family: My Struggle Book 1*, while curating the exhibition that explores Joëlle Dubois's oeuvre. *In My Struggle Book 1*, the first volume of a series of six autobiographical novels entitled *My Struggle* (*Min kamp* in Norwegian), Knausgård sets down a raw, razor-sharp dissection of his childhood and his tense, bewildering relationship with his father. His prose is unsparing, yet never baseless. What remains is not a caricature, but a shadow – something that settled quietly into who he became.

Dubois does something similar, though using a different language: that of the image. For *Rekindling*, her new solo exhibition at Be-Part in Kortrijk, she returns to the mother theme and the thread that connects but never breaks – not even through illness, decline or loss. The title refers to the rekindling of feelings, memories or love, just when the flames were about to go out. Through images, symbols and rituals, Dubois gives form to what we cannot grasp.

The exhibition forms the final part of a triptych about the mother-daughter bond, a cycle that began with *Forget Me Not*, was followed by *From Here On Out*, and now culminates in *Rekindling*. Each chapter marks a different stage of the process of letting go and, simultaneously, holding on. For what disappears from memory continues to exist in image, in colour, in movement.

For nine years the daughter cared for her mother. For nine years she continued to live in the same house close to her mother, and left her hair almost untouched – as a silent bearer of the past, as a tangible string tied to what was quietly slipping away.

As the mother faded away slowly, the daughter held onto images – as anchors, as resistance, as a quiet act of love. Just as Knausgård rewrites his past to understand it, so Dubois rearranges her images and memories to come to terms with them. Not in time, but in art.

Thus, this story ends where it began: with a bond that endures, despite everything.

Where memory fades, art offers form. Not to restore what was lost, but to give meaning to what remains.

Patrick Ronse,
Artistic Director at Be-Part, Kortrijk

Gloria Gatica, *I am my mothers daughter* (2013), https://allpoetry.com/poem/10590707-I-am-my-mothers-daughter-by-Gloria-Gatica.

75 × 55 cm

Self-Portrait as a Ghost

2025

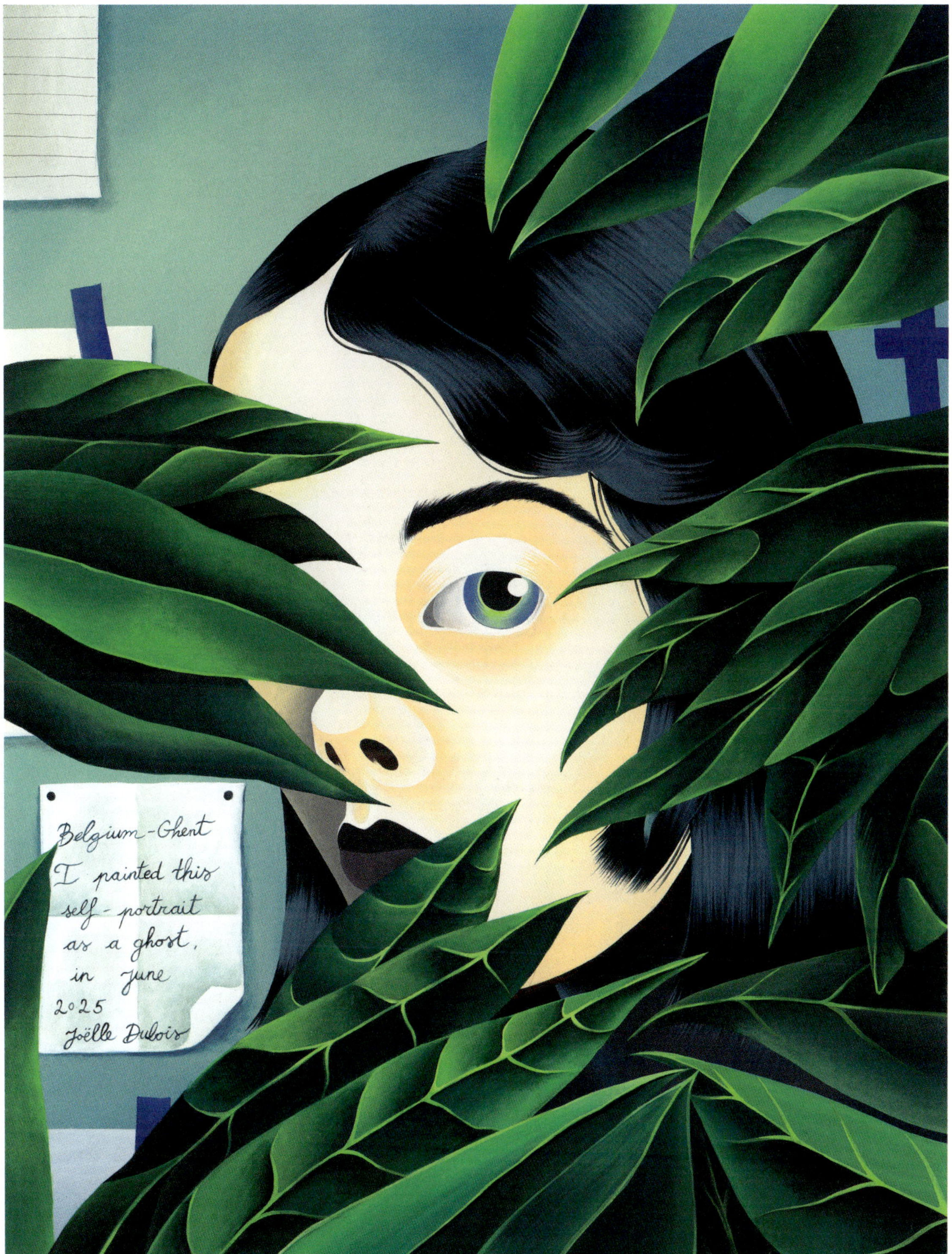
Belgium-Ghent
I painted this
self-portrait
as a ghost,
in June
2025
Joëlle Dubois

CREDITS

All works: © Joëlle Dubois

Photographs & reproductions of paintings, drawings, sculptures: courtesy of Keteleer Gallery, Antwerp. All photos by Alexey Shlyk.

Photos pp. 31–7 by Denis Decaluwé.

Photos pp. 7, 23, 16–7, 113: courtesy of Thomas Rehbein Gallery, Cologne. Photos by Simon Vogel.

Photo p. 191 by Dominique Provost.

All paintings are acrylic on wooden panel / pp. 12–3, 66–7 Ink on handmade paper / pp. 18–9, 26–7, 28–9 Ballpoint pen on handmade paper / pp. 32–7 Paint on mural / pp. 42–5 Fabric, lace, earth, UV-light. Soundscape by Joppe Tanghe / pp. 48–9 Acrylic and pencil on Japanese paper / pp. 52–9 Graphite on handmade paper / pp. 24–5, 64–5, 74–5 Ceramic vases by Jolien Holvoet, painted by Joëlle Dubois, glazed / pp. 96–7 Ballpoint pen on paper / pp. 109–11, 123–5 Mixed media on handmade paper 110g/m², A4 / pp. 139, 144–7, 150–1, 154–5, 158–9, 177–9, 182–3, 186–7 Graphite, dry transfer lettering on handmade paper. Poems by Precious Okoyomon / pp. 140–1, 156–7, 180–1 Bronze / pp. 149, 185 Stained-glass work produced by Veerle Verschooren, artwork and design by Joëlle Dubois / pp. 160–73: *The Memory Machine*, 2025. 2-channel video installation, length 25 minutes. Concept, sound, edit: © Joëlle Dubois, Florinda Ciucio. Camera: Karen Vazquez Guadarrama.

COLOPHON

Published on the occasion of the exhibition *Joëlle Dubois – Rekindling* from 6 September to 7 December 2025, presented at Be-Part, Kortrijk. Curated by Joëlle Dubois and Patrick Ronse and with the assistance of Lara Verlinde.

Texts
Christel Tsilibaris
Katrina Schwarz
Patrick Ronse

English translations
Yasmin Van 'tveld

Copy-editing
Derek Scoins
Yasmin Van 'tveld

Lithography
Pascal Van den Abbeele (Graphius)

Scans (drawings in *Rekindling*)
Fotoshop, Ghent

Project management
Stephanie Van den bosch

Graphic design
Tim Bisschop

Printing & binding
Graphius, Ghent

Publisher
Gautier Platteau, Hannibal Books

ISBN 978 94 9341 611 6
D/2025/11922/35
NUR 642

This book is published in collaboration with Keteleer Gallery, Antwerp & Be-Part, Kortrijk.

In honour of my mother Nicole Van Maldegem.

Joëlle Dubois would also like to acknowledge all her friends, collaborators and gallerists, in particular her father Hubert Dubois, Florinda Ciucio, Karen Vazquez Guadarrama, Barbara Vackier, Veerle Verschooren, Sarah Gevaert from ZarlarSwing Boerderie and all the animals, Buikgevoel, Elisa Maenhout, Femke Vandenbosch, Koen Leemans, Patrick Ronse and everyone at Be-Part, Bué The Warrior & Milo.

www.hannibalbooks.be
www.joelledubois.com
www.keteleer.com
www.rehbein-galerie.de
www.be-part.be

Cover: Joëlle Dubois, *Self-Portrait in Abundance*, 2025
Pp. 2–3: *I am My Mother's Daughter*, 2022, Neon Installation by Erwin (BE), 20 × 170 cm